I have observed the psychotherapy scene since the days when Freud was the main voice. Later brief psychotherapy took a mere 6 months. Now we have the 30 minute and even 5 minute cures of NLP. Speed is not the real issue. We must be closing in on the actual design of people. The Andreases are at the forefront of these discoveries. Their new book **Heart of the Mind** *is a needed presentation of these most useful methods. How cheering it is for me to find it is all so much simpler and easier than I had dreamed possible.*

—Wilson van Dusen, PhD, former Chief Psychologist
at Mendocino State Hospital, CA, and author of
The Natural Depth in Man

HEART
of the
MIND

Connirae Andreas PhD
Steve Andreas MA

Engaging Your Inner Power to Change
with Neuro-Linguistic Programming

Real People Press

Copyright © 1989
Real People Press
Box F
Moab, Utah 84532

ISBN: 0-911226-30-3 clothbound $14.00
ISBN: 0-911226-31-1 paperbound $9.50

Cover by Rene Eisenbart

Library of Congress Cataloging in Publication Data:

Andreas, Connirae.
    Heart of the mind : engaging your inner power to change with neurolin-
guistic programming / Connirae Andreas and Steve Andreas.
        p.   cm.
    Includes bibliographical references.
    ISBN 0-911226-30-3 : $14.00. — ISBN 0-911226-31-1 : $9.50
    1. Neurolinguistic programming.   2. Neurolinguistic programming—
Case studies.   I. Andreas, Steve.   II. Title.
BF637.N46A533   1989
158'.1—dc20
                                        89-27733
                                        CIP

Other books about Neuro-Linguistic Programming from Real People Press:

FROGS INTO PRINCES, by *Richard Bandler and John Grinder,* 197 pp. 1979 Cloth $11.00 Paper $7.50

USING YOUR BRAIN—FOR A CHANGE, by *Richard Bandler.* 159 pp. 1985 Cloth $11.00 Paper $7.50

REFRAMING: Neuro-Linguistic Programming and the Transformation of Meaning, by *Richard Bandler and John Grinder.* 220 pp. 1981 Cloth $12.00 Paper $8.50

TRANCE-FORMATIONS: Neuro-Linguistic Programming and the Structure of Hypnosis, by *John Grinder and Richard Bandler.* 250 pp. 1981 Cloth $12.00 Paper $8.50

CHANGE YOUR MIND—AND KEEP THE CHANGE, by *Steve Andreas and Connirae Andreas.* 187 pp. 1987 Cloth $12.00 Paper $8.50

The name *Real People Press* indicates our purpose; to publish ideas and ways that a person can use independently or with others to become more *real*—to further your own growth as a human being and to develop your relationship and communication with others.

1   2   3   4   5   6   7   8   9   10   Printing   93   92   91   90   89   88

to

Richard Bandler

and

John Grinder

Co-developers of Neuro-Linguistic Programming

and to

Leslie Cameron-Bandler and Judith De Lozier

and

Robert Dilts and David Gordon

Our teachers for so many years

Any sufficiently developed technology is indistinguishable from magic.

—Arthur C. Clarke

*The heart has its reasons
which reason knows nothing of.*

—Blaise Pascal

Contents

Introduction

Dr. Bernie Siegel's best-selling book *Love, Medicine and Miracles* grew out of what he had learned from his exceptional patients; those who lived much longer than expected, or who even became completely free of so-called "terminal" illnesses. He learned how some people were able to transform their lives to become free of disease.

In the same way, Neuro-Linguistic Programming has grown out of the study of the mental processes of those who can do something exceptionally well, or who have completely recovered from some difficulty. Most of us were taught to think of exceptional skills as the result of inborn abilities, traits, or talents. NLP demonstrates that by thinking about our abilities as learned skills, we open the door to understanding them more easily and teaching them to others.

The field of NLP is based on the realization that we create much of our experience by the specific ways that we see, hear, and feel things in our mind/body—what is usually lumped together and called "thinking." This is how it is possible for one person to feel terrorized by a simple task like public speaking or asking someone for a date, while someone else will feel energized or excited by it.

What's really new in NLP is that now we know *how* to explore a person's thinking in a precise way that actually allows us to take on that person's skills and abilities. When we really learn how to think about things the way someone else does, we automatically have similar feelings and responses. In problem areas in our lives, this ability to explore our thinking and feelings offers the keys to finding solutions.

In this book we give you a "front-row seat," so you can experience examples of how NLP works with people to make their lives better. All the cases we present to you were either participants in our seminars or private clients, and all names and identifying information have been changed, except for people who also appear in our videotapes.

In each case we point out the major features of what we are doing, and present some of the major ideas and techniques that guide our work. However, we will *not* be teaching in detail. While we encourage you to experiment with what you learn here, *we also ask you to be very cautious and gentle both with yourself and others. NLP is a very powerful set of methods, and anything so powerful can be misused. If you decide you want to learn to use NLP methods, we urge you to get thorough "hands-on" experiential training before becoming too ambitious.*

We have three major goals in presenting the cases in this book. The first one is to provide a message of hope, by offering glimpses of the wide range of problems that NLP can often resolve quickly and easily. Like so many things, change is only hard and slow when we don't know what to do.

Our second goal is to present examples of the different kinds of interventions that can be used to resolve problems and make a more satisfying life possible for you. Some of these interventions did not exist a year before this book was written, and by the time this book is published, even more methods will have been developed.

Our third goal is to offer you a new way of thinking about how minds work, and show you how you can use this information to guide your thinking and make life more enjoyable and satisfying—and probably longer, too.

—Steve and Connirae Andreas

Overcoming Stage Fright

1

Joan was a campaign manager for a local congressman. As part of her work she often had to make public presentations to groups of various sizes. Even though she was able to do this, she always suffered considerable discomfort. As soon as she stood up to speak, she got tense, her throat constricted, and her voice became higher and more shrill. She said she felt "disconnected" from the people she was speaking to. However, she enjoyed talking with small groups *after* the presentation: "Then I feel connected to them as individuals, and it's easy to respond to them; I really like that part of my job."

How Joan's Thinking Created Stage Fright

When I asked her if she had any idea how she created her tightness and discomfort, she said "No." Since the information I wanted from her was "unconscious," I asked her to imagine being back in the problem situation to see what she could discover:

"Think of one of the situations when this happened, and go back into it *before* you stand up to speak. See what you saw then, feel the chair under you, and hear the sounds around you there. Nod when you're fully back there."...[1]

When she nodded, I went on: "Now imagine that you stand up and walk to the front of the room where you will speak. As you do this, notice what you experience that creates the tension."...

---

1. Three dots (. . .) are used throughout this book to indicate a pause.

As she did this, I could see her shoulders rise as her chest became tense. When she spoke, her voice was indeed higher and shriller, so I knew that she was actually re-experiencing the problem situation. When she reported on her experience, she described her feelings of tension and discomfort in detail, but she still had no idea how she created it. She needed a little more help from me.

"Close your eyes and go back again to that situation of being in front of the group. As you stand there, notice any words you might be saying to yourself in your mind, or any pictures you might be making internally. . . . Try looking out at the group and notice if there is anything unusual about the people's eyes or their faces." Since I have worked with stage fright before, I know that often it occurs in response to imagining being watched, judged, or rejected by the audience, and this is usually most evident in how we see the eyes or faces of the audience.

After a few moments, Joan's body jerked slightly and she said, "Oh! They all have cartoon eyes! All those empty eyes are staring at me without any expression!"

If you imagine being Joan, looking out at a room full of life-size cartoon eyes, it's easy to realize how this would make her feel tense and "disconnected" from the group! Now that I knew how she created the problem, the next step was to change it to something more useful.

Creating Comfort

"As you're standing in front of that group, look past the cartoon eyes to see the *real eyes* of the people you're looking at. Start with one person, and when you can see his real eyes, let your eyes move on to another face and see her eyes. Continue to make eye contact with all the people in the group at your own speed, and then tell me how that changes your experience.". . .

As Joan did this, her shoulders and chest relaxed considerably, and she began to smile slightly. After about a half-minute she spoke in a voice that was almost as low as her normal voice: "It's much better now. I can see the people out there, and I'm more relaxed. But I still feel disconnected from them."

When I asked how she created this remaining feeling of disconnection, she said slowly and thoughtfully, "It has something to do with being higher than them. Even if I'm not on a stage, I'm always standing up and they're sitting down, so I'm still higher than they are. I don't like looking down at people. We can't meet eye-to-eye."

Since in the future she will actually be standing up, higher than the people she speaks to, I needed to find a way for her to *feel* as if she's communicating eye-to-eye, even when there is a physical difference in height. A first step in this direction is to convince her that this is possible.

"Joan, have you ever been at a presentation in which you felt as if the speaker was talking directly to you, person-to-person, even though he or she was speaking from a higher platform?"

Joan said thoughtfully, "Yes, I have."

"Good, so you do know it's *possible.* I want you to close your eyes, and go back to that presentation. Notice what that speaker does to establish that person-to-person rapport, even though he's physically at a different level."

After a few moments, Joan opened her eyes, smiled, and said, "He looked out into the audience and smiled, and some people smiled back. . . . Whenever I've presented I've been scared, and my face has been too tense and tight to feel like smiling."

"OK. Now that you feel more comfortable being in front of the group, you could easily smile at the people, right? Let's try it out. Close your eyes and imagine that you are walking up to begin your presentation. Before you begin, try smiling out at the group and notice who smiles back. Some will, and some won't; but either way it will be the beginning of your person-to-person interaction with the group."

After a few moments Joan smiled broadly and said, "That works. Some of them smiled back and that makes me feel connected with them. How could it be so simple?" The important thing was not just having Joan smile, but finding something that made *Joan* feel the person-to-person connection she wanted.

This session with Joan took about fifteen minutes. A few weeks later, Joan reported that in recent presentations she had felt relaxed, comfortable, and connected with the group.

Other Ways to Have Stage Fright

Few people will create their stage fright in exactly the same way Joan did, but they will do *something* internally that results in their discomfort. Some people will imagine not being able to speak at all; others may worry that the entire group will soon begin to snicker and get up to leave. Still others will remember a time in their past when they were humiliated by being ill-prepared for a presentation.

As soon as you understand how *this* person creates his problem, his response always makes perfect sense. Our responses aren't random; they are simply the consequences of how our minds work. It doesn't really matter exactly *what* each of us does to create a problem. As soon as you know what you do, you can begin to experiment with changing it to something more useful.

In the case of Joan, we directly changed elements of her internal experience. You can accomplish the same outcome by noticing what a person presupposes, and use purely verbal interventions to change how that person thinks, as in the following example.

Betty's Stage Fright

Betty also wanted to get over her stage fright. "I want to be comfortable in giving a seminar or presentation," she requested.

"So what has stopped you from just automatically being comfortable when you do a presentation?" I asked.

"Well, they know more than I do."

"They know more than you do?" I repeated. "How do you know so much that you know this?" I asked with a smile. Here I attempted to use Betty's own way of thinking to get her to recognize that her complaint actually results from her *own* knowledge, not the knowledge of others. But Betty's experience did not change.

"I don't." she responded.

"So you *imagine* that they know more than you do," I said. Now Betty was faced with an interesting dilemma. Either she can accept that she knew enough to know what others were thinking, or she can admit that she didn't know that much about the other's knowledge. In either case, her assumption that others know more than she does is likely to become a bit less real.

"Right. And everything has been said before, and presented before." Betty added.

"Oh. So are you one of these people that if you were an author, you wouldn't write a book because all the words in our language have already been used?" This metaphoric question takes her statement to an extreme in a context in which it is clearly absurd.

"Yes." Betty responded with a smile, amused, and not taking it quite so seriously.

"Is that a fact. Well, what makes you even want to make a presentation, if everything has been said before and everybody knows more than you? Why would you even want to bother?" Here I'm exploring the apparent contradiction between her motivation to present, and her assumption that "it's all been done before," so there's no point in presenting.

"That's a good question," said Betty, thoughtfully. "Well, I'm finding out now that I can say something in my way, and that other people can learn a different perspective even though it has been said before."

"So you have already come to the realization that sometimes seeing something in a different way gets a useful response from the listener. So you know that. Is there anything else that makes you want to do a presentation?"

"If I develop a passion for the material, then it shouldn't matter at all, because when I have that passion and that conviction inside—"

"Then what shouldn't matter at all?"

"That they know more and that everything has been said before. Because then I would have fun doing it, and I would feel comfortable."

Betty now had a conscious idea of what it *could* be like when she didn't have stage fright, but she clearly was not actually experiencing it yet. She was telling me how things *would* be, not how they *are,* so I knew I needed to go further.

"That sounds good to me. Now when you think about any audience in particular, what do they know *less* about than you?" Betty usually only thought about what others knew that she didn't. This asks Betty to think of when the opposite is true—when she knows more than the audience— to loosen up her thinking.

Betty thought for a few moments. "They know *everything* more," she laughed, clearly not completely believing what she was saying.

"EVERYTHING?" I teased her. "Look, if you are so good at imagining that others know so much, you ought to be just as good at imagining ways in which you know more than they do."

"Right, OK." Betty got serious. "I will come up with an answer. . . . What I have found is that a lot of people know less about their existence in terms of their worthwhileness and their self-esteem and self-concept." Betty's voice sounded hesitant, not completely convinced.

"So that is an area that you know more about than a lot of other people do. I noticed a little bit of hesitation as you said that. . . . I don't know if you already realize that for each person there are always areas in which you know more than they do, as well as areas in which they know more than you do. . . ."

I was making slow progress in loosening her all-or-none thinking, so I decided to try a different approach. "Now let me ask you something different. Do you think that the people who come to your group would be so stupid as to pick a presentation where they didn't think that they would learn something?" Rather than continuing to try to *change* Betty's belief that others know so much, now I was *utilizing* this belief to counter her stage fright.

Betty laughed, and I saw a strong physiological response. Color came into her face, and her muscles became a bit more smooth and supple—calm, yet livelier. This kind of physical shift is usually good evidence that a deep change in attitude has occurred—in contrast to an intellectual understanding. "Good point! Thank you. Thanks. That just pulls everything together," Betty stated with confidence and satisfaction. "I think I'll keep that one."

This brief interaction with Betty, which took about ten minutes, gave her a new way to think about giving presentations. It's important to recognize that this interaction was not a matter of my *convincing* or *advising* her that she was wrong and should think about things differently. I was able to enter Betty's own world and point out a way in which her *own* logic and beliefs provided her with a solution.

Betty's firm belief that "others are so smart" offered me a basis for changing her thinking about presenting. Since others were so smart, they *must* have the ability to decide whether they could learn something from Betty, and she could feel more comfortable about presenting. The *only* alternative is for Betty to change her mind about others being so smart, which would *also* lead to her feeling more comfortable about doing presentations!

This provides an example of one way to take an alternative point of view, so that someone has the opportunity to think about her own life in a way that makes her automatically feel good and resourceful. After this brief work with Betty, she felt very differently about giving a presentation— eager and self-assured, rather than uncomfortable and ambivalent. Her positive feelings were not a matter of effort—they were just there for her— as automatic as her previous response of discomfort had been.

I also want to point out that the new perspective I offered Betty was not "false confidence" that would blind her to her inadequacies. If I had gotten Betty to feel confident no matter who was in her group, she might have learned to just ignore the background and responses of the audience.

Instead, the perspective I offered her is one that I have when I teach. I assume that *everyone* in the room knows more than I do about *something*. Some people, some of the time, are even going to know more about what I am teaching than I do. That's inevitable, and it's also an opportunity for me to learn from them, which will benefit others the next time I teach. However, I also trust people's intelligence enough to select whether they want to be learning from me or not. I can have confidence in the judgement of the people who have decided they want to learn something from/with me and come to seminars.

One of the surprises for us as we have steeped ourselves in learning, using, and further developing NLP, is that the personal changes we make are usually fairly quick, as with Betty. This doesn't mean we can all completely transform ourselves in ten minutes. Sometimes it takes us *much* longer just to gather the information to find out what to do. Although for Betty only one change made the difference, sometimes a person needs two changes in belief or perspective, or five, or twenty, to get the desired overall change.

The field of NLP offers many ways to find out how our thinking creates limitations, and many ways to move toward solutions. If the first attempted solution doesn't work, we notice and move on to another possible solution.

Words don't have any energy unless they spark or trigger an image. The word in and of itself has nothing, nothing. One of the things I keep in touch with is, "What are the words that trigger images for people?" Then people follow the feeling of the image.

—Virginia Satir

2

Learning to Spell

Ben was a college student who had trouble with spelling all through his school years. He planned to look for a job that would require writing reports, and he was concerned that his poor spelling would be a serious obstacle. Spelling is a simple task, but like a lot of other simple tasks, it can cause misery and embarrassment if you can't do it.

When I asked Ben if he could spell the word "enough," he looked up and to his right, and then said uncertainly, "I think so." That gave me all the information I needed, to know *how* he spelled poorly. When most people look up and to their right, it indicates that they are activating the part of their brain that visualizes creatively. If you ask someone to visualize something that you can be fairly sure he's never seen before—such as a purple hippopotamus with large yellow spots on it—he'll almost always look up and to his right. (A small percentage of people—about 5%—are reversed, and consistently look up to their left. See Appendix I for an outline of these eye movements.)

Creative visualization is a marvelous skill that is essential in a wide range of creative activities. However, creative visualization is completely inappropriate for spelling, which is simply a rote memory task. In order to spell well, we have to spell words the way they have been spelled before, no matter how illogical that collection of letters might be. To do this, we need to activate the part of our brain that visualizes *remembered* images, not created ones.

8

If you ask someone to visualize a friend's face, or what her front door looks like, most people will look up to their left, because that gives them easy access to remembered images. (Again, about 5% will do the reverse, and consistently look up to their right instead.) Remembered images typically appear all at once, and they look the same as what the person saw when the remembered event originally occurred. Poor spellers are as capable as successful spellers; they simply access the wrong part of their brain. Like someone who searches for a cookie recipe in the "vegetables" section of a cookbook, they can't find the information they need. In order to spell well, we need to search in the part of our mind that has remembered pictures of words, and then simply copy them down. When a poor speller is taught how to use the part of his brain that has the appropriate information, he rapidly becomes a good speller—without the endless spelling tests that wasted so many hours of our lives in grade school.

Another important piece of information Ben gave me was that he was uncertain about whether he could spell the word or not. When a good speller looks at a remembered image of a word, he gets a feeling of familiarity that lets him know the word is correct. This feeling assures him that he knows how to spell the word. Since Ben was making up words each time, he couldn't get a feeling of familiarity that would let him know his spelling was correct.

Teaching Ben to spell well was simply a matter of rehearsal, training him to use the appropriate part of his mind to visualize remembered images, and then notice the feeling of familiarity that lets him know the image is correct. One of the easiest ways to teach this is to find a situation in which Ben already naturally does what I want him to do when he spells.

"Ben, I'd like you to think of someone who is a familiar friend.". . .

As Ben looked up to his left to remember his friend, I continued: "And then notice the feeling of familiarity you have that lets you know this is someone you know. . . .

"What you just did is exactly the same as the method that successful spellers use when they spell. They get a remembered image (gesturing with my hand toward where Ben had looked to remember his friend) and then they get a feeling of familiarity which lets them know the word is correct. Your brain actually already knows how to spell well; it just hasn't been applying this skill to the task of spelling.

"Now do the same thing with the word 'cat.' Look up there again (gesturing to Ben's upper left) and see the word appear all at once. As soon as you see the word clearly, notice the feeling of familiarity you have when you see that word."

Next I explained to Ben that his spelling problem had nothing to do with being slow or stupid. His grade school teachers simply had never been taught how to teach him to spell well. There are many skills schools still don't know how to teach well; many so-called "learning disabilities" are actually "*teaching* disabilities."

Since Ben had read lots of books, he already had many stored images of words that were spelled correctly. All he had to do to was look in the appropriate direction to see remembered images of them in his mind's eye.

I continued rehearsing Ben through another dozen words, gesturing each time to be sure he looked up and to his left. Then I continued asking him to visualize more words, as I stopped gesturing, to see if he would continue to look in the appropriate place automatically. Ben did, so I knew the new method of spelling was becoming automatic for him.

I had deliberately started with short words to make it easy for Ben. Before going on to longer words, I wanted to prepare him to think that long words will be just as easy as short words. Again, I do this by asking him to think of experiences that confirm this.

"Ben, can you make a picture in your mind's eye of the house or apartment you live in? (Ben: Yes.) Good. Now can you see some mountain you've seen, in the same way? (Ben: Yes.) Good. So it's just as easy for you to make an internal picture of something large as it is to make a picture of something small, right?"

"I guess so. I never thought of that before, but sure."

"And in the same way, it's just as easy to make a picture of a long word as it is to make a picture of a small word; it's still only one picture. Now I'm going to ask you to do the same process with some longer words, words that many people might assume are more difficult to visualize." I then went on to rehearse Ben through the same process with some longer words.

Then I asked him if he had any questions, both in order to answer them and to distract him temporarily. After talking a while, I asked Ben, "How do you spell 'rhythm'?" He immediately and automatically looked up to his left, indicating that his new way of spelling was automatic. If he hadn't looked up left, I would simply have gone back to rehearsing him through more words until it became automatic and unconscious. This process took about fifteen minutes.

More About Spelling

Notice that I never actually asked Ben to spell any words out loud. At this point I'm not concerned whether he can actually spell words well.

Once he has learned the ability to look for remembered images and check for the familiar feeling, he will quickly *become* better and better at spelling.

Since he has been spelling "creatively" for years, he now has in his mind lots of incorrect remembered images of the words he has misspelled. For a while he will continue to make some mistakes due to this. However, as he reads more and more words that are spelled correctly, his memory will become more and more accurate. And as he relies on remembered images and on his feelings to know when words are correct, he will also begin to notice when he is uncertain. (Previously he was uncertain most of the time.) That uncertainty will motivate him to ask someone or to look up the word in a dictionary. Each time he does this, the accuracy of his store of remembered images will improve, and his spelling will improve with it.

When Ben was a "creative" speller, it did him absolutely no good to look up a word, because the next time he'd just make it up again anyway, and not refer to his remembered image from looking it up. If you ask good spellers what they experience when they see a word misspelled, they'll usually say they're powerfully motivated to correct it. That same motivation is activated whenever they're uncertain about how to spell a word—they *have* to find the correct spelling!

An adult like Ben has already learned everything he needs to be a good speller except what I taught him. With small children, teaching successful spelling takes somewhat longer, because they have more to learn about letters and words, etc. However, using this method no child ever has to be a poor speller, and no child ever has to take a spelling test. When children learn to rely on remembered images, they will learn to spell correctly as long as they have lots of books to read. At least 90% of the many hours we all spent on spelling in grade school were probably totally unnecessary. What we *do* need to spell well is knowing how to use the part of our brain that stores remembered images, and a lot of time to read.

Other Ways to Spell Poorly

In addition to "creative spelling," there is one other major way to be a poor speller: to search in *auditory* memory. People who do this try to "sound out" words. Since about 40% of English words do not look the way they sound, the best you can do with this method is about 60%.

Yet despite this, most remedial spelling programs teach children to sound out words, what is called "phonics," or "phonetics." What makes this mistake particularly ironic is that you can't even spell "fonix" or "fonetiks" phonetically! (There is an old joke: "How do you spell "fish" phonetically?"

The answer is "ghoti"—gh as in enough, o as in women, and ti as in motion.)

One woman to whom we taught the NLP spelling strategy wrote in a letter afterwards, "I learned spelling by phonics almost exclusively. It is truly a wonder that now, at age 63, I catch my mistakes almost exclusively by the sense of sight—an NLP miracle."

In the Spanish language, *every* word looks exactly the way it sounds, so an auditory way of spelling could work. However, with only one exception all the Spanish-speaking people we met on a South American tour also used remembered visual images, and were good spellers. (The *only* poor speller we found tried to feel out the words kinesthetically!) We assume this is because it is so much faster to spell using a visual image than to sound out words. Images are almost instantaneous; sounds are sequential. When you hear a song, you hear the words and sounds in sequence. When you see sheet music for the same song, you can see it all at once.

Some people, of course, combine the two major ways of spelling poorly. First they sound out part of the word, and then they use creative visualization to try to change the sounds into letters!

Once I found a poor speller who said he felt bad anytime he was asked to spell a word. When I asked him to spell a word, he looked up left and then felt bad. I was puzzled at first, because the sequence he used—remembered visual image, followed by a feeling—was the sequence that all successful spellers use. When I asked him what he saw up there, he looked startled, and said, "I see my third grade teacher scowling at me," something he hadn't been consciously aware of before.

I asked if the part of him that made the picture of the third grade teacher would instead be willing to show him a picture of the word he had been asked to spell, and he got a positive indication that it was willing. (See chapter 8 for more about working in this way with "parts" of a person.) When I asked him to spell another word, he looked up left and then comfortably spelled the word out loud. Although he already was using the appropriate part of his brain for spelling, the content (the image of the teacher) was inappropriate to the task.

Once we found a good speller who used a unique way of spelling correctly. As a small child she had spontaneously decided on a color code for each letter of the alphabet. (She had also spontaneously color-coded the numbers from one to ten, and when she was later given a set of Cuisenaire rods, they were all the "wrong" color, which was very confusing to her!) When she spelled a word, she first saw all the letters in their individual colors. Then she knew the spelling was correct when all the letters changed to be the same color! Although she was accurate, this method was also *very* slow. She had always run out of time on spelling tests.

School districts and teachers are beginning to use the NLP spelling method to enhance their effectiveness. After June Jackson taught teachers in an Idaho school district the NLP spelling method, district-wide spelling scores for 1800 students improved in one year. The Director of Special Services reported the results: "The spelling subtest scores (on the Stanford Achievement test) gained 15 percentile points, moving from the 62nd to the 77th percentile! Prior to your workshops, we had been unable to influence this score favorably with any other methods."

Nancy Gaudette, a Washington middle school teacher who has been using the NLP spelling strategy both in her classroom, and to teach other teachers, commented: "It's turned non-spellers into spellers, and they love it. It's fascinating that now they enjoy something they hated so much before. It made such a difference on spelling test scores for our school that the state department noticed and became interested in our spelling program."

Although spelling is a simple task, there is considerable variety in the ways that people attempt to accomplish it. The same variety appears when you study how people learn, make decisions, or motivate themselves. Their success or failure at these more complex tasks is also a direct consequence of the mental sequence they use, and that sequence can also be changed to make the task easy. (See chapters 15 and 16.)

3 *Becoming More Independent in Relationships*

Ann and Bob had been married for seven years. Although most things were going well for them, they asked for help with a problem that had been an irritation ever since they met. As Bob described it, Ann was insecure about their relationship, and was continually asking for reassurance. In order for Ann to be reassured, Bob had to tell her that he loved her eight or ten times a day. If he didn't, Ann would start asking him if he loved her, and wouldn't be satisfied until he told her, in an appropriately warm and soft tone of voice.

Bob found this irritating, and sometimes even a bit insulting. He showed his love in many ways, and he touched her lovingly many times a day. If they had a serious disagreement about anything, Ann would be sure that Bob didn't love her, and for days after the argument was over she would need an extra dose of reassurance.

On the surface this seemed like a simple case of using different evidence for being loved. Ann needed to *hear* loving words in order to know that Bob loved her, while Bob relied on *seeing* Ann's smiling face and *feeling* her loving touch. Many couples have different ways of knowing they are loved. As Bob put it, "I know she loves me just by the way she looks and feels; I don't know why she has to hear it ten times a day. Anybody can say words; it's the actions that count." For Ann, on the other hand, Bob's words mattered almost more than his touch.

14

Even though it felt unnatural to him, Bob had gotten into the habit of telling Ann that he loved her throughout the day, and this had helped a lot. However, when they got angry at each other—as all couples do—he found it hard to feel loving. And if he did tell Ann that he loved her, his tone of voice was unconvincing until the dispute was completely resolved. This is what made their arguments so devastating to Ann.

Ann agreed that Bob often touched her lovingly, and did many considerate things for her. However, it was only when he told her that he loved her that she really felt loved. "I feel really wonderful when he tells me he loves me in that warm low tone he has; I feel safe and complete." As she said this, Ann smiled, her face softened, and her shoulders settled slightly. "The good feeling lasts for a time, but then after a while the feelings start to fade, and I start wondering again."

This gave me important information. The problem wasn't just the different kinds of evidence that Ann and Bob used to know that they were loved. The problem was that for Ann, this sense of being loved didn't last very long, and it seemed to leave Ann in a more vulnerable position. When Bob was feeling loving and said so, Ann could feel good, but what about when he *didn't* feel loving right then, or didn't *say* so?

Self Concept: Knowing Who We Are

Many of us seek reassurance from others for something we seldom or never experience within ourselves. If we don't think we are capable, or sexy, or lovable, or worthwhile, we often continually look for others who will tell us that we are. It can be important to develop an inner sense of having these qualities, so that we don't desperately need the external verification. I decided to find out if this would make a difference for Ann.

I asked Ann if she thought of herself as a lovable person. Ann looked a little startled and confused, and said, "Lovable isn't something you *are!* Love is something you *get* from other people."

Obviously being lovable was not part of Ann's self-concept, and I was on the right track. If Ann thought about being lovable as a characteristic of *herself,* then the good feelings would probably stay with her through time.

When I asked Ann, "What would it be like if you thought of yourself as being lovable?" she replied, "That's weird!"

Ann's response was further evidence that being able to think of herself as lovable would be useful to her.

Maintaining Balance with Couples

At this point some readers might wonder if by focusing on Ann, I'm acting as if she is "broken" or "at fault." Indeed this is always an important concern to keep in mind when working with a couple. If the change process *isn't* handled carefully, one or the other might get the message that they are "at fault." To prevent this from happening, I shared some of my approach to working with couples with Ann and Bob.

"When couples get together and stay together, my assumption is that each member of the couple has a *different* set of resources—that's what attracts people to each other—and each has about the same *amount* of resourcefulness. *Each* of us also has areas in which we can become more resourceful. The more we take advantage of opportunities to do that, the more we can get what we want in our lives. I want to make sure I'm available to assist *both* of you in gaining the new choices you want, so that no one gets 'left behind.' This is an area where it seems, Ann, that you might want more empowering choices. Is that right?" (Ann nods emphatically.) "And while I go ahead with Ann, I'd like you, Bob, to keep in the back of your mind the question 'Where do *I* want more choices in this relationship?' so you make sure you also get what you want."

Creating a Durable Sense of Self

The easiest way for me to assist Ann in creating a durable way for her to think of herself as lovable is to find out how she already does this with something else. By asking her about something that *is* part of her self-concept, I can go on to find out how she thinks of this.

"Ann, what is something you know within yourself is true about you—no matter what someone else might think?"

"Well, I guess I'm persistent. . . . I'm intelligent. . . . I know I'm kind."

When Ann talked about being persistent, she qualified it with "I guess." In contrast, when she spoke of being kind, she expressed her certainty with, "I know."

"How do you know you're kind, Ann? What internal experience gives you that knowing that you're kind?"

"Well when I think of being kind, I feel soft and warm."

"That's the feeling you associate with being kind, but I'm asking you a different question. How do you *know* you're a kind person?"

Ann paused for a moment. "Well, I think about times when I've been kind." As she did this, she glanced to her left and gestured briefly with her left hand. This was an indication to me of where in her personal space she sees these images of being kind.

"Good. How do you think of those times that you've been kind? Do you talk to yourself, do you see pictures, or do you feel the movements that you make when you've been kind?"

"Well, I see pictures of when I've been kind to someone." Ann gestured again with her left hand. There's a whole bunch of them, sort of in a row. They're fairly small, about arm's length."

"Good. That's the information you use to know you're a kind person. Now, what happens to your sense of yourself as a kind person if you find that you've been unkind to someone, either by accident or because you were irritated or something?" By asking this I'm testing to find out if her sense of being a kind person persists through time, even in the face of occasional lapses.

"Well, I'm concerned, and I do what I can to try to clear up the situation, but I still know I'm a kind person."

"Good. The fact that you try to make things right when you've been unkind is further evidence that you're a kind person, right?"

Ann looked thoughtful. "Well, I never thought about it that way. I guess that's true. I think I usually just think of all the other times I've been kind."

"Would you have any objection to thinking of yourself as a lovable person in the same way that you think of yourself as a kind person?"

"It still seems strange. . . . I've just never thought of being loved that way before. I guess if I had that same kind of sense of being loved, it wouldn't matter as much whether Bob says he loves me, would it? . . . No, I have no objection. That might be a good idea." As Ann carefully thought through the implications of my question, I saw no nonverbal indications of any objections. She was just carefully thinking it through.

"Good. Close your eyes and think of one example of your being lovable and loving, a time when you created an experience of loving and being loved.". . . (Ann nods.) "Now put that picture into the *same place* as one of the pictures of your being kind. Make it exactly the same as the picture of kindness; the same size, the same distance from you, etc.". . . (Ann moves her head to the left, indicating that she is moving the picture to the appropriate location, and nods again.) "Now think of another example of loving and being loved, perhaps with a different person or in a different situation.". . . (Ann nods.) "Now put this one over there with the other picture. Continue doing this until you have a whole bunch of pictures sort of in a row, fairly small, at arm's length." I deliberately used the same words and phrases that Ann initially used to describe her pictures of being kind, to help her create the same inner knowing that lets her know she is a kind person. "Let me know if you need any assistance, and let me know when you're done.". . .

Ann spent a minute or two patiently assembling pictures of herself being lovable and loving, and then said, "OK. I'm done."

"OK. Open your eyes. That seemed to go smoothly. Do you have any questions?"

"No. It was interesting. At first it still seemed strange, but it does work. With each picture I put over there, I felt a little more solid about it. For some reason, it seemed much better to think of being *loving,* than being lovable. I'm more in charge if I'm loving, and I can't *be* loving unless I'm also lov*able,* in a way."

"So are you a loving/lovable person?" By asking this I'm making a first test to see if the change is still there.

Ann's eyes flicker to the left briefly. "Yes, I am. I can see that now." As always, her nonverbal behavior—her eyes looking to the left, and her matter-of-fact tone of voice—are more important indications than her verbal answer.

"Now Bob, in a moment I want you to tell Ann that you love her. Ann, when he does that, I want you to notice if anything is different from before. Go ahead Bob."

(Softly) "Ann, I love you."

Ann smiled, while tilting her head slightly. "It's still nice to hear him say it, but it's like I already know it. It's like sometimes when I know I've done a good job and then someone compliments me. It's nice to have someone else notice, but I already know it."

"Now, Ann, close your eyes and imagine it's three weeks from now. During all that time Bob has acted the same toward you in every way, except he hasn't said 'I love you' once in those three weeks. What is that like for you?"

Ann smiled broadly. "That's funny. I heard an internal voice say sort of huffily, 'Well! It's about time he did!' But it was kind of like a joke. It's no big deal."

It's now over two years since this session, which took about a half-hour. Both Ann and Bob agree that it's no longer an issue. He tells her he loves her a few times a week, and she almost never asks. With her inner knowledge of being loved, Ann is no longer dependent on Bob for reassurance, and they both enjoy each other more. When they get into

— Focus on *giving* love, instead of *receiving* love,

arguments, it's still unpleasant, but Ann isn't devastated, and responds much more resourcefully.

Developing our Sense of Self

In further work with Ann and Bob, we assisted both of them in making other shifts to enable them to have an even better relationship. In this example, Ann was the one who gained an additional choice. Whenever working with a couple, it's important to maintain balance by adding to *both* their choices, for several reasons. If we only gave Ann new choices, she and Bob might both conclude that Ann was the "problem" in their relationship. This view could get in the way of their developing a better relationship. Another possible consequence is that Ann might become so capable and resourceful, that if Bob didn't also gain new choices, she might become less satisfied with him as a partner. Most partners are quick to perceive the advantages for *them* in gaining additional choices, as well as the ways in which their relationship will improve.

Not everyone has a row of self-image pictures off to the left the way Ann does, but everyone has *some* way to think of their personal abilities or characteristics. It is this kind of internal structure that gives every person a sense of self that continues through time. In Ann's case, we simply built a representation of the quality of being loving/lovable that she didn't previously have.

Although it's not always as easy to change the self-image as it was with Ann, the principle is the same: find out *how* the person thinks of herself, and change it directly. We have used this effectively with many people who want to feel lovable, sexy, or any other characteristic.

Ann just *didn't have* a way to think of herself as lovable. Some people go farther, and have a vivid and complete representation of themselves as *not* lovable or *not* something else. They may have a self-image that is filled with pictures of failures, mistakes, humiliations, etc. Whether it's a child who assumes he will fail in school or an adult who believes she can never have a fulfilling relationship, a "poor self-image" typically results in familiar self-defeating behavior. In that case, it's not simply a matter of building a positive sense of self. We need to change these negative images before giving the person a more positive and useful self-image. A method for directly changing limiting beliefs is presented in chapter 7 of *Using Your Brain for a Change,* by Richard Bandler.

On the other hand, some people are completely convinced they are wonderful, but others don't agree with them. They have a self-concept that lasts through time—but it's inaccurate, and it doesn't respond to feedback.

A person may think he's kind, yet continually do cruel things without noticing it. A person may think he's a wonderful joke-teller, yet no one ever laughs. This same process can be used in reverse to help these people, though it's somewhat harder, and the people who need it most are the least likely to ask for it!

If we recognize this in ourselves, we may find it useful to use the same process in reverse to *weaken* our self-concept for that trait. We can find something we're *not* so convinced of, and make the images of our joke-telling ability like *that.* We can also build in a way to notice how other people respond when we're "unfunny" as well as "funny."

Our self-concept affects our behavior in powerful ways. The key is to notice *how* adjusting it affects our behavior, and make only adjustments that result in making our lives better. Does *knowing you are lovable* make you a more loving, responsive, resourceful person? Or does it make someone into a "princess" who ignores complaints from her friends and family? Does *knowing you are sexy* make you enjoy your sexuality more, and make you act in ways your partner also enjoys more? Or does it make you ignore your partner's wishes, and lead to arguments? When this inner knowledge makes us more the person we want to be and makes our relationships better, it is useful. As I was working with Ann, I observed closely to notice whether or not the shift would make *her* more resourceful and also have a positive impact on her relationship with Bob.

Codependence

In a curious mirror-image, many people are actually dependent on someone *else* being dependent. This "codependent" behavior is often seen in spouses and children of alcoholics and other drug-abusers. In some ways, the label "codependent" makes the problem harder to change. Like categories such as "teenager," "delinquent," etc., it *can* make what is actually a changeable behavior pattern *seem* like an unchanging trait. Our experience is that when we understand the structure of any difficulty, including codependence, adding new choices is usually easy.

With Ann, we worked directly with the mental structure of her self-concept. However, it's possible to make the same kinds of changes conversationally, without taking the time to discover the details of the mental structure.

Sarah was a warm and sensitive person who hated to hurt others' feelings. For most of her married years, she had been very accepting of her husband, who had a drinking problem. Sarah asked for help in being able to have more of her own life, instead of always helping others.

"I would like to continue having a relationship with some people, but I would like it to have some separation from my private life and my social life."

"So what stops you from already having that?"

"I have a real sense that I don't want to hurt their feelings. They end up showing up at my house, and I find it hard to say 'No' to them. . . . I also tend to have a strong sense about who is pretty centered and who isn't. If I know someone can take care of themselves, I don't feel this way."

"Oh, I see. You only do this with the people who are weak and dependent!" I said, joking yet serious. (Sarah nods.) "So it's the people who are *already* weak that you make into *more* of a dependent person, is that it?" (Sarah laughs, nods, and puts her hand on her chest.) "So you don't do this with the people who can take it."

"No, I don't."

"You just do it to people who can't handle it."

"Yeah. Right!" Sarah laughs and nods.

"So with people who are dependent already, you're going to make them worse, is that it?". . .

"I'm not really clear how I do it, though."

"Well, think how many people you've hurt in that way, in the past. . . . How many people have you really made into groveling, sniveling, totally dependent and incapable people? They may have *started* doing this on their own, but you helped them along the way."

"It's *not* that bad!" Sarah laughed. "It's just that there are times that—"

"How bad is it?"

(Still laughing) "It's, . . . it's getting better, *instantly!*"

"So how is it that now you're going to be more respectful of these people by setting your own limits, . . . in a more respectful way, in a way that really respects them as human beings who can take care of themselves, . . . rather than make them more dependent?". . .

"Yeah, I'm not real clear about that."

"You're not clear about exactly how. So, *consciously* you don't know just yet how that's going to occur."

"Right."

"How many times will you do this before you realize exactly how it is that you did it?"

(Laughing) "*One* more time!"

"When you look back on it, do you think that you'll understand just how that shift occurred? . . . Or is it something that'll be a more intuitive kind of thing that will forever be a puzzle to you?"

"No, it won't forever be a puzzle to me. Yeah, one piece is being more conscious about what I'm doing, what the interaction is."

"OK. Now, how can someone's feelings being hurt in the moment be helpful to that same person in the long run and make them into a stronger and better human being?" Although I was asking a question, I stated it emphatically.

Sarah nods her head and takes a deep breath. "Bingo! Yeah. That's— Yeah. That's the key piece right there. Because that opens it up." Sarah's expression shifted, and she looked more relaxed and calm, indicating that she was seeing things differently.

"Being nice now can be really nasty later, because you set people up for a life of dependency. A lot of parents have done that. They try to be nice to their kids and they raise children who don't know how to be grown-ups. They thought they were being nice, but they didn't prepare their children for standing on their own two feet."

(Nodding and laughing) "I'm not nice to my kids."

"I'm glad that at least you've been a good mother, even though you haven't been a good friend to some of these other people."

"Hard Rock Cafe, Yup! OK." (nodding)

"So, you're all set?"

"Yes!"

"I'm glad that you're so sure of this. Now, think of one of the worst of these people, a real 'cling-on.' When you imagine that person in the future, is there anything that could get you to be inconsiderate again in the same way you were in the past? Or will you have those ways of respecting yourself in the same way that you really respect who they are, and who they are going to be.". . .

"Survival. A life-and-death situation would make me very disrespectful of myself."

"Well, but then it's not disrespectful!"

"But then it's not disrespectful. Yeah. It would have to be critical."

"Yeah. And that's the time when people really *do* need your help, and it's not insulting. If somebody's just been run over by a truck and broke both legs, it's not insulting to ask, 'Can I help you onto the stretcher?' That's not the time to say 'I'm sorry, I want you to stand on your own two feet.' Right? It's when their legs are intact and you do that that it's disrespectful."

"OK." Sarah nodded. "That's a real different way to look at it. Thanks."

The key intervention was to broaden Sarah's time frame, pointing out that her "being nice" in the moment actually harmed people in the long run.

However, this comment was only effective because of the groundwork I had laid earlier in this conversation: bringing to her attention that she was catering to others' dependency, and probably harming them by making them more dependent and less capable. "Being nice" is very important to Sarah. Rather than try to change her mind about being nice, I *utilized* it to get her to do what would benefit others in the long run, even if they might have "hurt feelings" in the present. This allows Sarah to have more of a life of her own, freeing her of having to respond to everyone else's needs and wishes.

Although this was a significant change for Sarah, she had already benefitted from earlier sessions in ways that supported her making this shift, and there was more to be done. After this session she continued moving forward in other related areas of her life.

Many people in Sarah's situation are still responding to having been abused or mistreated in the past (see chapter 7) and often they are troubled by shame (see chapter 14) and a poor self-image as well. For Sarah, and for many others in this situation, dealing with these other areas is useful in arriving at a more complete resolution.

Self: A Source You Can Always Count on

As we explored her goals, Gail became aware of an issue that was keeping her more tense and nervous than she wanted to be. She had a deep fear of being abandoned. This kept her from feeling secure, enjoying herself, and acting spontaneously in many situations. Since Gail felt most afraid of losing her husband, we worked with that.

"What would you lose if you lost your husband?" I asked. With a few more questions, it became clear that Gail was most concerned that if she lost her husband, she would lose his love. As Gail talked about her husband, and her feelings that she needed certain things from him, she always looked off to a particular spot, a little to her left.

"Being loved is very important," I agreed with Gail. "It's important enough that it's worth making sure you get it. And the way you can make *sure* you get it, is to get it from someone who you can count on to always be there, and that's *you!*" Gail was smiling. The idea obviously appealed to her.

"Now, you know that spot in front of you where you've seen your husband in your mind's eye?. . ." I gestured to where she had been looking and Gail nodded. "Notice what it is like when instead of seeing your husband there, you imagine yourself giving you the love you want. What happens as you see yourself giving you this love, and you enjoy getting it?"

Gail's face gained color, and her tense shoulders and back began to relax. "I like that."

"You may want to move that other you in even closer. . . . And now you can explore stepping into the you over there who is doing the loving, and feel what it is like to *be* her, loving Gail. . . . You can enjoy that position, too."

Now Gail looked even more resourceful. "I want to come a little closer and put my arm around myself," Gail responded.

"Great. And when you've enjoyed that completely, you can merge back into yourself, with all of these good feelings extending even more around you."

After this session, Gail described feeling more secure, and more able to give her husband love instead of focusing on needing love *from* him.

Alternative to Abandonment: Giving to Oneself

Much has been written in the literature on codependence about the overattachment or "enmeshment" many people experience, and the resulting fear of abandonment. If we consider ourselves dependent on others for something essential, as Gail did, it can be very frightening to contemplate the possibility of losing them. What they need is a positive replacement that enhances their sense of self, as I offered Gail.

One of our colleagues, Robert McDonald, noticed in his work with codependency that many people complaining of this problem quite literally have inner images of being physically attached to a parent, spouse, or other important person. One man said it was as if his father was attached to his chest. A woman said it was as if her mother was small and curled up, attached to her right side like a barnacle. Other people imagine cords connecting them to someone else.

While at first this may seem strange, it also makes perfect sense. Feeling dependent, like every experience we have, must have an internal mental structure. When someone is codependent on someone else, it makes sense that they need to experience a close connection. A tight cord or a body connection are typical ways people experience codependence.

If these people imagine disconnecting themselves from the other person, they typically become worried about abandonment. To accomplish what these people really want, Robert and I developed the following process. He has been using this process in workshops, with powerful results.

— must her, an internal mental structure,

Releasing Codependence: Reconnecting with Self

Find a quiet, private location where you can let your attention turn inward for 15 to 20 minutes without distraction, and go through this process standing up.

1. Identify the Other. Think of someone you think you are codependent or overinvolved with. For most people this is a parent or a close loved one. Whether the overinvolvement is minor or major, you can benefit from this process.

2. Become Aware of Your Overconnection to this Other. Imagine that this person is standing in the room with you. If you don't see internal images, just "sensing" or pretending that you are doing these steps will work equally well. Walk all around the other. Notice what she looks like. Touch her to notice what she feels like, and sense your feelings of being with her. Especially pay attention to your feelings of being overly connected with this person. Now notice *how you* experience yourself as being connected. Does it seem like you are physically attached somehow? Is it a direct connection between your body and hers, or is there a cord or other means of connection? Notice where the attachment is; where does it connect with your body, and where does it connect with the other person's body? Many people experience this connection in the stomach, chest, or groin area. Let yourself get a full experience of the quality of this connection—how it looks and feels.

3. Temporary Independence. Now try severing this connection for a moment, just to notice what it would be like. You could do this by imagining that your hand was a razor-sharp knife, and you could cut the cord, or dissolve it or sever it in some other way. . . . Most people are very uncomfortable thinking of separating at this point, and this is a sign that this connection has served an important purpose. You don't need to really disconnect yet, because you aren't ready to do that comfortably until you have a solid replacement ready.

4. Find the Positive Purposes. Now ask yourself on the inside, "What do I really want from the other person that would satisfy me?" . . . Then ask "And what would that do for me that's positive?" until you get a really core answer, such as security, safety, protection, love or being worthwhile. . . .

5. Develop Your Evolving Self. Now turn to your right (some people will prefer to turn to the left), and create a full three-dimensional image of the you who has evolved beyond your current level of resourcefulness. This is the you who is several steps ahead, who has already resolved the issues you are now dealing with, who loves, appreciates, and wants to nurture and protect you. This is the you who can provide what you learned you really wanted in Step 4. You can notice how she moves, her expression, how she sounds, what it's like to touch this you. If you don't "see" this resourceful self, you can just "sense" what she's like. Some people sense a warmth or a glow around this resourceful self.

6. Transform the Connection with Other into Connection with Self. Turn again to the attached "Other." See and feel the connection. Then sever the connection with this "other person" and immediately reconnect with your Evolving Self in the same way that you had been connected to the other person. Enjoy the feelings of being interdependent with someone you can really count on: yourself. Thank this you for being here for you. Enjoy receiving from yourself what you had wanted from the other person. This is the you who can go forward for you into your future, making way for you—your constant companion who is with you to check things out for you and to make sure you are safe.

7. Respecting the Other. Look back at your "Other," and notice the severed connection. See that the other person has the option of reconnecting the cord to herself. You can imagine her cord attaching itself to an appropriate spot on herself. If the cord came out of the navel, you might see it go up to the other person's heart. If there was no cord, you can envision this "Other" as physically connected to her own "evolving self," just as you now are. This can give you the secure knowledge that this other person will also now be better off with a greater sense of themselves. Notice how you can now be more fully present with this person.

8. Adding to Your Connection with Self. Now turn back to your evolved self, with whom you are now connected. Actually step into this evolved self, so that now you are looking back at yourself. Feel what it is like to be resourceful and giving to yourself. After enjoying the feelings of being this self, you can bring the resourcefulness of this self back into you, as you step back into the you of the present.

9. Going into the Future. Notice what it's like to have this new resourcefulness with you as you imagine relating to other people on this more solid footing. Imagine what it will be like to go into your future with your evolving self as your companion. You may get a sense of how this evolving self goes about handling difficulties.

Not Magic, But Powerful

After seminars, Robert has received many positive reports from participants. One woman who had experienced a heart-to-heart attachment to her husband with a cord joining their chests, said:

"There has been a definite change in my life; I'm not as needy of my husband. Before I had abandonment feelings whenever he would go away for a while. My heart is now filled with a lot of love where a lot of ache used to be whenever my husband was gone. I automatically see my wonderful glowing self. It automatically comes in if I start to hang on him."

Becky had an attachment to her mother, with the cord going through her left side and into her back, along her spine. The cord was connected to her mother's body in the same way. Then Becky noticed that this same kind of attachment went from her mother to her grandmother, and from her to her great grandmother and so on, with the cords attaching in the same place on each. Becky called this "the lonely martyrdom of being female" in her family, and said:

"Doing this exercise was successful. I now catch myself 'doing mom' and stop. I notice myself doing something like that attached line, and think, 'Oh, that's her, that's not me.' So on a daily basis I reaffirm the connection with my new self. Issues come up, but now I have choice. This pattern was not magic. It doesn't come out of the sky. I have to be responsible for myself on a daily basis. But it was very powerful to be able to see that line.
"It has been a known fact that throughout my family's history, the women have had a physical back misalignment. I have had that also. When I noticed that, I said, 'It stops with me.' What was powerful was the full understanding of the actual physical back misalignment that was cross-generational. I don't have to do that. It's ending with me."

The processes in this chapter can help us build a healthy ability to stand on our own feet and feel our own sense of self. This does not mean learning to be alone. Rather this is what allows us to be together with other human beings in ways that are fully respectful of everyone.

4 *Healing Traumas*

When Sally was away from her eight-year-old son for more than a day, she became anxious any time she thought of him. This was especially true if she talked to him on the phone, and she wanted to have a more resourceful response. Since I had met her at a professional conference that was far from her home, it was easy to test her response. When I asked her to think of her son, she became tense, and her breathing stopped temporarily.

When I asked her how she thought of her son, she said it was a dim, still picture, far away, "with a lot of air in between him and me." When she saw that image, she felt as if she were losing him, which created her anxious feelings. When I asked her to try moving the picture of her son closer, Sally felt much better.

I could have eliminated her anxiety by directly changing this image of her son. However, Sally had already told me that she knew her anxiety stemmed from a traumatic experience she'd had when she was seven years old, which continued to bother her. At that time her father disappeared unexpectedly for about five days. No one had any idea where he was, if he was ever coming back, or whether he was dead or alive. Sally said she felt totally abandoned, lost and frightened. This experience had "imprinted" itself in Sally's emotional life, and now she had this same feeling when she was away from her son.

If I had simply changed the way she thought of her son, only that one isolated experience would be changed. She would still be left with her unpleasant childhood memory, and it is likely that this memory also caused other difficulties in her life. If I can change the childhood memory, then all the experiences that it affects will also be changed. By doing this, I can give her the change that she is asking for, and many other additional benefits as well.

How Sally Sees a Positive Imprint Experience

The first step is to find out how Sally thinks of a powerful *positive* memory that also strongly affects her behavior. These impactful experiences are often called "imprint" experiences. "Sally, I want you to think of a memory that is a really positive resource for you now. It might have been pleasant or unpleasant at the time it occurred, but somehow you learned something that made that memory have a powerful and positive impact on your actions in the present. It doesn't matter what it is, as long as you experience it as powerful and positive now. . . . When you have selected one, I want you to think of that memory the way you think of it when it has that powerful impact on you. Notice how you experience it."

When Sally went back to the memory she had selected, she smiled, her breathing deepened, and her back straightened a bit. Clearly this was exactly the kind of powerful memory I wanted her to find.

"Now, Sally, I want you to think of an ordinary memory that is of little consequence. It could be brushing your teeth this morning, putting on your clothes, or anything like that.

"Next I want you to compare those two memories. As you compare them, you can notice the differences that make one powerful and the other ordinary. For instance, one might be a movie while the other is a still picture. One might be in color while the other is black and white. One might have sound, while the other is silent."

"The ordinary one is small and still, like a black-and-white snapshot. The powerful one is all around me, like I'm actually there in it. It's moving and the colors are very soft pastels like a Monet painting; I love them. And there's a pleasant sound. There's no sound in the ordinary one."

Creating a New Positive Imprint

"Now I want you to set those experiences aside temporarily, while I ask you a very important question. What experience could you have had *before* your father's disappearance that would have made it much easier for you to go through his disappearance? What specific experience could have prepared you for it, so that you didn't need to feel those awful feelings of being lost and abandoned?"

"My father was everything to me at that time. I think if someone I trusted had told me that he would always be there and protect me no matter what else happened, that would have made it much easier—maybe if my brother had said that to me."

"Good. That's certainly the kind of thing that can make a big difference, so let's try it. Close you eyes and go back to being six or seven years old, well *before* your father left. *Build* a detailed experience of your brother talking to you and reassuring you. As you do that, be sure to make that experience just like the positive powerful memory you recalled earlier. Build this new experience so that it's all around you, moving, with sound, and with those soft pastel colors that you love so much. You can keep revising and adjusting that experience as much as you like, in order to make it the kind of memory that will allow you to respond resourcefully to your father's unexpected absence later. Take all the time you need, and nod your head when you have finished building it to your satisfaction.". . .

As Sally began to build this new memory, her breathing deepened, she smiled, and her back straightened in the same way as when she recalled the original positive memory. This let me know that Sally's *new* memory would be an equally powerful resource. After about a minute, she nodded.

Using the New Imprint for a Powerful Change

"Next I want you to come rapidly forward through time, bringing the impact of this positive experience with your brother along with you. As you move forward through time, you can notice how all your later experiences are shifted and reevaluated in the light of that experience with your brother. Realizing that much of this will happen at an unconscious level, come rapidly up through time. When you reach the present, stop and see yourself moving on into the future, seeing how you will be different as a result of this experience with your brother. Again, take all the time you need, and open your eyes when you're done.". . .

After about a minute, Sally opened her eyes. "That was interesting," she said. "Coming forward in time was sort of like that part at the end of the movie *2001* where all the stuff is shooting past on both sides. When I came to the time when my father left, I just sort of sailed through it. . . . And when I think about it now, it's very different. I was still concerned, but I knew my brother would be there. I feel bigger, somehow; I feel more powerful."

"That all sounds good. Now think about your son, and find out how you feel.". . .

"I feel fine now. He doesn't seem so far way any more. I even tried making that small, dim, far-away picture, but it doesn't affect me."

This process took approximately fifteen minutes. The next day Sally told me that she had called her son the previous evening and she had felt fine. The anxiety had not returned.

Although I have been unable to reach Sally for long-term follow-up, I know from using this method with many other people that the results usually last, and sometimes even become more powerful over time.

Sexual Response

Beverly was unhappy with what she called her "phobia of sex" and reluctance to get involved with a man. She had struggled with this aversion to sex and involvement ever since she'd gone through a very difficult experience with an earlier relationship. Beverly had been living with a man when she accidentally became pregnant. The man withdrew, leaving her to deal with it alone. Even though Beverly had been opposed to abortion, and thought she would never consider it, she made the difficult decision to have one. This experience left Beverly avoiding intimacy and sexual involvement.

Since Beverly's complaint stemmed from an earlier traumatic experience, I utilized the same process that I had used with Sally. When choosing a resource experience, Beverly decided to build a previous experience of having caused a friend's death through her error, and then having come to terms with her mistake and its consequences. When she first told me that this was what she wanted to build as a resource, I was a bit surprised, since most people would choose a more "positive" experience. After some thought, I decided that she was wiser than I; she had chosen exactly the experience that would prepare *her* to deal with the abortion.

When I talked with her about two months later, she said that she definitely felt a new openness and willingness to form a relationship with a man, but no one she knew at the time seemed right for this. After two more months, she called and left this message: "The acid test arrived, and I passed with flying colors." She had found someone special to love, and was enjoying her intimacy and sexual involvement, with no trace of the old fear and reluctance.

The Method

This process, called the "decision destroyer," was recently developed by Richard Bandler, one of the co-developers of NLP. It utilizes a major assumption that most of us have about our lives: that the past influences the present and future. If traumatic past experiences can cause problems later, it also makes sense that positive learning experiences can serve as resources later.

All of us make "conclusions" or "decisions" based on the experiences we have in life. These conclusions can strongly affect how we respond to later experiences. Many of our beliefs were formed by one intensely significant experience in the past; others by a series of less intense experiences.

For example, Sal had an early experience that made him conclude he couldn't learn. When Sal was three, he grabbed a puzzle off the shelf and tried to put it together. The puzzle was for six-year-olds, but Sal didn't know that. He didn't even fully comprehend that six-year-olds could do things that three-year-olds couldn't. He was only aware that he tried and tried, but couldn't get the puzzle together.

Sal's parents were in the room observing his growing frustration. They were disconcerted by Sal's whimpering about the puzzle and didn't know what to do. Finally his father said, out of his own frustration, "Oh, just put that puzzle away. You can't seem to learn anything anyway!" The next time Sal tried to put a puzzle together and got stuck, he remembered the last time he had tried and failed, and what his father had said. "He's right. I can't learn," he thought. He put the puzzle away without trying very hard, and turned to something "easy" to do.

Later young Sal was trying to take apart an old clock with a screwdriver. He liked unscrewing things. Sometimes it takes a little figuring out to determine what to unscrew in what order, and Sal soon encountered something he couldn't immediately see how to take apart. Thinking back to his earlier experiences of failure, Sal didn't try very hard. He quickly put the clock down, thinking this was more evidence that he couldn't do things.

Over the years, Sal had many more experiences supporting his conclusion that he couldn't do things. Based on Sal's early experience, he was prepared to think of later events in the same way—strengthening his early conclusion about his limitations.

In contrast, Glen had an early experience that colored his entire future, in a much more positive way. When Glen was four, his family moved from the desert to Ohio, where there were lots of trees. Glen wasn't accustomed to all the trees and was eager to climb them. After selecting his first climbing prospect, Glen moved up from one branch to the next, excited about this new activity. When he was quite high up, Glen looked around, pleased, and decided it was time to get down. That was the first time it had occurred to Glen to look down, and he became terrified. He clutched the branch, and screamed to his mother who was around the corner of the house. "Help, I can't get down!"

Glen's mother came running, and was a bit nervous herself at seeing

Glen so high in the tree. However, she calmly said, "Glen, you're holding on tightly, and that's good. Now you managed to get *up* that tree, and if you can find a way to get up, you can find a way to get down. Can you reach down with one foot and feel for a branch that feels solid, and will hold your weight?" Glen felt calmer just hearing his mother's voice. He had a sense of competence about himself as he realized that he *had* climbed all that way up by himself. He settled down to the job of finding his way down, slowly and carefully, until he was safely at the bottom. Although he was more careful about climbing trees in the future, Glen came down with a sense of competence—that *he* could figure something out on his own.

This experience stuck with Glen. When he started school and encountered tasks that were difficult, Glen would think about climbing the tree, realize that he could figure things out, and kept trying and asking questions until he *did* figure them out. He kept working at things until he succeeded, sometimes long after his friends had given up. Each success became further confirmation that Glen could learn and succeed at things.

When we form unuseful conclusions, as Sal did, it's usually because at the time we didn't understand that *other* people are limited in some way. Sal's father certainly didn't *mean* to make him feel like a failure. He was just frustrated and didn't know what else to do. In situations like this, children often think badly of themselves, rather than just understanding that someone else is limited. Understanding how these formative experiences work gives us the key to knowing how to produce powerful changes in traumatic experiences in our own past history.

It can be very difficult to try to change a traumatic experience directly, because the person has such a strong response to the trauma. That's like trying to build a house during an earthquake. However, when you create a positive healing experience *before* the trauma occurs, there is no interference. If you build a house well, it can easily stand up to a later earthquake. By giving the new memory the same characteristics of a powerful positive memory, you make sure that it will have the strength to influence later events in a positive way. Even though the person consciously knows he created this memory, those characteristics still give it the unconscious power of an actual memory. Our audiotape "The Decision Destroyer" includes another complete example, as well as discussion (see Appendix II).

Changing an Abusive Past

Although Sally and Beverly had only one traumatic experience, this method is particularly useful for people who had a series of traumatic experiences over a long period of time. Building one powerful new memory can revise a long history of unpleasantness for someone with an abusive or exploitive childhood, and be a step toward creating a more resourceful self.

Kristen had repeated experiences of abuse in her childhood, and wanted to gain more resolution. When she tried to think of a new imprint experience to place in her past, she couldn't think of one that seemed strong enough to overcome the impact of the abuse. Instead, she imagined being the wiser, more evolved *her* that she wanted to be in the future. When she took this experience back into the past with her, and then came up through time, it was a dramatic experience for her. Afterwards, she noticed that her interactions with other people were different in an interesting way. When she had talked with someone previously, she felt as if the other person was not only seeing her, but was also seeing all her past experiences of abuse at the same time. Kristen had always thought other people saw her as "that kind of a person," and this limited what she thought was possible for her. In contrast, after this experience, Kristen said, "Now it's like they're just seeing *me,* and what I'm doing right now." Kristen felt freer, no longer limiting herself to being "that kind of person."

Recovering Hearing

Dick wore a hearing aid in one ear, and an artificial tuning fork had been surgically installed in the other. Even with the hearing aid, Dick sometimes didn't hear voices and sounds that were within hearing range for others. Dick's hearing problems had begun after an experience years earlier, when he'd been flying over the Persian Gulf. Dick's plane had been cruising at 40,000 feet, when a window blew out, causing an immediate and complete loss of pressure. The plane was not equipped with the convenient oxygen masks of today's airliners, so the pilot quickly dove to 10,000 feet where there is breathable oxygen.

This rapid loss of pressure, followed by the 30,000-foot drop, was more than Dick's ears could stand. On that rapid descent, a pocket of air had gotten trapped in Dick's eustachian tubes. Afterwards, Dick had ear surgery in an attempt to correct the problems that resulted, and a tube was placed in his ear to drain the air pressure. According to Dick, his doctors later told him that this procedure had further traumatized his ear, causing otosclerosis, or early aging of the ear.

In response to medical recommendations, Dick then had ear surgery on his right ear, and a metal tuning fork was installed to bypass the hardened anvil. This restored Dick's hearing in that ear to its pre-trauma level. However, he frequently had ringing or pain in his ears.

Dick's hearing in his left ear had worsened gradually over time. He first noticed that his left ear didn't hear as well when he was listening to a cassette player with stereo headphones. He realized that he needed to turn the volume for his left ear up to 9, while the volume for his right ear was set on 1. When Dick had his hearing tested, his left ear tested in the "hard of hearing" range at 60-70 decibels. Prior to the airplane experience, Dick had several hearing tests, with both ears in the ten-decibel range. Ten decibels is a little less than average, but within normal range. For comparison, the sound level right in front of a speaker of a big rock band is about 90-100 decibels.

Dick had left his hearing aid at home the day I was teaching the decision destroyer in an advanced training group. To learn the method, each person in a practice group rotates between three positions: client, guide, and observer. When it was Dick's turn to be client, regaining his hearing was far from his thoughts. He was hoping to gain a general sense of health, well-being, and balance in his life.

First, he chose a time when he was healthiest. He went back to a time during his teenage years when he considered himself to be in excellent shape, both physically and emotionally. He picked a time of life when he had energy, concentrated well, learned quickly, and was as strong emotionally as he was physically. It was also a time when he had the capacity to make good decisions. As Dick went back to reexperience that time, he gave himself instructions not to make the changes too specific, ". . . so that all kinds of pieces can tie together. Let it synthesize as it will." Dick reported visualizing this experience of health like a wave. He had an image of a sand "sculpture" that you can turn over, and notice how the sand resettles in new patterns. Health for him was "rolling with the wave" of sand.

When Dick was fully immersed in that experience, he let himself move quickly forward through time, bringing his experience of full health along with him, all the way to the present. Dick then held onto that experience of health in the present, while seeing himself going on into the future, still with the experience of health.

When Dick was finished, he was puzzled by hearing the sound of falling water. Looking around, he realized it was a nearby water fountain, which he hadn't noticed before. Then he noticed he was hearing it with his *left* ear! Most of us found it difficult to believe that Dick had regained his hearing so suddenly. Several people in the seminar tested Dick by whispering to him behind him—something he couldn't have heard only a half hour before. Later medical tests have verified Dick's subjective experience: his left ear, which had tested at 60-70 decibels, now tests at 10 decibels—the same that it was before the airplane incident.

A year later, I asked Dick what difference this has made in his life. He now has no need for his hearing aid—and in fact has lost it. His ears feel comfortable; he no longer has any ringing or pain. "Just recently I went to a conference and enjoyed being able to sit in the back row," Dick said. "Before, I always had to sit in the front row, even with my hearing aid. I sang one of the lead parts in a community theatre play recently. I wouldn't have done that before, because I couldn't have noticed whether I was on or off pitch.

"And on an added note, I use my voice now to communicate in ways I wasn't aware of before. I use voice tone and rhythm—I adjust the volume and pitch of my speaking voice more than I did before. It helps me get results in my consultations with my clients. I hadn't recognized how important sound was."

The decision destroyer is one of the most widely-useful methods presented in this book, and has produced some of the more striking results. It is particularly useful when a person has had a long history of unpleasant experiences, which is often the case for someone who has been abused over a long period of time. As the person comes forward through time with their powerful resource, *all* those problem experiences become transformed at once, rather than having to laboriously change them one at a time, as most conventional therapy would. In addition, it typically results in the person gaining a more powerful sense of themselves as a person—something that serves them well in future challenges.

Eliminating Allergic Responses 5

When Maria was eleven years old, she was stung on the foot by a bee. For most of us this would be a painful, but unremarkable occurrence. However, the events which followed made this an unforgettable experience for Maria and her family. About ten minutes after the sting, Maria noticed that her throat felt prickly and itchy inside, and seemed to be swelling. Soon she had considerable difficulty breathing. Her frightened family rushed her to a nearby emergency room. By the time she arrived, Maria could barely breathe. The doctor on duty immediately gave her three different injections to counteract her symptoms. He said that she probably would have died from suffocation without rapid treatment. Maria was warned to stay away from bees to prevent a life-threatening recurrence, and she made every effort to do so.

After ten years of this, Maria was tested to find out if she was still sensitive. The doctor who administered a skin test told her that she was still very sensitive, and advised her to take weekly shots of bee antigen, to gradually build her tolerance to bee stings. To be safe, she should do this for the rest of her life. Maria self-administered this treatment for the next twelve years. About four years before I worked with her, changes in the procedure made self-administration of the shots impossible, so Maria decided to stop taking them.

When Maria learned that NLP had a method that can eliminate allergic response, she was interested. "Maria, first I want to give you an idea of what we'll be doing here. For many years now it's been known that allergies are essentially a 'mistake' of the immune system. When the immune system is functioning well, it identifies truly dangerous substances and responds to them in order to protect your body. This is the way your body protects you from harmful bacteria or viruses.

"But sometimes a person's immune system makes a mistake and identifies a harmless food, pollen, dust, or a bee sting as being dangerous, when it really isn't. If your immune system *thinks* something like that is dangerous, you end up with an allergy instead of protection. In your case, your immune system made a very serious mistake which nearly killed you. And, of course, the sensible thing to do when you make a mistake is to clear it up.

"The process we're going to use will simply retrain your immune system to respond more appropriately to bee stings. It will let your immune system know that although a bee sting is a bother and a nuisance, it's not something to be concerned about. The purpose of your immune system is to protect you. Once your immune system knows that bee stings are harmless, you'll actually be much *safer* because you won't have that dangerous allergic response. Your immune system will be able to respond the way it does to anything else that is innocuous.

"First I'd like to have you get *just a little bit* of your allergic response, so I can observe your current response, and be able to know when your response is different." Since Maria's response had been life-threatening, I needed to be *extremely* careful to get only a partial response. I emphasized wanting only *a little bit* of the response, and was prepared to watch closely and interrupt before the symptoms got intense. "I'd like you to close your eyes and go back to being eleven years old, just after being stung by that bee, when you were first beginning to notice those symptoms in your throat—OK, that's enough! You can *open your eyes and look at me now,* as you feel your body return to normal."

As Maria recalled that experience, her expression had shifted in a variety of ways. She became tenser overall, especially in her face, which became whiter. She also showed a variety of other symptoms of stress. By having her recall the allergic state I could notice how she looked in that state. This information will be essential later when I want to test to see if this problem state has been altered.

"Maria, the next step in this process is for you to think of something that is similar to a bee sting, but to which your immune system *already knows how to respond appropriately,* without an allergic response. What seems similar to you? How do you respond to ant bites, for instance?"

"How about wasp stings?" Maria asked. "I've been stung by wasps, both before and after I was stung by the bee, and I never had anything other than local pain, reddening, and swelling."

"That's perfect. Since your body already knows how to respond appropriately to wasp stings, we'll use this as a resource to retrain your immune system. Now close your eyes again, and recall a time when you were stung by a wasp. As you feel the sting, and experience what that is like, you can realize that your immune system knows exactly how to respond appropriately to this situation. Notice what that is like."

As Maria responded to imagining being stung by a wasp, her posture and expression shifted in a variety of ways. Her back straightened up, her breathing was regular, etc. As I saw these nonverbal changes, I reached over and placed my hand gently and firmly on her shoulder, so that my touch will be associated with her appropriate response to wasp stings.

"Maria, I'm going to keep my hand on your shoulder to stabilize the healthy response you are now experiencing. Your body already knows how to respond appropriately to a wasp sting. Now I want you to open your eyes and imagine there is a thick plexiglass screen across the whole room in front of you, from floor to ceiling. You are here, completely safe, protected from anything that might occur on the other side of the screen.

"Now see yourself on the other side of the plexiglass. Watch that Maria as she responds to a wasp sting, her immune system responding normally and appropriately. . . .

"Now you can watch and notice what it's like as that Maria over there *responds in the same way* to a bee sting. Just as with a wasp sting, her immune system knows exactly what to do."

I was watching Maria very carefully to verify that her nonverbal response continued to be her normal response to the wasp sting, and not the response I saw at the beginning when she recalled being stung by a bee. If she had fallen back into the old allergic response, I would have interrupted her, backed up, and started over again.

"Now take the plexiglass shield away, reach out and bring the Maria you see in front of you back into you, so that you can gain her knowledge of how to respond appropriately to bee stings. . . . Now, with your immune system knowing what to do, imagine being stung by a bee, right here, noticing what it's like to now have the resources to respond appropriately.

You can have a sense of appreciation that your immune system has learned something so important so quickly, and enjoy your new response."

As she did this, Maria's nonverbal expression remained resourceful; she maintained the same normal response when thinking about being stung by a bee. Throughout this process, I had stabilized this response by keeping my hand on her shoulder. Next I want to test to see if she can respond in the same way without this assistance, so I take my hand away from her shoulder. When I asked her to close her eyes and vividly imagine being stung by a bee again, her nonverbal expression continued to indicate a normal response. I went one step farther in my testing. "Maria, now imagine that you take this resource of your immune system knowing how to respond appropriately, and relive being stung by a bee when you were eleven years old, as it would have been, now. . . ." As Maria did this, her old stress response was no longer there. In its place I saw all the nonverbal signs of Maria's normal resourceful response. This process took approximately ten minutes.

When we were finished, Maria was unconvinced—as most people are—that she was any different. However, I had seen a marked shift in her nonverbal response to imagining being stung by a bee at the end of the process, so I was sure it had worked. Given the seriousness of her previous allergic response I recommended that she *not* test this by being around bees and getting stung, but that perhaps she get a skin test. However, life soon provided a more complete test, uninvited.

About two months after I worked with Maria, she was stung by a bee while she was at home alone. She was frightened, and immediately called an emergency clinic to get advice about using an epinephrine kit she had recently bought. She didn't want to use the epinephrine kit unless it was necessary, so she called a nearby friend, told her the situation, and then continued to talk with her until twenty minutes had passed. Except for the local redness and swelling that is normal for a bee sting, she had no reaction to it. Although Maria was very pleased, she is still skeptical, and is wisely cautious, carrying her epinephrine kit with her on outings as a safety measure.

The Method

This process was adapted by two of our colleagues, Tim Hallbom and Suzi Smith, from a method originally developed by Robert Dilts, one of Bandler and Grinder's earliest and most capable colleagues.

Extensive clinical experience indicates that this allergy process is completely effective in approximately 80% of cases in which the specific

od is dependent on the ability to use words skillfully to elicit states in
lient. Nonverbal congruence is also an essential factor, as with all NLP
ods. It is possible that some failures are simply due to limits in the
l and nonverbal skills of the person carrying out the procedure.

Another factor, often called "secondary gain," may be the reason for
times when this method has not been effective. Secondary gain is just
er way of saying that all our behaviors have positive purposes. For
ce, when someone has an allergic response to sugar, very often the
y has the positive function (secondary gain) of keeping the person from
g weight. If we were successful in eliminating the allergy, the person
then be faced with a new problem: eating too much sugar and
g weight. If some part of the person recognizes this, it will wisely and
usly oppose the elimination of the allergy.

he solution to this conflict is to teach the person *more effective*
ative ways to control her weight. Then when the allergy is no longer
ary to serve the positive function, there will be no resistance to
ating it. Similarly, someone may unconsciously prefer to remain
c to cigarette smoke because he doesn't have other ways to comfor-
nsist that others not smoke, or because the allergy is the only way
to get attention from others. Saying "I prefer that you don't smoke
me" or "I want some attention from you" may be awkward, so the
"speaks for" the person. If someone who doesn't want cats in his
ost his allergy to cats, he might no longer be able to enforce his

hen the positive functions (secondary gains) are known, it is usually
to find effective alternative ways of achieving them. However, our
functions are often unconscious. If they are not identified, they will
be powerful obstacles to change, no matter what method is being
hapter 8 includes a method that can help us identify these positive
s in an affirming and respectful way, so that we can find better
ive solutions.

cientific Background

recent years so much experimental scientific evidence has been
ating regarding the intimate anatomical and biochemical interrela-
ween the nervous system and immune response that a new field,
neuroimmunology," has been created. Earlier reports had demon-
hat emotions, mood, and stress affected the immune response.
r, the link was previously thought to be only hormonal and
fic.

allergen has been identified. It also works well for ma
metals, chemicals, etc., that are not considered true alle
Eliminating Allergies (1) includes three complete ses
Tim and Suzi, with follow-up interviews. On this videot
as three clients lose their allergies or sensitivities to ca
and darkroom chemicals.

Although most people need the assistance of sor
method, we have been surprised to find that some p
allergic response just by listening to a tape. One man

"I played your allergy tape for my wife, and two
allergies. After just listening to the tape, all three noticed
gone! My wife had been allergic to goldenrod and many ot
me with a bouquet of goldenrod on the table."

Non-specific Allergies

The method works much less often for non-s
which the specific allergen is unknown, presumal
difficult to identify a sufficiently similar situation v
However, we have sometimes been able to get resul

Anna, who had suffered from asthma since chi
her asthmatic symptoms increased significantly dui
pollen seasons. She thought her asthma might be pa
response. When I used the allergy process with h
anything to which she was certain she *didn't* have
instead, I asked her to think of *an earlier time in*
symptoms.

"Watch *that* Anna—the Anna who knows I
wide range of things—pollens, molds, dust, and
just automatically responds appropriately." Thi
from her; she looked very resourceful as she thou

Several days after completing the process, *I*
report that her asthma symptoms had dropped
half their previous level. Since she was a
thoroughly educated herself about asthma and h
could safely reduce her medication on her own.

What if the Method Doesn't Work?

As we previously mentioned, for reasons
method does not work for about 20% of people

Bernie Siegel's book *Love, Medicine and Miracles* (2) and Stephen Locke's *The Healer Within* (3) are excellent sources for the growing evidence—both anecdotal and scientific—for the mind's ability to affect the immune system.

For those who would like more direct access to a few of the sources on the influence of psychological factors on immune system activity, we refer you to several recent articles in *Science,* the journal of the AAAS. A 1985 report (4) summarizes the findings of the "First International Workshop on Neuroimmunomodulation" held at the National Institutes of Health. In part, this article states:

"Investigators have shown that stresses, both severe or more mundane, can alter immune responses and that classical Pavlovian conditioning, a form of learning, also influences them. Moreover, there are both anatomical and chemical connections between the immune and nervous systems that may serve to integrate their activities. Not only can the nervous system influence immune responses but, the new work shows, immune responses can alter nerve cell activities. In fact, the cells of the immune system may function in a sensory capacity, relaying signals to the brain about stimuli, such as invading foreign pathogens, which would not be detected by the more classical sensory system."

In a 1984 double-blind experiment (5), guinea pigs were injected with a foreign protein to stimulate the immune response, and these injections were accompanied by an odor. After only five pairings with the odor, the animals' allergic response, as measured by histamine release, could be stimulated by the odor alone. The average histamine levels in response to the conditioned odor were thirty times higher than levels in response to a neutral odor. In another more specific study (6) rats were trained to have an allergic response to a light and sound. The level of a specific enzyme known to be an essential link in the allergic response was approximately four times the level in untrained animals.

Some researchers consider this to be the same process by which *people* acquire allergies. An event or emotional response may trigger the person's immune system response at the same time that a cat, cigarette smoke, pollen, or some other "allergen" is present. Just as the guinea pigs learned to have an allergic response to an odor, the person learns to have an allergic response to this substance that happened to be present at the time.

The method described in this chapter also uses a simple conditioning technique to change the immune response. When the client imagines a situation in which the immune response is normal, this results in a normal physiological response, which is then substituted for the inappropriate allergic response. The intermediate step of seeing yourself with the new desired response is not absolutely necessary in all cases. This step makes it easier to learn the new response, while at the same time reducing the possibility that the person will revert back into the old allergic response.

Since this method demonstrates that the human immune response can sometimes be reconditioned in minutes, there are enormous implications for treatment of a wide variety of diseases in which the immune response is inappropriate. Using the same kind of process, it may be possible to reduce or eliminate the destructive autoimmune responses in such diseases as Multiple Sclerosis, Rheumatoid Arthritis, and Lupus. Our experience with this method also supports the growing body of evidence that it must also be possible to psychologically increase the immune response to other diseases such as cancer.

Cautions and Suggestions

If you are interested in trying this method, we would like to offer you two important precautions. First, if the allergy you are dealing with has any possible life-threatening consequences—as it had with Maria—use this method only under direct supervision by a medical doctor. Then if you were to accidentally trigger a severe allergic response, the doctor could deal with the consequences medically. We suggest that anyone with an allergy of any type obtain medical input in addition to utilizing this method.

Secondly, we would like to remind you that this method is based on the body's ability to condition and decondition an allergic response. If someone were careless about applying the method, it would be possible to condition the allergic response to other cues, instead of eliminating it. Presumably this is what has occurred spontaneously with people who are allergic to a wide variety of stimuli. Although this has never happened in our application of this method, it is a possibility if someone were not carefully trained.

If reading this chapter, or watching the allergy videotape, stimulates you to comfortably and automatically recover from an allergy, as it has for some others, congratulate your unconscious mind. If you want a "guide" to assist you in eliminating an allergic response, we recommend finding someone who is thoroughly trained in this method. Before attempting to guide others in this process, we encourage you to get thorough training, so that you are able to get results in a way that protects your clients.

References

1. "Eliminating Allergies" videotape (see Appendix II).
2. *Love, Medicine, and Miracles,* by Bernie Siegel, 1986.
3. *The Healer Within,* by Stephen Locke, 1986.
4. "The Immune System 'Belongs in the Body.'" Pervasive anatomical and biochemical links between the immune and nervous systems help explain how moods might influence disease susceptibility. *Science,* 8 March 1985, pp. 1190-1192.
5. "Learned Histamine Release." *Science,* 17 August 1984, pp. 733-734.
6. "Pavlovian Conditioning of Rat Mucosal Mast Cells to Secrete Rat Mast Cell Protease II" *Science,* 6 January 1989, pp. 83-85.

6 *Responding Resourcefully to Criticism*

All of us encounter criticism from others; the *way* we deal with it can either significantly enhance our lives, or it can make us depressed and sour. It's easy to "take it personally" when someone criticizes what we do, or to magnify the importance of the criticism. In this chapter you can learn a specific process that has enabled many others to respond resourcefully to criticism.

Randy, a college professor, noticed that criticism of any kind irked him. "I've usually found ways to avoid it," Randy revealed. "I've worked myself into a position professionally where not many people criticize me. But my wife isn't intimidated by my credentials, and she is overly critical. All this criticism at home upsets me. It also leads to arguments between my wife and I. I feel like she's attacking me, but she says she has something important to say and I'm not listening. I was hoping she would come to see you, so that she could learn to be a little more tactful. She won't do it, though, so I want to find out if you can help anyway."

My first job was to shift Randy's focus of attention to something *possible for him.* Perhaps he was right that his wife was overly critical and could benefit from learning how to be more tactful. However, even if Randy's wife didn't choose to add to her own personal choices, there is still much Randy can gain by having a different *response* to his wife. If Randy had a way to listen to his wife without taking it personally, he would be able to feel better himself, as well as be more compassionate about *her* limitations.

One of the first things we modelled a number of years ago was how some people are able to respond well to criticism, when others are devastated at a hint of disagreement. When we studied people who responded resourcefully to criticism, we were careful about who we selected. We searched for those who could *consider whether there was any useful information in the criticism.* We didn't want an approach of just ignoring criticism, and feeling good; we wanted to assist people in feeling good while considering the valuable information in the criticism. We also selected people to study who kept a feeling of compassion or goodwill toward the person offering criticism. Some people are only able to keep their own self-esteem by "counterattacking." They come out of criticism feeling good, but they insult or demean the other person. When someone counterattacks, they usually don't benefit from criticism—they just deflect it. In contrast, even harsh criticism *can* benefit us, if we have a way of feeling resourceful while we consider, "Is there something I can learn here?"

We discovered that a key distinction between people who respond well to criticism and those who feel devastated when criticized, is in *how they see the meaning of the criticism.* People who remained resourceful *saw themselves* doing the behavior that was being criticized. The criticism was "out there," "at a distance." From this distance, it was easy for them to calmly make their *own* evaluation of the criticism, and decide what was useful in it, and what to do about it.

In contrast, those who are devastated by criticism "take it right in." Many people literally imagine that the "negative meaning" of the criticism goes right into their chest, like a piercing arrow or a dark beam of light.

Out of these discoveries we developed a "Strategy for Responding to Criticism," which can easily be taught to others. This has been useful to many people, and it seemed like just the thing for Randy.

"Randy, I'm guessing that some of the time your wife's criticisms are delivered badly. And I know that if a person has to listen to a lot of criticism, it can certainly be annoying and hard to listen to. Would you like to have a way to feel resourceful yourself, even if she uses a bad tone of voice, or points her finger at you, or whatever?"

"Sure. If that's possible."

We then guided Randy through the Strategy for Responding to Criticism, which we describe in detail later in this chapter. When we had finished, Randy looked and felt different when he imagined criticism from his wife.

When we spoke to Randy several months later, he was very happy with the results. "I noticed the difference right away," Randy commented. "When I got home from my appointment with you, my wife complained that I was late, and that I hadn't let her know my schedule so she could plan. Before I would have just felt bad about it. This time I just thought about it, and I realized there was something I could do about this next time. She seemed kind of surprised when I asked her more questions to find out what parts of my schedule she wanted to know about. This strategy has been working so well for me that I've taught it to some of my students, too. I think a lot of people could use it. Another thing I've noticed," Randy continued. "My wife seems nicer in the way she criticizes me now. I don't know if I'm just hearing her differently, or if she has really changed, but it's nice."

Randy noticed something that many people notice when they gain new personal choices that really work: suddenly those around us also seem more reasonable and resourceful. Many people comment after gaining new choices that their parents, friends, and co-workers seem easier to get along with. While this doesn't always happen, frequently when one person gains more choices, others around them also respond more positively.

Outline for Responding to Criticism

Learning this process is fairly simple and straightforward. Before you begin, make sure you will be uninterrupted for about a half hour. We suggest finding a comfortable, quiet spot, so that you will learn most easily.

The major key to this process is to maintain distance between yourself and the criticism. You can do this very literally by keeping the critical comments at a comfortable distance from you, perhaps behind a plexiglass barrier, so that you can view them objectively as if you were watching a movie of someone else. This keeps you from automatically feeling bad, and allows you to calmly evaluate the meaning of the criticism *before* responding to it.

As you go through this process it's very important to keep your resourceful feelings all the way through. Before beginning, think of a time when you felt particularly capable, or a time when you knew you were loved and safe, or some other time that is a powerful resource for you. Go back *into* that experience and *relive* it for a few moments, so that you regain the good feelings you have there, and maintain them throughout the process. If at any time during the process you begin to feel bad, simply stop whatever you are doing and return to this resource experience, so you can regain these positive feelings before proceeding again.

Step 1: See yourself at a distance. Out in front of you somewhere, you can see yourself. You don't have to *really* see yourself, you can pretend to see yourself, or "sense" that it is "as if" you see yourself out in front of you. This you out in front of you is the one who is going to learn a new way to respond to criticism. Since this you is out in front of you, any feelings about being criticized will be out there in front of you, too. If you want to, you can imagine putting up a plexiglass shield between yourself sitting comfortably in a chair, and the you out in front of you. You can see and hear through this shield, yet you know it's a strong protective barrier.

As you go through the next steps, you can enjoy feeling pleased that you are learning something that will serve you well in the future.

Throughout the rest of this process you can continue to observe this you in front of you, making sure that he also looks comfortable and resourceful as you go through each step.

Step 2: See yourself being criticized. That you over there in front of you is about to be criticized. Watch him over there as he immediately *sees himself being criticized.* This may sound a little strange, since most people don't ordinarily do this. You are watching *him* in front of you, and this you in front of you is also watching himself as someone criticizes him. It's as if you can see the pictures he is making in his mind, out in front of him. If this is a little difficult to do at first, keep going. The things that are already easy for us to do are usually the ones from which we get the least benefit. If you don't already do it, this will provide a powerful new choice.

Make sure that the you in front of you stays feeling resourceful, while he sees himself get criticized out in front of him. If he doesn't immediately feel resourceful enough, let his image of himself being criticized get smaller and farther away until he feels resourceful.

When we asked Randy to do this, he saw "Randy" in front of him, and that Randy watched his wife criticize another Randy in front of him. You will be watching yourself watch yourself be criticized. Again, if you aren't aware of seeing pictures, just pretend to.

Step 3: See yourself picturing the meaning of the criticism. Now watch that you in front of you as he makes a movie out in front of him of the *meaning* of the criticism. For example, Randy's wife sometimes criticized him for being too lenient with the kids. He watched Randy make a movie in front of *him* of what his wife was talking about. He watched himself disciplining the kids.

Make this movie small enough and far away enough that you can comfortably observe it, feeling resourceful, perhaps with a bit of curiosity. Notice whether you can make a complete picture of what the other person means, or if your picture is fuzzy or incomplete. If the other person just says "You are rude," or "You always act superior," you don't really know yet what the other person means by that. You can't make a complete picture of what this means, unless you ask questions. Always begin by acknowledging the other person: "I'm concerned about that." "I'm glad you brought that up." Then you can go on to ask, "What exactly did I do that you consider rude?"

Watch the you in front of you ask the other person questions, until that you can make a clear movie of what is meant. Make sure the you in front of you looks comfortable and resourceful throughout this step.

Be careful to find out what the *other* person means, and not "fill in your movies" with what *you* think. For example, Randy could easily make a picture of what *he* thought "being too lenient" meant, but he needs to find out what his *wife* means by those words. Since in the past Randy had just felt bad, he hadn't asked her for details. When Randy saw himself watching this unclear movie of himself "being too lenient," he knew he needed to ask his wife what she meant, so he rehearsed doing this in his imagination. "I want to be sure I know what I did that you think is too lenient. What did I do or say, and what do you want me to do instead that you think would work better?" Then he imagined what she might say in reply.

As Randy rehearses this process in his imagination, it doesn't really matter if his guess about what his wife might say is correct. Once he has learned this process he will actually ask her, and she will actually tell him.

Step 4: Decide what you think. Now that you have full information, while still feeling resourceful, you are in a good position to decide what portion of the criticism you agree with, and what part you may have another opinion about. The easiest way to do this is to compare the movie you've just made of the criticism, with your own remembered "movies" of the same events. Again, you can watch as the you in front of you does this. He will comfortably watch both these movies out in front of him, and compare them.

Now watch as that you checks whether the two movies match. This will let him know if he agrees with all of the criticism, or none of it. Usually, there will be at least some of the criticism that you can agree with. If your memory of what happened is significantly different from what the criticizer is saying, it is time to ask more questions. Watch the you in front of you ask the other person for more information. For example, the person may have complained: "You are disinterested in my opinions." After asking, you may find out that she concluded this because you looked away when she was talking to you. You may agree that you did look away, yet know this was so that you could carefully think over what she was saying to you— actually evidence of interest, not disinterest.

Step 5: Decide on a response. So far you've only been acknowledging the other person and gathering information, while feeling resourceful. Now you have the information to decide what to do. You know what you agree with, and what you disagree with. Exactly what response the you in front of you selects depends upon your goals as a person, your values, your relationship to the other person, etc. You can notice how much easier it is to select a response that is more respectful of both you and the other person, when you feel resourceful rather than attacked. Here are some possible responses for you to consider:

a. Begin by letting the other person know what you agree with. "I'm glad you brought that to my attention. I hadn't realized the impact of what I was doing, and now I'll be able to do something better next time."

b. Your response might include an apology: "I'm very sorry. Certainly what I did was tactless and shortsighted." A sincere apology can go a long way to regaining rapport, particularly when you are prepared to act differently in the future.

c. After agreeing or apologizing, you may want to add information that helps the other person understand your different opinion. "Thank you for being direct with me about something that concerns you. I know I look away a lot when people talk to me. Looking away really helps me think more clearly about what you are saying. Actually I do that *more* when I think you're saying something important, and I need to take a little time to understand it."

"I agree that I have been too lenient with the kids. I hadn't been aware of the impact, since I'm home mostly in the evenings, and you're with them all day. I think of you as being in charge of them, since I don't know what went on earlier. I think what will help me with this is if we decide together who is in charge of the kids each evening. If we've agreed that I'm in charge, I'll know it's my job to do the disciplining if any needs doing."

d. Ask the other person what will make a difference: "What would you like me to do now to clear up this situation?" This doesn't mean you have to do it, but it may give you valuable information. Sometimes people ask for something difficult or unreasonable. But more often when the other person lets you know what will satisfy them, it's something simple that you would be willing to do.

    e. Let the other person know what you plan to do differently in the future: "You're right. I did plan the family vacation without consulting you. Let's scrap these plans and start all over. And the next time I plan something major like this, I'll be sure to consult you."

    f. If you disagree completely with the other person, even after significant information-gathering, you may decide to let the person know: "Thanks for sharing your point of view with me. Here's the way I think about it. . . ." "We have a very different opinion about this, and certainly each of us has the right to think of things the way we do."

    g. Occasionally you may decide that the other person's world view is so different from yours that you don't want to waste your time discussing it. "With our completely different opinions, I don't think there's anything to be gained from our discussing this any further."

    Step 6. Rehearse using the information you learned to make it easy for you to act differently next time. In Step 5, you may have already decided to do something different in the future. If you haven't, watch the you in front of you ask himself this question, "Do I want to use the information I got from this criticism to act differently in the future?" If so, first watch yourself decide what to do differently next time. Then observe as he actually imagines *doing the new behavior* when and where he wants to.

    Repeat these six steps several times with different examples. It's useful to go through this process with different people offering different types of criticism. For example, you can make one criticism very vague, so you can practice asking questions to understand what the person really means. Use another example where you completely agreed with the criticism, and also one where you disagree with all or part of it. *Make sure you select examples of criticism that have been difficult for you in the past.* For some people, criticism from close friends or family seems hardest, while for others criticism from co-workers, an employer, or from employees, may seem most difficult.

    Usually three or four rehearsals are enough for this new process to become an automatic part of your behavior.

    Step 7: Incorporate the part of you that learned this process. This may seem a little strange to some people, but it's a very important step. You have just watched a part of yourself learn a new way of responding to criticism in a useful way. Now you are going to take him into yourself in order to make this process an automatic part of *you.* First let the plexiglass shield melt away. Then thank him for being a special resource to you in this way. . . . Now you can actually reach out with your hands and arms, and imagine embracing that you in front of you, and gently bring him back into you, taking all the time you need, so that all those learnings will be immediately available to you any time you find yourself being criticized in the future.

Many people who have learned this process at seminars, from our previous book (1), or from watching our videotape (2) have offered reports on how it has made a big difference for them. Besides finding it easier to deal with criticism in the office and at home, some have commented that it has also been very useful in dealing with internal self-critical voices. They just did the same process with what they said to themselves.

The same process can also be used with compliments, to make you less susceptible to the flattering opinions of others. After evaluating the compliment, you can courteously acknowledge it. If the person has complimented something that is very important to you, you can respond with more depth.

Use With Veterans

Peter Gregory, a psychology technician at the Veterans Administration Medical Center, Fort Harrison, Montana, called us recently to thank us for the NLP methods he had learned from us, because he has been finding them so useful in working with veterans. Also a former team leader of a Vet Center in another state, he has worked with hundreds of veterans since 1973. Peter said:

"Besides the phobia procedure, I use your strategy for responding to criticism frequently. In addition to being good at desensitizing people's response to authority figures, it's really useful for people who are violence-prone. Some of the guys can now listen to criticism from their wives better without being abusive. They don't get offended so easily. I have many veterans who tell me, 'I just didn't realize I was coming across aggressively.'"

Learning how to respond positively to criticism is only one of many skills that can make our living easier. Each such skill adds to our self-esteem at the same time that it makes more choices available to us, and allows us to connect with others at a richer level when we want to.

References

1. Andreas, Steve & Andreas, Connirae. *Change Your Mind—and Keep the Change,* Chapter 8, "A Strategy for Responding to Criticism."
2. "A Strategy for Responding to Criticism." Videotape (see Appendix II).

I do not resent criticism,
even when, for the sake of emphasis,
it parts for the time with reality.
                                        —Winston Churchill

Phobias, Traumas, and Abuse

7

When Lori was eleven years old, she fell into a wasp's nest and was stung hundreds of times. Her whole body swelled up so much that her rings had to be cut off. None of her clothes fit, so for several days she had to wear her father's bathrobe. Since then, she had a severe phobia of bees. As she put it, "If a bee is in the house, *I'm not!*" If a bee got in her car, she had to pull over, stop, open the doors, and wait until the bee left. She also avoided flower beds because of the likelihood of bees. A participant in one of our phobia workshops knew of Lori's phobia, and asked her if she wanted to be a demonstration person.

Since many of the examples in this book are partially summarized for your convenience, we offer a complete verbatim transcript of this session. Some readers may want to skim through the following transcript; those who are interested in the details of a complete session can enjoy the opportunity to read through it more carefully. This session is also included in our videotape "The Fast Phobia/Trauma Cure (1).

Lori, whom I hadn't met before, had walked into the room a few minutes before I asked her to join me at the front. In order to emphasize the method, I did not tell the group what Lori's phobia was about. The method will work with most specific phobias, regardless of what the person is phobic of. I began with some "small talk" to gain rapport.

"Lori, I haven't spoken to you at all."

Lori: "No."

"You talked with Michael, I guess."

Lori: "Umhmm."

"I don't know what kind of outrageous promises he's made." (smiling)

Lori: (laughing) "I won't tell you. I won't tell you what he promised."

"Anyway, you have a phobia, which we won't tell them (the group) about, OK.?"

Lori: "All right."

"And, it's a very specific thing, right?"

Lori: "Umhmm."

"Is it just one thing, or is it kind of a class of things?"

Lori: "It's one thing."

"Just one. OK. And what I'd like you to do first—Well, think of it right now. If one of these were flying around right now. . . ."

Lori: "Ohhh!" (She rolls her head around in a counter- clockwise circle, laughing tensely.)

Now that I have seen Lori's phobic response, later I will be able to recognize when her response is different. Now, however, I need to get her *out* of this state before proceeding with the technique. I do this with specific instructions, distracting, reassuring, and asking her about her friend Michael.

"This is what we call a 'pretest.' That's fine; come back. (Lori is still laughing nervously). . . . Look at the people here. . . . Look at me. . . . Hold my hand."

Lori: "Thank you. . . . OK."

"We're not going to do stuff like that, right? OK."

Lori: "OK. Whew!"

"Now look out at the folks here. How is it just being in front of these folks?" (Lori looks out at the group.) "Is that a little nervous-making too?" (Lori breathes out strongly, and says, "Not bad.") "Is that OK?"

Lori: "Yeah, that's fine."

"OK. You've got a friend over there, right?"

Lori: "Yeah."

"He's got a nice smile."

Lori: "He sure does. He's a great friend."

"Yeah, good."

Now Lori is back to a pleasant normal state, so I can begin the method. "OK. Now what I'd like you to do first, before we do anything—the whole procedure by the way is very simple, and you won't have to feel bad and stuff like that. But we need to make a few preparations. What I'd like you to do first, is imagine being in a movie theater."

Lori: "OK."

"And this might be easier with your eyes closed. . . ."

Lori: "All right." (She closes her eyes.)

"And I want you to see a picture up on the screen, of yourself—a black and white snapshot. And it could be of the way you're sitting right now, or something you do at home or at work. . . . Can you see a picture of yourself?" (Lori nods and says, "Umhmm.") "Is that pretty easy for you?" (Lori: "Uhhuh.") "Good."

"Now I want you to leave that black-and-white picture on the screen, and I want you to float out of your body that's sitting here in the chair, up to the projection booth of the movie theater. Can you do that? Take a little while.". . .

Lori: "OK."

"OK, so from now on I want you to stay up in that projection booth. Can you see yourself down in the audience, there?" (Lori smiles slightly and says, "Umhmm.") "And you can also see the black-and-white picture up on the screen?"

Lori: "Yeah."

"OK. Of yourself?"

Lori: "Yeah."

"Pretty interesting." (Lori laughs and says, "It's good.") "Do you know you could go to a workshop on 'Astral Travel' and pay $250 to learn how to do this?" (Lori laughs.)

"OK, now I want you to stay up in that projection booth, and see yourself down in the audience, and see that black-and-white picture on the screen of yourself."

Lori: "Umhmmm."

"Got that?"

Lori: "Umhmm."

"OK, I want you to stay up in that projection booth, until I tell you to do something else."

Lori: "OK."

"So you can kind of see through the glass, and there are holes in the glass so you can hear the movie, because we're going to show a movie pretty soon. What I want you to do is run a movie of yourself in one of those bad times when you used to respond to that particular thing. And run it from beginning to end, and you stay back in that projection booth. You might even put your fingers on the glass and feel the glass. Just run a whole movie, clear to the end. See yourself freaking out over there, in response to one of those situations. That's right. Take all the time you need, and just let me know when you get to the end."

I am watching Lori closely for any nonverbal signs that she might be falling back into the phobic response, but she remains resourceful.

Lori: "It's hard to get to the end."

"OK. What makes it difficult?"

Lori: "It just seems to stop. The thing seems to go over and over." (Gesturing with her right hand in a circle.) "The particular incident goes over and over and over and doesn't seem to have an end, although I know it ended."

"OK. So it tends to go over and over and over."

Lori: "Umhmm."

"OK. Let's speed up the movie. How many times does it have to go over and over before you can get to the end?". . .

Lori: "Um, half a dozen."

"OK. So let it flip through half a dozen, so it'll let you get to the end. . . . And when I say 'end,' I mean after the whole thing happened and you're back normal again.". . .

Lori: "OK."

"OK. Got to the end?"

Lori: "Umhmm."

Although I have not seen any sign of her phobic response, I want to check by asking her. "Was that fairly comfortable for you, watching that?"

Lori: "A little uncomfortable, but not bad."

"A little uncomfortable, but not bad. Not like the real thing."

Lori: "No."

"OK. Now in a minute I'm going to ask you to do something, and I don't want you to do it until I tell you to go ahead. What I want you to do is to get out of the projection booth, and out of that chair in the audience, and go into the movie at the very end, when everything's OK and comfortable. And then I want you to run the whole movie backwards, including those six times around. Have you ever seen a movie backwards, in high school or something?"

Lori: "Yeah."

"OK. I'm going to have you run it backwards in *color,* and I want you to be *inside it,* so it's just like you took a real experience, only you ran it backwards in time, and I want you to do it in about a second and a half. So it will go 'Bezzzoooouuuuuurrrrrrpppp,' about like that."

Lori: "OK."

"OK. Go ahead. Do that.". . .

Lori takes a deep breath, shudders, and then says, "Whooof!"

"OK. Did you come out on the other side all right?"

Lori: "Yeah." (laughing)

"A little weird in the middle there, eh?"

Lori: (shaking her head and continuing to laugh) "Ooooh."

"OK. Now I'd like you to do that a couple more times, and do it *faster*. So go into the end, right at the end, jump into it, and then go 'Bezourp,' real fast, through the whole thing.". . .

Most people only need to run the movie backwards once, but because of Lori's momentary discomfort, I thought it would be helpful to do it several more times. This time Lori responds much less, sighing a little at the end.

"Now do it a third time, real fast.". . .

Lori: "OK."

"OK. Was it easier the third time?"

Lori: "Umhmm."

"OK. Now, that's all there is to it."

Lori opens her eyes, looking *very* skeptical, grabs the chair with both hands, shakes her head, and then starts laughing loudly. After about eight seconds of laughter, she says, *"I'm glad I didn't pay for this one!"* and continues to laugh for another twelve seconds. Although Lori has been very willing and cooperative throughout the process, this demonstrates that she certainly has no belief in what we have been doing. Lori's skepticism is very familiar to us. Even though we have guided literally hundreds of people through this process, *we* are still amazed that such a simple process can have such a profound impact. My next comments are both to acknowledge her disbelief, and to allow a little time to pass before testing her response to bees again.

"Fine. It's all right. We love to joke. Joking is one of the nicest ways to dissociate. Think about it. When you're joking, when you're having a humorous response to something, there's really no way to do it other than popping out for a while, looking at yourself, and sort of putting a different frame around what's happening, such that it's funny. It's a really valuable way of dissociating. We believe that dissociation is the essence of a lot of humor—not all, there are different kinds of humor, and so on. But we definitely recommend it."

"Now, Lori, would you imagine now that one of these little critters— came." (gesturing with one finger, like the flight of a bee, toward Lori) Lori pauses, looks momentarily worried, then thoughtful, but does *not* go into the fear response that she demonstrated at the beginning of the session.

Lori: "OK."

"What's it like?"

Lori: "Um hay de hay." Lori is at a loss for words, and begins laughing. "Um.". . .

"Do you still have it (the phobia)?"

Lori: (Looking down, surprised.) "No!" She laughs and puts her hand on her chest.

"This is a nice response because it looks like, 'What?' Consciously she's expecting to have this (old) response. She's had it for—how long have you had this?"

Lori: "Twenty years."

"She's had the response very, very dependably for twenty years. It's been a very unpleasant and overwhelming response. There's a very strong conscious expectation. And what you saw there, was this conscious expectation, 'Ooooh! It's going to be terrible, . . . What?'"

Lori: (laughing) "It's true."

"Now let's make it a real bad one, you know. Have one come in and land on your hand or something." (Lori looks down at her hand.) "Can you imagine that?"

Lori: "Umhmm." She shakes her head in disbelief. "Whew!"

"What's it like?"

Lori: "Ummmm. . . ." (Neutrally, shrugging her shoulders) "It's like having one sitting on my hand."

"That's a typical answer—is what's so funny 'It's like being in an elevator, you know.' Isn't that a mind-boggler?"

Lori: "Yeah, it is! Because I had that happen within the first year after the first incident, I had one land on me, Woof!"

"And it was different, right?"

Lori: *"Yeah!"* (looking down at her hand again.)

This session took less than seven minutes, in January 1984. Lori's nonverbal response to bees in her imagination was clearly *very* different at the end of the session than it had been at the beginning. Several times during the next summer we asked if she had seen any bees, because we wanted to know what her "real world" response had been. Each time she said she hadn't seen any bees. Finally in December 1984, we took a jar with about a dozen honeybees to her house. In a videotaped follow-up interview she comfortably held the jar with bees and examined them closely. When we let several of them out of the jar, she watched them crawling on her living room window without any reaction. A bee was in her house, and this time, so was she. Now it is more than five years since the session, and Lori reports that she still hasn't noticed any bees, though she admits, "They must have been around me."

It's actually fairly common that people become completely oblivious to what had been the stimulus for their phobia. What used to terrorize them becomes so normal and ordinary it's not worth noticing. When we called one woman a few weeks after eliminating her elevator phobia, she realized she had ridden in several elevators without even noticing!

When to Use the Phobia Method

This method was developed by Richard Bandler (2) as an improvement on an earlier method he had developed along with John Grinder (3). It works very consistently for any phobia in which the person responds instantaneously to a specific stimulus: insects, heights, birds, snakes, water, closed spaces, elevators, etc. Although it has worked for some cases of agoraphobia, it is not usually the method of choice.

Phobic responses are typically *instantaneous* responses to a particular situation or stimulus. Other fear responses, often called "anxiety," develop more slowly over a period of minutes or hours. This method is not usually effective for anxiety responses. However, the swish pattern (see chapters 17 & 18) is usually effective for these.

In addition to specific phobias, you can use this method effectively for many problems that are not generally thought of as phobias, provided that they are quick responses to unpleasant memories. This includes a wide range of traumatic responses to past accidents, abuse, serious illness, drug "flashbacks," and war experiences, including most "post-traumatic stress disorder" (PTSD).

Although some people with severe traumatic experiences need the assistance of someone trained in this method, many others have been able to use this method by themselves to neutralize fears. The process is outlined below for your convenience.

We suggest that you first use it on one or more *mildly* unpleasant experiences to learn the steps of the method and verify that it works. With this knowledge and practice it will be much easier to deal with more severe experiences.

Post-Traumatic Stress Disorder

One man I worked with, John, had been struggling with PTSD for twelve years. He had tried every kind of therapy he could find, including Transactional Analysis, Gestalt Therapy, Reality Therapy and Rational-

---

Fast Phobia Method: Outline

First select an unpleasant memory, phobia, or traumatic experience you want to neutralize. You can review the example of Lori for a more complete description of each step.

1. Imagine you are in a movie theatre. *See yourself* doing something neutral on a small black-and-white screen.

2. Float out behind yourself and watch yourself watching yourself on the movie screen.

3. Staying in this position, now watch a movie, in black and white, on that small screen, of *yourself* going through the experience you've selected to "neutralize."

4. After you finish *watching yourself* in this movie, when things are again OK, stop the movie so it's a still picture. Then step *into* the still picture, turn it into color, and run the movie backwards, very rapidly. It will be like seeing a movie backwards, with you *inside* it, as if time had reversed direction.

5. Now test. Think of the event or memory, and notice if you can think of it more comfortably. If so, you are done. If not, you can go through the process another time, or get assistance from someone trained in these methods.

Emotive Therapy. John had been a marine MP in Vietnam. When he returned home, he found that—like many other Vietnam Veterans—he could not leave his war experience behind him. John found himself waking up from nightmares in which he was back in Vietnam, screaming and thrashing around in bed. Sometimes his wife had to sleep somewhere else or risk being hit. After such a night, John would "wake up ten times as tired as when I went to bed." If someone came up behind him and touched him or spoke, John would jump, and had to restrain himself from a violent response.

John had avoided all things Asian because they stimulated his nightmares. He even had one waking nightmare. At an outdoor flea market he heard Vietnamese voices, and looked up to see an extended family of ten Vietnamese all walking toward him. This "clicked me right back to the most violent incident that occurred to me in Vietnam," and when he looked around, "*everyone* was Vietnamese." John panicked and ran.

I worked with John for about forty minutes. Most of this time was spent convincing him to try the method. Since he had been through so many therapies that hadn't solved his problem, he was reluctant to try again.

About a month after the session, in a videotaped follow-up interview (1) John reported that he finally had the results he wanted. He was now sleeping well and waking up rested. He had even become good friends with two Asian people, and had gone to a Japanese restaurant and ordered the meal in Japanese, a language he had not used in twelve years. Deeply moved, John told me how grateful he was for his renewed ability to connect with Asians as people, rather than only as reminders of past horrors.

John also said that the day after the session he had gone to a two-day seminar with his wife. At the end of the first day, his wife said to him, "What's happened with you? You're different. You used to jump when people came up behind you, and you're not doing that any more." Thinking back, he realized that she was right, but he hadn't noticed it.

He had also seen a rerun of a Vietnam movie, "The Boys from Company C," without any problems. The first time he had seen it, "It was hell for two weeks."

This is the kind of report that clearly indicates change has occurred at deep unconscious levels, and is not just superficial. I recently called John, who verified that he was still doing fine five years later. As an additional test, I asked him to describe to me the worst incident he had experienced in Vietnam. In a normal voice, he told of being in the marketplace in Pleiku waiting to pick up his troops when an older child grabbed for his wallet. As he grabbed the child's hand he heard someone shout "Grenade!" behind him, and felt something push hard against his back. When he regained consciousness, he was leaning against a tree, still holding the child's arm. "That's all I was holding, because the rest of him was gone." As he finished, he said, "That's interesting. I've still got some 'willies.' That's to remind me of my mortality. I want to keep that." John is now a drug and alcohol counselor. He is someone who savors his life deeply.

John went through some horrible experiences—experiences we would prefer never happened to anyone. When things like this have happened to people, we are glad to be able to assist them in getting beyond the terror of these events. No one deserves to have this kind of experience the first time. They certainly don't deserve to live with it the rest of their lives.

Sexual or Physical Abuse

The fast phobia method forms the foundation for another method we've developed which has been an important part of our work with people who have been sexually or physically abused. Recently, our society has begun to recognize how many have experienced some form of abuse, and the problems that abuse can cause later in life. While some have recovered on their own from the emotional impact of these experiences, many others need assistance to become free of this trauma.

Leroy had a background filled with experiences so traumatic that many of them had been blanked from his memory. If anyone talked to him about anything that reminded him of his past experiences, he found his mind wandering immediately to something else, or he became frightened and left the room. Leroy was so intent on avoiding the pain of his past that it interfered with his day-to-day experience. He wanted to do something to resolve this.

I gave Leroy a brief overview of a method we have used to assist others in recovering from abusive past experiences, and asked if he wanted to find out if it would help him. He was eager to try.

First I guided Leroy through the phobia procedure with three events from his past that had been unpleasant, but not so extremely traumatic that he had blanked them from his memory. After this, he was able to think about these unpleasant experiences comfortably.

Then I explained, "Leroy, you've had many other experiences in your past that were extremely unpleasant. Some of them were so unpleasant that they have been blocked out of your awareness, to protect you from any bad feelings. And it's a good thing that your unconscious wants to protect you. This process can teach your unconscious a way to protect you even more fully. There is really no need for you to remember these experiences consciously, because we can guide your unconscious mind in re-sorting and recoding those experiences so that at the unconscious level you will no longer be bothered by them. When things happen that shouldn't have happened, it's better to leave those things in the past. Your unconscious will still know what those experiences were, so that you can keep any possible learnings from those experiences, and be able to make sure that nothing like that happens to you again, but you can have a sense of comfort when you consider them, even at the unconscious level. And your unconscious can decide if and when it's appropriate for you to know about any of this consciously."

Recoding Past Unpleasant Experiences.

"So what I'd like your unconscious mind to do first, is to sort through all your past experiences, at the unconscious level, and separate the unpleasant experiences from those that were neutral or pleasant. Because we are going to do something special with the unpleasant experiences. Your unconscious can give you a signal to let you know when it is done sorting. You might hear something on the inside, or see something, or just get a feeling of being finished."

Leroy closed his eyes and went into an altered state to do this. Since it became difficult for him to speak to me in this state, I asked him to nod his head "yes" and "no" to communicate with me. When Leroy gave me a "yes" nod, I proceeded to the next step.

"Thank your unconscious for sorting those experiences. And now it is time to recode those experiences, so that you can keep any learnings you want to keep from them, but have new feelings associated with them. You know what happened when you recoded the three unpleasant experiences that we worked with using the phobia method a few minutes ago. When you *saw yourself* at a distance having those experiences, you could feel comfortable watching them, as if they were happening to someone else, or as if you were watching a movie. And they did happen such a long time ago. Consciously you have experienced the phobia method, and unconsciously too. Now your unconscious can use that same phobia method on all those unpleasant experiences in the past. It's a good thing that your unconscious knows how to do the phobia method, because things happen so much faster at the unconscious level.

"And I don't know how quickly your unconscious mind will thoroughly recode all of your unpleasant past experiences, making them into smaller pictures in which you see yourself at a distance. And you might find that the color goes out of these memories as well, as they seem to be farther away. At the unconscious level, you can notice how even if these memories are all sequenced in time, so that you can see them all at once, they don't seem very significant any more, because *your unconscious now knows how to deal with unpleasant things.*"

As I was talking, Leroy was giving me ample signs that he was fully following along. He showed the many small muscle movements throughout his body that people typically make when they go through a major internal reorganization. When Leroy was finished, I continued, "And there's one more thing your unconscious can do so that you can *completely disconnect* yourself from the feelings you *had* about those experiences. Because any unpleasantness belongs in the memory, not with you. Any remaining unpleasantness that *was* connected to you can *go into the memory,* over there.

"To do this, your unconscious can have all your past experiences from conception to now, lined up in order. And all the unpleasant experiences which you've just recoded can be marked out, perhaps to the side of the others. . . .

"Now you can notice as your entire line of past events floats around *behind* you. You are here in the present, and when you are ready, you can let yourself very quickly go *backwards* through *all* of the unpleasant experiences you've ever had, doing the last bit of disconnecting from each of those unpleasant experiences, as each one undoes itself very quickly." Since this is an unconscious or semi-conscious process, it reorganizes experience very rapidly. In fact, if someone does this step slowly it usually doesn't work. It took Leroy about five seconds.

Reconnecting with Past Resources.

The next step was designed to make sure Leroy regained the full benefit of all his pleasant past experiences. Many people who have been abused try to forget their *entire* past, cutting off pleasant past memories along with the unpleasant ones.

"It's also important to make sure you can fully experience and enjoy all the *pleasant* and *resourceful* experiences you have had in your past. You can begin to notice now, either consciously or unconsciously, all your pleasant past experiences. And it doesn't really matter if a pleasant experience was a day long, a minute long, or a fraction of a second. All of those pleasant experiences are yours, and you deserve to keep them with you in a way that you *feel connected to them* at the unconscious level, whether you consciously remember them or not.

"So when you have sorted out all your pleasant past experiences, you can make sure they are larger, colorful movies, so you will *feel* their impact. And you can be *in* them, fully enjoying the experience of being there. Even when you think of all of your pleasant past experiences at once, you can feel solidly connected to each one, as if you are in each experience, because these are your experiences, and an important part of the learning from these experiences is to enjoy the powerful feelings of resourcefulness they provide."

Leroy glowed as he did this. His face looked almost ecstatic as he reconnected with the pleasant parts of his past in a way that allowed him to enjoy and appreciate them more. As well as being enjoyable, this ability to *thoroughly feel* our pleasant past experiences helps provide a basis for knowing our own self-worth.

"Leroy, to enable you to connect even *more* fully with your past pleasant experiences, once again your unconscious mind can order all your past experiences from conception until now. . . . This time you'll be marking out all your pleasant experiences for special attention, because we're going to do one more thing with them. . . .

"When your pleasant past experiences are all lined up, you can float up and go right back to the moment you were conceived and drop down into your body. When you're ready, you can have the full experience of going very rapidly *forward* through all those experiences from conception on, connecting with the resources in each experience with your entire body, so that the resourceful feelings sink into every cell. And it can be as if you are gathering resources into yourself, so that as you move forward through each of those resourceful experiences, it remains in you as you move on to the next.". . .

Recoding the Present.

"You have reorganized your past in a major way. And you can also bring this recoding that you have done with your past, into your present. So that if something unpleasant is happening, it is almost as if it is happening to *him, over there,* allowing you to feel resourceful in dealing with whatever is happening. . . . And when something pleasant is happening, of course you can enjoy the full feelings of being in the experience." As he followed my suggestions, Leroy's head orientation shifted from looking to his left to looking straight ahead, indicating that he had shifted into present experiencing (see chapter 19 on Timelines).

Bringing the Learnings into the Future.

"And we all have things we know are going to happen in the future, and you can also code the future in a similar way. Even though you don't now know most of what will happen in the future, and even though you are doing things to make your life more and more positive, we all will have some pleasant experiences, and some not so pleasant. Without knowing exactly what it is, anything unpleasant that might happen can appear smaller, more black-and-white, while your unconscious image of the positive future you are moving towards is more colorful and larger." As I said this, Leroy turned slightly to his right, indicating that he was thinking of his future.

Respecting Personal Ecology.

After completing this process, I asked if any part of him had any objections to what we had done, but there were none. Since this is a fairly major recoding of experience, it is important to be alert for any individual need for adjustment. Sometimes people have beliefs about themselves not being worthy of this change, for example.

"Leroy, give yourself all the time you need to completely integrate this recoding, making certain that your new coding is fully ecological for you as a person, and your relationships to those around you, because the unconscious mind *can always make adjustments* to make the new coding work even better, and be even more appropriate for you as an individual. Your unconscious mind may choose to further integrate this way of coding your experience in your dreams tonight, allowing you to awaken tomorrow morning feeling refreshed and well-rested. And if your unconscious wants any assistance in any way, it can signal you by giving you a tingle up your spine, or perhaps an image to let you know."

The next morning Leroy felt a sense of well-being, and did not need any further assistance. He reported several months later that he had been able to recall his past more comfortably, and the sense of well-being remained. "Several other issues came up for me, and I've been able to deal with them more easily," Leroy said.

The Impact

This method neutralizes the intense bad feelings that often accompany the actual memories of abuse, and makes it possible to take any further steps that may be necessary. When someone has an essentially phobic response to abuse, as Leroy did, this method will fully resolve those bad feelings. In addition, it helped him *reconnect* with past resources, which is equally important.

Many others have given us reports similar to Leroy's after using this method: "I feel more resourceful, more centered." "I can think about the past without it bothering me." Sometimes people remember past incidents that were so traumatic that they hadn't been able to remember them before knowing how to "see them at a distance." Even though they were unconscious, these incidents are often the basis for forming limiting beliefs about ourselves, so having them available to deal with can be very useful. (See chapter 4 for a method for transforming limiting beliefs resulting from past traumas.)

How it Works

What makes this method work is understanding some important facts about our mental images. When we imagine something big, bright, colorful, and close to us, we usually have strong feelings in response to it. This is how I asked Leroy to recode all of his *resourceful* experiences, so that he would have full and robust feelings for each of them.

In contrast, when we imagine something small, farther away, in black-and-white, and we *see ourselves* in the picture, as if we are watching ourselves on TV, we don't have the feelings of the experience; instead we have the more "objective" feelings an observer would have. This is how I asked Leroy to recode all his unpleasant or traumatic experiences.

Rapidly going backwards through unpleasant experiences also has a predictable impact. Most people report that more color washes out of their negative experiences after doing this. Sometimes people report that their experiences become transparent, fade, or "fall off of" their Personal Timeline (see chapter 19). Rapidly going forward through pleasant experiences usually strengthens the positive experiences we have and often brings color and intensity back to the memories.

Although this process is much easier with the assistance of someone trained in this method, you may be able to successfully do this on your own. The outline below is provided for those who would like to do this. Be sure to gain ample experience with the phobia cure in Step 1 before proceeding. If you encounter any internal objections to this process, give your unconscious instructions to put things back the way they were, and read chapter 8 to learn how to deal with objections before proceeding.

Next Steps with Abuse

People who have experienced abuse as children often have other difficulties, such as continuing to be abused as adults. Often they need some additional assistance in sorting out how to know who they can trust in the future. Now that they can comfortably look at their old memories, they can go back and notice what "warning signs" they can be alert for. If they were beaten or sexually abused, they need to know what cues they can notice in future situations in order to protect themselves. Identifying these warning signs can help someone who has been abused to both *be* safer as well as *feel* safer in the present.

Other methods in this book can also be used to fully resolve other consequences of abuse. In addition to the unpleasant memories themselves, many people also form beliefs about not being worthwhile as a person, or suffer from shame. You'll find methods for changing unuseful beliefs about the self in Chapters 3 and 4, and a way to recover from shame in Chapter 14. A variety of NLP methods can help develop stronger feelings of self-worth, which usually make people unwilling to be abused in the future.

Recovery from Abuse and Trauma: Outline

This process enables you to rapidly reprocess multiple experiences of abuse or other trauma. The example of Leroy offers more complete instructions for each step.

Step 1. Preparation. Do the fast phobia process with three unpleasant experiences from your past, to form a foundation for what you will do in step #3, below. (See the Fast Phobia Outline earlier in this chapter.)

Most people find it easier to do the remaining steps thoroughly if they first close their eyes, relax, and enter a meditative state.

Step 2. Memory Sorting. Ask your unconscious to separate your past pleasant and unpleasant experiences.

Step 3. Recoding Your Unpleasant Past Experiences.

a. Ask your unconscious to use the phobia cure to make all your unpleasant past experiences smaller, less colorful, and farther away. Your unconscious can also give you the visual perspective of *seeing yourself* in all these experiences, rather than seeing them from your original point of view.

b. Line up all your past experiences in order, and mark out the unpleasant ones. Stand with your back to your past, and then go *backwards* very rapidly through all the past unpleasant experiences, to completely disconnect from them. Return to the present.

Step 4. Reconnecting with Your Pleasant Past Experiences.

a. Ask your unconscious to recode them all in living color, perhaps make them larger, and to have you be *in* them rather than observing from the outside, so that you can experience them fully.

b. Line up all your past experiences in order, and mark out the pleasant ones for this process. Float up over your past experiences, dropping back down into yourself at conception. Move rapidly forward through all of your pleasant experiences, reconnecting fully with each, all the way to the present.

Step 5. Bringing the Learnings into Your Present. Bring this way of thinking about pleasant events and unpleasant events into the present.

Step 6. Recoding Your Future. Bring this way of thinking about unpleasant events and pleasant events into your future.

This completes the process. You can now enjoy further integrating this way of processing your experiences into your life.

Some people who have been abused become abusers themselves as adults. For some, this is the only kind of family behavior they have seen. They may want to learn more loving ways to interact, but haven't had any alternatives. Becoming an abuser can also be due to an unresolved conflict or "split" between an internal "abuser" and "abusee." This conflict can be healed using the method described in Chapter 13.

Many people believe they are "slaves to the past," and that "psychological wounds scar for life." I have quite a few physical scars that never hurt a bit; when I look at them, they're only reminders of what happened in the past that let me know what to avoid in the future. Fortunately, the mind can heal itself even faster and more completely than the body can. We hope these examples give you an experience of how unpleasant past events can be transformed into resources for present and future well-being.

References

1. "The Fast Phobia/Trauma Cure" videotape. (see Appendix II)
2. *Using Your Brain—for a CHANGE,* by Richard Bandler, Chapter 3, pp. 37-48.
3. *Frogs into Princes,* by Richard Bandler and John Grinder, Chapter 2, pp. 109-125.

8

Positive Intentions

During World War II, at the height of Japanese expansion in the Pacific, there were Japanese garrisons on literally thousands of tiny islands scattered across an enormous expanse of ocean. When the tide of battle turned, many of these were overrun and defeated, but some were entirely missed. On other islands, small groups of soldiers or isolated survivors hid in caves in inaccessible areas. A few years later, the war was over. But since these survivors didn't know this, they continued to struggle on, maintaining their rusting weapons and tattered uniforms as best they could, totally isolated, yearning to be reunited with their command.

In the years immediately following the war, many of these soldiers were discovered when they shot at fishermen or tourist boats, or were found by natives. As the years passed, these discoveries became less frequent. The last one we can recall was about fifteen years ago, some thirty years after the war had ended.

Consider the position of such a soldier. His government had called him, trained him, and sent him off to a jungle island to defend and protect his people against great external threat. As a loyal and obedient citizen, he had survived many privations and battles through the years of war. When the ebb and flow of battle passed him by, he was left alone or with a few other survivors. During all those years, he had carried on the battle in the best way he could, surviving against incredible odds. Despite the heat, the insects, and the jungle rains, he carried on, still loyal to the instructions given to him by his government so long ago.

How should such a soldier be treated when he is found? It would be easy to laugh at him, and call him stupid for continuing to fight a war that had been over for 30 years.

Instead, whenever one of these soldiers was located, the first contact was always made very carefully. Someone who had been a high-ranking Japanese officer during the war would take his old uniform and samurai sword out of his closet, and take an old military boat to the area where the lost soldier had been sighted. The officer would walk through the jungle, calling out for the soldier until he was found. When they met, the officer would thank the soldier, with tears in his eyes, for his loyalty and courage in continuing to defend his country for so many years. Then he would ask him about his experiences, and welcome him back. Only after some time would the soldier gently be told that the war was over, and that his country was at peace again, so he would not have to fight any more. When he reached home he would be given a hero's welcome, with parades and medals, and crowds thanking him and celebrating his arduous struggle and his return and reunion with his people. (We offer this story with thanks to Greg Brodsky, who told it to us in 1977.)

Who Are the Soldiers?

In one view the lost soldiers were acting in ways that were bizarre and crazy, by fighting a war that had long been over. Yet their intention was positive—to protect and defend their country. Although they were doing the best they knew how to do, and however useful their behavior may have been initially, once the war was over it no longer served a purpose.

At times all of us are like these lost soldiers. We all have feelings or behaviors that were developed to serve a useful purpose when we were younger, and we continue even when they are no longer useful to us.

Some people find themselves still fighting battles with their parents long after they have died. We may find ourselves responding in the workplace with behaviors developed to deal with an older brother, or the school bully. People who have been abused sometimes learn to mistrust others so well that they have great difficulty trusting others who love them deeply.

All of us sometimes do things that we consider stupid or limiting— that get in our way. Sometimes we feel angry, inadequate, or something else, when we think that's a dumb thing to feel. We also occasionally see our friends and relatives doing stupid or bizarre things. "If only they knew better," we think.

We usually try to "get rid" of these behaviors or feelings, criticizing ourselves roundly. "You ought to be able to stop smoking!" "You should feel self-confident, there's no reason not to." "I'm so annoyed that I get migraine headaches!" Usually we don't know the useful purpose behind these behaviors or feelings. We just know that these responses get in our way.

Rather than just "trying" to change, it is now possible to utilize an NLP method called "Six Step Reframing." The most important part of this method is that you begin by making an unusual assumption: that *every behavior or feeling you have, no matter how bizarre or stupid it seems, has some useful and important positive intention or purpose.*

This often seems ridiculous to people at first, but it is a powerful assumption that makes much inner healing possible. It helps us turn problems and limitations into assets and allies, and lays the foundation for easy behavioral change. This assumption also helps each of us gain greater rapport with all parts of ourselves—with our entire being.

Reframing with Pseudo-endometriosis

When we were first learning this method years ago, I worked with a woman, Martha, who had physical symptoms that had not yielded to standard medical practice. Martha's doctors described her symptoms as "pseudo-endometriosis," meaning that they were like endometriosis but also different. To put it simply, her menstrual period never quite stopped or started. She had light, intermittent bleeding all the time, and her blood pressure was elevated. Her doctors wanted her to undergo a hysterectomy if her symptoms did not clear up soon.

After making sure she was making full use of these medical resources, I proceeded on the working assumption that some part of her was producing these symptoms. Using the method described more fully later in this chapter, I found that a part of her did not want her to have another child. It wanted her to enjoy her own life and not spend so much time taking care of others.

Martha had been a "super-mom" most of her life, having taken care of a depressed husband, as well as her ten-year-old daughter. About a year previously she had thought about having a second child, even though she was now single and would have to raise it alone. However, at that time she was overweight, and she wouldn't consider getting pregnant unless her weight was normal. She began losing weight, and when her weight reached normal range, she began to seriously consider becoming pregnant. That's when her symptoms began. These symptoms effectively prevented her from becoming pregnant, because she wouldn't consider trying to become pregnant as long as her periods were abnormal. It is possible that her symptoms even made pregnancy physically impossible.

As Martha digested the message that she already had enough responsibilities, and it was time for her to enjoy life more, she realized that this part of her was right. Although there are pleasures and satisfactions in raising a child, there were also many other activities that she could enjoy fully without taking on additional responsibilities. This part of her had been wiser than she, and she agreed with it.

The next week, at a regular medical checkup, her blood pressure had dropped by 50 millimeters, surprising Martha as well as her doctors. Two weeks later her period became normal, and stayed normal. The last time I saw her, five years later, she had experienced no recurrence of her symptoms.

Although we have been successful using this method with a number of other physical symptoms, we want to emphasize that we insist that people also make full use of medical resources. With another woman who had very similar physical symptoms, Six Step Reframing did not affect her symptoms. However, Reframing *did* make some valuable shifts in her overall well-being. She contacted an inner part of herself that wanted her to take better care of herself. After the process, she was pleased to find herself responding to her own needs more naturally and automatically. Doctors eventually identified a rare deficiency in Vitamin K, which promotes blood-clotting and healing. Injections of this vitamin completely cleared up her symptoms.

Inner Parts

When we speak in terms of "inner parts," or "parts" of a person, it's important to understand that we're not talking about little people running around inside of us, or of a particular body part. "Parts" is just a convenient way of talking about the experience we all have when we are divided, or in conflict; we kind of want to do one thing, and also want to do another at the same time. For example, perhaps I want to stop losing my temper, but I still automatically get mad in certain situations. Since I still *have* my temper, it's as if a less conscious "part" of me continues to get angry, while another more conscious part of me doesn't like it. If I want to stop smoking but haven't, it's as if a part of me wants to smoke, while another part of me doesn't like smoking. Whenever someone is in conflict like this, we can use the word "part" to refer to a certain set of feelings or behaviors we have, that represents part of us but not all of us.

Overcoming Shyness

Jerry wanted a way to become more assertive in meeting women. He was typically shy and nervous around women—particularly women who were attractive to him. Jerry hoped to meet someone he would really like, and eventually get married and have a family. All this seemed very unlikely if he didn't get over his shyness. He rarely got to step one—meeting a woman—unless someone else set things up for him.

For years, Jerry had been trying to overcome his shyness. He thought of himself as "nervous" and "lacking self-confidence." Yet Jerry was clearly an intelligent man who had a lot to offer.

In working with Jerry, I first talked with him about thinking about his shyness in a more positive way. I suggested that the part of him that made him shy actually had an important positive purpose for him. It was a part that wanted something very valuable and useful for him, even though we didn't yet know what that was. Up to this point, Jerry had only fought with that part of himself and told himself how stupid it was. Now I was telling him it had a kind of wisdom that was valuable for him in some way. The part of Jerry that made him shy felt acknowledged and appreciated.

In guiding Jerry through Six Step Reframing (presented later in this chapter), we soon learned that the part of him that made him shy actually wanted to keep him from embarrassing himself in front of attractive women. This part was afraid that if he said or did anything, it would be something "stupid." When I asked this part, "And what are you trying to accomplish *for* Jerry that's *positive* by keeping him from embarrassing himself? What do you want instead?" the part responded, "I want him to get close to people." Jerry was very surprised to hear this, because although he had consciously been fighting against this part, it turned out that the part wanted exactly the same thing that Jerry consciously wanted—more closeness. The *way* Jerry had been using to try to get close—shrinking into the walls and feeling shy—was not working very well. However, we clearly had conscious and unconscious agreement about the desired goal. At the level of *intention,* Jerry's conflict had vanished.

One of the most powerful aspects of Six Step Reframing is that it provides a way to find this conscious and unconscious agreement. Even when we find ourselves *doing* the exact opposite of what we want to do, when we look at the *positive purposes* that these parts of ourselves have, they become transformed into valuable and powerful allies. Usually these parts of ourselves developed at an early age. Although they have positive purposes, their *methods* are often childish, outdated, and counterproductive.

Once you have reached agreement about the positive intention, you can then go on to find new choices in behavior and feelings that get better results. All the energy that had gone into the conflict is redirected in a fulfilling way.

This was the next step for Jerry. We knew the positive intention for the part of him that had been making him shy, and Jerry completely agreed with this intention. Now it was just a matter of utilizing Jerry's unconscious resources to generate new and better solutions. I asked Jerry if he was already aware of a creative part of himself, and he was. The next step is to use his creative part to generate alternative behaviors to reach the positive intention.

"Jerry, go inside and ask the part of you that wants closeness to go to your creative part, and ask your creative part to generate many other possible ways to get closeness. Some of these ways will not work well at all; some will only be mediocre, while others will be very effective. Your creative part's job is not to judge the effectiveness of these ways but just to generate possibilities. The part of you that used to be shy, and wants closeness, will select *only* the ways that it likes at least as well or *better* than making you act shy. This part will give you a 'Yes' signal when it has three new ways."

With a little more guidance, Jerry's part soon gave the "Yes" signal, indicating that it had three new ways to get closeness that it thought would work better than shyness.

"This is kind of interesting," Jerry said. "One of the ideas that came up was simply seeing things to do when I see an attractive woman. It's like I see a little movie of walking over and doing something. Before I just thought about her frowning, or something like that. The second idea seems to be a voice inside that tells me to go introduce myself and say something. The third idea took a little longer but I really like it. It's laughing at myself. I don't mean laughing out loud, but just having a different attitude about making little mistakes.

"You know," Jerry continued, "These things don't seem very profound, but I think they'll work. I feel very differently about this now."

What Jerry said makes sense. What makes this method work isn't having profound solutions, it's that the "formerly shy part" of Jerry is now redirected toward finding better ways to satisfy its intention. This part is no longer limited to being shy—the only choice it had before. This part has been "welcomed home" and given updated choices. Jerry's conscious mind may even have tried the same choices earlier, but since the unconscious part of him would have opposed them, they wouldn't have had much chance to work. Until this unconscious part of Jerry is integrated back into Jerry's behavior, even a good solution would fall on its face.

Jerry later reported that he was comfortably meeting women and getting to know them.

When You Can Use Six Step Reframing

Reframing can be used with literally any behavior or feeling response that you would like to change.

1. Behaviors and Habits. Each of us does things that we don't like. Some people have habits like smoking, drinking or overeating that cause problems.

2. Feelings or Emotions. Occasionally we all have feeling responses we don't like: feeling angry, depressed, intimidated, impatient, resentful, etc.

3. Physical Symptoms. Six Step Reframing can also be very effective when physical symptoms have a useful message for us. Sometimes a backache, for example, can be a message to slow down. A shoulder ache may be telling us we are taking on too many burdens. A migraine headache may be telling us we need to take it easy and get more rest. Many people who have learned Six Step Reframing have told us later that they are physically healthier because they now have a way to pay more attention to the messages their bodies offer. They respond to these messages by reducing physical stress—taking a break, getting more rest, getting more exercise, standing up for themselves better, etc. Of course, any time you have a physical symptom, we recommend also making use of appropriate medical resources.

Using the Six Step Reframing Process for Yourself

To gain the advantages from Six Step Reframing for yourself, settle into a comfortable chair and guide yourself through the steps below. You may be able to get complete results by following this process. Even when people don't get all the way through, they typically experience beneficial results from the parts they do complete. Usually it's even easier to get results by being guided by someone trained in the method. Additional instructions on making this method work easily are available in two earlier books (1,2).

Some of the steps in this process may seem a little bit strange to you. They certainly did to us at first. We always tell people, "The only reason we do something as strange as this is that it gets results—usually quickly and easily." The worst that can happen is nothing, and frequently people gain new choices for problems that had bothered them for years.

Step 1. Pick a behavior or feeling that you have but you don't like.

Perhaps you smoke, overeat, procrastinate, or feel inadequate or angry at times, or have some physical problem. Pick something specific (X), and then think about "the part that makes me X."

Step 2. Set up communication with the part. First turn inward and apologize to this part of yourself for not appreciating it in the past. Tell it you now realize that this part wants to do something important and positive *for* you by doing X, even though you don't yet know what this positive purpose is. The more kind and gentle you are to this part of yourself, the more willing this part will be to communicate with you.

Now close your eyes and ask a question inside. The question is, *"Will the part of me that makes me X, communicate with me in consciousness, now."* After you've asked the question, notice what you see, hear, or feel. This often seems a little strange to people, and that's fine—just notice what happens. People get a wide variety of signals from their unconscious parts. You may get an image of a person, or an animal nodding its head; you may see a color or shape. You may hear sounds or words. Many people feel a body sensation—a tingling in the spine, warmth in the hands or face, an increase in heart rate, or something else.

You may experience some aspect of your response in the actual problem situation. For example, if you are working with a part that makes you feel angry, you may feel tension in your stomach or feel your heart speed up slightly as the signal. Some signals are so unique and surprising that you *know* immediately that another part of you is communicating with you. At other times, the signal may seem like your own ordinary thoughts and images. As soon as you get a signal, pause to *thank the part for communicating with you.*

Since reframing works by communicating with "unconscious" parts, it's very important that the signal is one that you *can't* duplicate by conscious effort, to be sure you aren't just fooling yourself. It's a simple matter to consciously try to create the signal you got. If you can't, you have a good signal; go on to the next step. If you *can* duplicate it, you can simply tell your inner part, "In order to be sure that I'm communicating with you, I need to have a signal that is clearly outside my control. Since I can duplicate the signal you just gave, will you please choose another signal that I can't duplicate exactly," and wait for a new response. Each time the part communicates, thank it for its response—even if you don't understand it yet.

Whatever you see, hear, or feel in response to the question, you need a way of knowing what this signal means—when this part of you wants to say "Yes," and when this part of you wants to say "No." Go inside and tell your part, *"So that I will know exactly what you mean, if you mean 'Yes,' you are willing to communicate with me in consciousness, please increase the signal"* (in brightness, volume, or intensity). *"If you mean 'No,' you are not willing to communicate, please decrease the signal"* (in brightness, volume, or intensity).

Typically the signal will increase or decrease, and it doesn't really matter which it does. If the part signals "No, I don't want to communicate," *that is still a communication.* Almost always this simply means that there is certain *information* that the part doesn't want to communicate, and that's fine, because it doesn't need to.

Step 3. Separate the behavior from the positive intention. Now it is time to make the distinction between the part's behavior or response and its *positive intention* or *positive purpose.* Remember, our assumption is that even though this part is doing something you don't like, it is doing this for *some important positive purpose.*

Go inside and ask your part, *"Are you willing to let me know what you want for me that's positive by doing X?"* Your part can use the same yes/no signal you established in Step 2 to give you an answer.

If your part signals "Yes," thank it and then ask it to go ahead and tell you. If your part signals "No," also thank it, and tell it you are assuming it has a positive intention that you are better off not knowing right now. You can go on to Step 4 even when you don't consciously know the positive intention.

It's very important *not* to "second guess" your parts and decide what they are telling you. Reframing provides a way to find out *from the part.* If you're not sure what the part is telling or showing you, you can use your yes/no signal to find out. For instance, you can say internally, "I think your positive purpose is to help me succeed. Please give me a 'Yes' signal if this is true, and a 'No' signal if this isn't correct." Each of us has unique messages, which may be entirely different from someone else's. One person's migraine often has a very different message than someone else's. (It's even worse to second guess someone else's parts, and tell another person what message their unconscious is offering them.)

If you first get a "positive purpose" that you don't like, or that seems negative, thank the part for giving you this information. Then ask "What do you do for me that's positive by doing that?" Keep asking this question until you get a positive purpose you agree with.

Until now we've been calling your part "the part that makes you X." Now we'll start calling this same part "the part that *wants Y,*" to acknowledge and ally with its positive purpose.

Step 4. Find new behaviors or responses. Turn inward and ask your part to use its yes/no signal to answer this question: *"If there were ways that you* (the part that wants Y) *thought would work as well or better than X to accomplish your positive intention for me, would you be willing to use them?"* If your part understands what you mean by this, you will always get a "Yes" answer. You are offering *better* choices for the part to get exactly what it wants, *without taking the old choice away.* If you get a "No" answer, this only means that the part doesn't understand what you are offering. You can back up to explain more clearly, so the part can understand and agree.

Now take a moment to become aware of a creative part of yourself. All of us have a creative part. It's important to be clear that we're not talking about exceptional artistic creativity. It may just be the part of you that thinks of a new way to write out a shopping list, or a new way to arrange your furniture, or that thinks of something different to do for fun. If you prefer to use a different word than creative, that's fine. Whatever you call it, you'll be utilizing this part to generate alternative ways to satisfy the positive intention.

Turn inward, and ask the part of you that wants Y to *"Go to the creative part, and communicate to the creative part what your positive intention is for me, so that my creative part understands."* Then invite your creative part to participate in the way creative parts most love doing: *"As soon as you understand the positive intention, please begin to make up other possibilities for accomplishing that positive intention, and communicate these to the part that wants Y."* Some of these possibilities won't work at all, some will work a little, and others will be superb. The creative part's job is only to "brainstorm" possibilities for the other part to choose from. *"The part of me that wants Y can then select only those new ways that it thinks will work as well or better than X in achieving its positive intention. Each time it selects a new choice, it can give me a "Yes" signal so that I'll know."*

When you've gotten three "Yes" signals, you are ready to go on to the next step. Thank both your creative part and the part that wants Y for helping you in this way. You may know consciously what your three new choices are, or you may not, and it doesn't really matter.

Step 5. Gaining commitment and testing your process. Ask the part that wants Y, *"Are you willing to actually use these new alternatives in the appropriate situations, to find out how well they work?"* Again have the part use its yes/no signal to answer.

If you get a "Yes" response, go ahead to Step 6. If you get a "No," find out what the objection is. You may need to back up to Step 5 and get additional choices that will satisfy the objection.

Step 6. Checking for personal ecology. The part of you that wants

Y is now satisfied. It has three new choices it likes. Now turn inward again and ask of all your *other* parts, *"Does any other part of me have any objection to any of my new choices?"* If you receive no internal signals, you have completed the process.

If you do get a signal—by seeing, hearing, or feeling something inside yourself—you first need to find out if you really have an objection, or if some part of you is just excited about having new choices. Say "If you have an objection, please *increase* that signal for 'Yes'; if you don't have an objection, please *decrease* it for a 'No.' If you do have a part that objects, you can cycle through this same Six Step Reframing process with both the new part *and* the part that wants Y, to find three new choices that satisfy *both* their positive intentions.

If you get several signals that are objections, you simply go back to step two, and ask *all* objecting parts to form a "committee" to identify each part's positive purpose and select new choices from the ideas the creative part generates. Make sure each new choice satisfies *every* part involved. A consensus, rather than a majority vote, will result in gentle and lasting change. Once *all* your internal parts agree, you will find yourself automatically acting in new and better ways.

Learning to Love and Respect All of Ourselves.

Six Step Reframing is a very rapid and elegant way to gain useful changes in behaviors and feelings. Even more important than getting a solution for a specific personal problem, reframing creates a new positive *attitude* toward ourselves and others.

For centuries, saints and sages have advised us that learning to love ourselves is important, making us more able to lead fulfilling lives and love others. Yet few are able to offer specific and efficient *ways* to learn how to do this. It is presented as something we are just supposed to achieve by will power or grace.

Having used Six Step Reframing many times with ourselves and with others, we have found that the method provides a *way* to love ourselves. After all, if we are focused on the behaviors and feelings we don't like, it's easy to dislike ourselves and others. Reframing teaches us how to welcome each of these feelings and behaviors for their positive purposes. If we feel unhappy, guilty, angry, or embarrassed, rather than criticizing ourselves for these feelings, we can welcome them and find the positive purpose in them. As we find other ways to achieve these *positive purposes,* we no longer need to experience the unpleasant feelings or troublesome behaviors.

Other Examples

We have utilized Six Step Reframing to assist people in reaching a wide range of personal goals and outcomes. When Elna wanted to stop smoking, Six Step Reframing made this easy for her. The entire session with Elna, along with an introduction, discussion, and follow-up interview, is available on videotape (3).

Jack wanted assistance because he feared he would lose his wife. Jack was a highly successful businessman, but complained that his personal life wasn't going very well. His wife complained that he was constantly judgmental and critical. Jack didn't want to be, but couldn't change; the criticisms just popped out of his mouth. If Jack restrained himself, he still looked and felt critical, and his wife wasn't fooled. She knew he was being critical even when he didn't say anything. Jack had an inner voice that criticized *himself* constantly as well, and he frequently felt inadequate or imperfect.

Six Step Reframing helped Jack regain rapport with his internal critical voice. He found that the voice really wanted his life to be better, and—like so many parents—criticizing was the only method this voice knew to try to improve things. After the Reframing process, this voice became Jack's ally, offering positive suggestions and ideas in a soft and inviting tone of voice, instead of criticisms. Jack noticed himself naturally becoming more positive with his wife and with others, too.

Anna had been raised in a very conservative religious home, and though now married, still felt very guilty every time she and her husband had sex. Somehow sex just seemed wrong. She found herself avoiding sex, so that she wouldn't have to face her feelings of guilt and confusion. Anna wanted to be able to enjoy her sexual relationship with her husband, but "fighting off" her feelings of guilt hadn't worked, and Anna wasn't sure what to try next. Through Six Step Reframing, Anna became reconnected with the part of her that had been making her feel guilty. This part wanted her to be a good person, so that she could have a sense of self-worth. Another part of Anna also soon became involved in this Reframing process—a part that as a teenager had rebelled against Anna's background, and had led her to be promiscuous for a time. This part wanted Anna to be her own person—to have independence. Through Reframing we found new choices that fit with the positive intentions of both parts, so that Anna could feel comfortable about enjoying sex in her marriage.

One of our employees got a reputation for being "stuck up" because she didn't say hello to everyone when she walked into the office. It turned out that her positive purpose was to respect each person's work time. She didn't want to disturb anyone in the middle of a project.

Improving Family Relationships

The same process is useful in family relationships. In fact, the basis for this process was originally developed by Virginia Satir, one of the pioneers of Family Therapy. She used it for many years, both before and after Bandler and Grinder delineated the Six Step process. The next chapter describes how to use a variation of this approach with children.

Realizing positive intentions can also help us deal with adults who act in ways that disturb us. The person who yells at you in traffic is using the only way he knows to vent his frustration and try to feel better. The person who deceives you believes she has to in order to survive in a world she perceives as confusing and untrustworthy.

We invite you to experiment with taking on the assumption that each of us always has positive intent. Notice how you feel and act differently if you assume that a person who had been annoying to you has some positive purpose for his behavior. Even if you don't know what it is, you can assume there is one. And do the same for yourself. Each of *your* feelings and behaviors also has a positive purpose for you to welcome and turn into an ally.

References

1. *Frogs into Princes,* by Richard Bandler and John Grinder, chapter 3.
2. *Reframing: Neuro-Linguistic Programming and the transformation of meaning*, by Richard Bandler and John Grinder.
3. "Six Step Reframing" videotape, Connirae Andreas (see Appendix II).

Can your learned head
take leaven from
the wisdom of your heart?
— Lao Tze
(Witter Bynner translation)

Parenting Positively

9

Many of the methods in this book are useful in healing or changing difficulties after they have begun. It is also possible to utilize the same principles to help children get a good start in life. NLP principles make parenting more enjoyable, as well as more effective. In our own parenting we have gained both from the specific methods in NLP, and from general methods designed to help each of us tap into our inner wisdom to guide us.

Parenting can often seem overwhelming, making us want to turn to experts for advice so we can just follow "good rules of parenting." Even more valuable than this advice is knowing how to use our own experience—our inner expert. We all have more information than we know we have about our child's situation. Gaining access to what we know, but don't know we know, can help us generate possible solutions to problems.

Accessing Your Own Parenting Wisdom

First find a comfortable, quiet place where you won't be disturbed for a few minutes. Take a moment to relax and get comfortable, so that it's even easier for you to benefit from this process.

Step 1. Think of a difficult situation with your child. Perhaps your child has been doing something that you haven't known how to handle, or that drives you up the wall. Are you worried or concerned about some aspect of your child? Perhaps you will select something your child does, or it might be something about your child's feelings. You will get the most value from doing this if you pick something that happens repeatedly.

Step 2. Run your movie of this situation from your own point of view. Reexperience the episode. Imagine you are going through this situation with your child again. Start at the beginning, looking out through your own eyes, reexperiencing what actually happened. Notice what information is available to you, how you feel, and what you see and hear. If you are someone who doesn't "visualize," that's fine. You can just "sense" that you are reexperiencing this from your own point of view, and this method will work just as well. You may want to go through several examples of this situation.

Step 3. Reexperience this *same* situation again, but *as your child*. Run your movies of this situation from your *child's* position. Go back to the beginning of the same situation you reexperienced in Step 2. Stop your "movie" right before the situation started. Before you play the movie, *this time* look over at your child. Notice your child's posture, the way your child is moving, breathing, etc. Listen to the sound of your child's voice. Now *step into your child*. Take a moment to *become* your child. You are now moving like your child, breathing as your child, sounding the way your child sounds, seeing out of your child's eyes, and having your child's feelings. Let yourself take on this experience as you now let the movie of this situation go forward. If you're not sure you're "really" being your child, that's OK. Just let yourself do it, and notice what you can learn.

Take as much time as you need to go through this situation *as your child,* and notice what new information is available to you. Do you become aware of feelings your child may be having that you weren't aware of from your adult point of view? As your child, do you notice something your child wants or needs that you hadn't been aware of? What else do you learn by being your child? What sense do you get about what your child is experiencing in his/her own world, and how she is dealing with it?

What do you notice about your own behavior as you watch and listen from your child's position? Does your behavior seem different to you from this vantage point? For now, just take note of what you learn from doing this. If you notice that part of your own behavior seems very inappropriate from your child's position, you can be pleased that you got new and useful information. If you learn something about what your child may be feeling, you can be similarly pleased.

Step 4. Reexperience this situation as an "Observer." Run the same movies again, but this time from an outside position. Watch and listen to that experience from a point of view that is off to the side, allowing you to see *both* yourself and your child at the same time. Observe the experience as if you were watching a movie of someone else.

Notice what you learn from this position. Do you notice something about the way you and your child respond to each other? How do things look and sound to you as an outside observer? What do you see more clearly about yourself and about your child?

Step 5. Making use of your information. You've just experienced your problem situation from three very different and very important positions. What information do you have now that you didn't have before? What ideas do you have about your child and what you can do, given this new information?

Most parents gain a lot of interesting information by becoming their child in Step 3. You may have a new sense of what your child feels or wants which you didn't have earlier. This information is a gold mine for parents.

At the same time, we recommend being very tentative about using what you learn this way. No one ever completely knows what another person is thinking or feeling, so when we do this we are "making it up," and need to check out our hunches carefully. This process can help us tremendously in gaining better intuitions about what others are experiencing, but *they* are still the experts about themselves.

For example, if you sense that your child wants to feel safe, you may want to provide more experiences of safety for your child. You may decide to try out having a quiet time each evening before bed when you just hold and rock your child. Then you can notice how your child responds. Does your child act more relaxed and comforted at the time? Does his behavior change the next day in ways that you like? If so, you will probably want to continue your new ritual until the child loses interest in it. But if your child prefers to get off your lap and play on the floor, you may want to try something else.

It is almost never helpful to tell your child what you think your child feels. Even if you are right, it usually annoys children (as well as adults) to have someone else tell them what they are feeling.

Self, Other, and Observer:
A Key to Wisdom in many situations

The essence of this method is to guide ourselves through three major "positions" or "viewpoints" in our lives. We can experience any event as ourselves (Self), as another *person* in the experience (Other), or as someone else might view it (Observer). As most of us go through our lives, we usually experience things from our own point of view. This gives us access to some information, but not to all that is available. If we take the time to notice what information is available when we become the "Other," or when we become an "Observer," we gather much more data upon which to base our actions and feelings. In essence, we become much "wiser" as we gain access to much more information. This ability is a tremendous asset, not only in parenting, but in creating lasting intimacy with someone else, and in building respectful and successful business relationships.

You may have found one or two of these positions more familiar than the others. This, too, can be valuable information for you. Some people rarely or never take the "Observer" position. This means that for them, most new information will come from taking the "Observer" position more frequently. Many people like to talk about difficulties with a friend in order to get an "outside perspective." When we take the "Observer" position to look at our own lives from this stance, we can offer this perspective to ourselves.

Some people rarely or never experience the "Other" position. These people are often accused of being rude or offending others, or of having "poor social skills." Often this is just a matter of not knowing how to literally "become someone else," so that they can realize how their behavior affects another person. Someone in this situation will gain most by trying out the "Other" position more often, because this is where more new information will become available. For centuries, people have described the value of "walking in someone else's shoes." This process gives us a direct way to do it. With a little practice, it can become a detailed and finely tuned ability to notice other people's responses.

Although it may sound a little strange, some people rarely experience life as themselves. It is as if they are almost always an outside observer, seeming "distant," or "unemotional" to others. Others are always thinking about things from someone else's point of view, never their own. These people can gain a lot more from life by learning to experience their own position.

Each of us can gain by noticing which position or viewpoint is least familiar to us, and practicing that position more often. By gaining more balance in our ability to take the position of "Self," "Other" and "Observer," we have three times the information and wisdom than if we took only one position.

Nonverbal Rapport with Your Child

Most parents want to have a deep connection with their children, and some succeed. You can utilize a nonverbal rapport process to help you establish that connection with your own child—and you may be surprised about other benefits you notice as well.

nviting Gradual Change

Out of the connection and acceptance that comes from nonverbal ιatching, your child may feel more receptive to small shifts in behavior. ou will be in a better position to invite gradual changes in your child's ehavior.

When our children were infants, we often held them and matched their eathing to gain rapport. It's difficult to breathe as fast as an infant breathes, instead we gently placed a hand on the child's stomach or back, and owed this hand to follow the child's up-and-down breathing movements. netimes we stroked his head or back *in time with his breathing,* stroking wnward with each exhale. Nonverbally we were responding to the d—letting him know we were "with him." This usually had a noticeable ning effect. When our children cried or were agitated, we began by ching their breathing, and then very gradually made our movements other and slower, inviting the child to follow to a calmer state. If the was not ready to follow, we did not insist.

It's possible to match breathing and movement with newborns. As ren get a bit older, we can also match voice tone and tempo, and in ways. Sometimes you'll want to just match. If you want to help your enter a calmer or more resourceful state, you can first match, and then lowly change your own behavior to being more calm or resourceful. uideline we use is to change your behavior only as fast as your child s. When your child follows you into a calmer, more resourceful state, s if your child is first experiencing, "Oh, I am understood, he is ng me. I must be OK because he is matching me. And now he is ng a tiny bit, and it feels good to follow. If he can be me, then I can and follow to a new state."

g Your Child's Positive Intentions

the previous chapter, you read about Six Step Reframing, and how positive purposes or intentions in even the most "negative" rs can start us on the path to finding new choices.

s is particularly important and useful in parenting. When our misbehave, it can be very easy to assume negative intentions. In nting classes I sometimes hear parents say things like, "My child ower struggle with me—he just wants power." or "Sometimes it e my child is just trying to get to me. He figures out exactly what t me and does it." It's easy to label children's behavior as mean

Early in the development of the field of NLP, it was disc
people who are in deep rapport with each other match
nonverbally. For instance, when two people are sitting in
deeply involved with each other, they are usually matching
body posture, voice tone, and tempo. If one suddenly started
louder or much softer, or faster or slower than the other
communication cycle would be interrupted.

A baby in the babbling phase is thrilled to have
conversation with someone who will use the same sounds,
rhythm and tempo. When a young child is in a shy phase, if
to quickly establish rapport by being "shy" along with h
hides behind mom or dad, you can "hide" behind your
can cautiously peer out at the child, and quickly pull your
your hands as soon as the child notices you. Usually the
very interested in *your* shyness, rather than being so focu

You are probably already matching your child son
can experiment with nonverbal matching at other tim
impact it has on your relationship. Sometimes it seem
first, but as it becomes automatic, most parents find
connected to their child in a new way. You can
breathing, your child's voice tone, or your child's mov

As you do this, your child unconsciously experie
edgement. We have all experienced the "brush off"
"Yes," but nonverbally shouted "No." What can
acknowledging than having someone nonverbally r
we say, but *all* of our communication—the way
move? When we match our children's communic
saying, "I am noticing you. I am responding to y
you as unique, and different from any other h
responding. I am changing who I am for this mo
being with you in a very basic and core way."

I have attended a number of parenting cla
"being with" a child when you don't know wh
advice. And when you know how to mate
behavior, you have a specific *way* to be with
deep connection of respect for who your chil
are not doing anything to your child or tryin
are just acknowledging who your child is.
demonstration of acceptance than *being* your
breathing, voice tone, etc.

or aggressive or even "bad." If we think of our children as having negative intentions, we become adversaries.

In contrast, when we assume our children always have *positive intentions,* it makes our job easier. Rather than assuming our child wants power, we can ask ourselves, "What would having power do for my child that is positive?" Having power might be a way for the child to feel safe in the world, to feel worthwhile, or some other positive purpose. Even when we don't know exactly what our child's positive purpose is, knowing that there always is one changes our feelings and actions toward our child. We no longer need to be at war with our children's misbehavior. Instead, we can ally ourselves with our children's positive purposes and assist them in finding better ways to get what they want—ways that are also more acceptible to us and others. Here's an example of how this works:

When our children were much younger, I walked into the living room one day and saw Mark, 3, hitting Loren, 1. Since Mark was being quite forceful, I moved quickly to keep Loren from being injured.

"Mark, NO!" I said clearly and firmly, as I moved the two of them apart. "I don't want you to hit Loren."

Kneeling beside Mark, and shifting my voice tone completely, I asked gently, "Mark, what were you trying to do?"

"I want Loren off my blocks."

This made a lot of sense. At one, Loren was quite mobile, and thought knocking down towers was a fun activity. "That sounds like a good idea." I agreed completely with Mark's positive intention. "Let's think of how we can make sure your tower stays safe. Do you want me to help you move this tower to the table, so Loren can't get it?"

"Yes." Mark thought this was a good idea.

"Now, that will work much better! Now you can build your tower and it will be safe!"

Many children's quarrels are variations of this scenario. When children don't get what they want, they tend to push, hit, shove and yell. From the outside it may look like one child is being mean. From the child's perspective, it's the only way she can think of to get something she wants. Our job as parents is to respect the positive intention, and offer better ways to achieve it.

Positive Intentions Respect Both Children and Parents

When a child misbehaves, many parents only use Step 1; they try to stop the unwanted behavior. If I had done this with Mark, he would feel frustrated and resentful because he still has no way to protect his block

---

Finding the Positive Intention With Children

To use when a child is "misbehaving"—likely to hurt himself, another person, or abuse property.

1. First interrupt, limit or stop the unwanted behavior, as quickly and calmly as possible.

2. Find the positive intention of the unwanted behavior. "What is it that you are trying to do?" "What is it that you want?"

3. Agree with or acknowledge the child's positive intention. "It's important to protect your toys."

4. Help the child find other ways to achieve his positive intention. "How else could you accomplish that?" With young children it can be useful to mention possibilities for the child to consider.

---

tower. That's what he really wants. Hitting and shoving was only a way for him to try to get it.

If we only stop unwanted behavior, children often gradually learn to think of themselves as "mean" or "bad." They feel in conflict because as they see it, they can either hit and shove and get what they want, or be "nice" and lose something important to them.

In contrast, using all four steps enables you to help the child identify her positive intention and find another solution. Three of the long-term effects are:

• The child thinks of herself as having good intentions, in contrast to being "aggressive" or "bad." This adds to a positive self-concept.

• The child eventually will come to think of other children in the same way—that even when they do things he doesn't like, they are acting out of good intentions.

• The child learns to automatically think of alternative solutions and use her creative resources whenever there is a problem to be solved.

Building Self-worth: Self vs. Behavior

It's important to know how to talk about our children's behavior so that we make it easy for them to behave well and feel good about themselves. Unfortunately, the way parents often speak to and about their children makes it more difficult for the child (and the parent, too).

Have you ever heard a parent say things like, "Johnny, I wish you weren't so inconsiderate!" or "I don't know how you got to be so hyperactive!" If we talk this way to our children, we are acting as if being "inconsiderate" or "hyperactive" are permanent personality traits. We are talking as if this is who our child *is*. "Johnny has brown hair, two arms, and *is* hyperactive." We call this "Language of Self." When Johnny hears this, he may feel bad that he is inconsiderate or hyperactive, but since he hears this as something that he *is*, it isn't something he can do anything about.

Rather than speaking about Johnny's Self, we can simply comment on Johnny's *Behavior* in a way that Johnny knows he has choice: "Johnny, Grandma doesn't want anyone running in her living room. If you feel like running right now, you can do that in the back yard, or you can think of something quieter to do in here with us." If you imagine that you are Johnny, you can get a sense of how this is much easier to respond to positively. We're not calling Johnny an inconsiderate or hyperactive *person;* we're simply talking about Johnny's *Behavior* and telling him what choices he has. The guideline is that when we want to *shift* our child's behavior, we make our job easier if we talk about it as a separate *Behavior,* not as part of our child's *Self.*

By using "Self" language when your child is behaving well, you can help your child identify with personality characteristics that will serve your child, and build a positive sense of herself. This is what is often called "self-worth" or "self-esteem." Here are examples: "Sara, thanks for giving a toy to Allison; you really know how to share." "That's a great idea for how to get up onto the rock; you're good at solving problems."

We recommend starting with the specific behavior, so that your child knows what you like: "Thanks for setting the table." Then you can help your child think of this as something characteristic of him or her: "I'm glad you're so helpful." This helps your child think of this as an example of the way she *is,* and to take pride in this.

Of course, it's wise to use this kind of praise in moderation. Overdoing this could encourage a child to rely too much on external praise and support, rather than noticing the pleasure that is inherent in acting in ways that are cooperative and respectful of others.

Temporary vs. Permanent Language

Similarly, we have a choice about speaking of our child's misbehavior as something temporary, or acting as if our child's misbehavior is permanent. Here are some examples of using "Permanent" language: "You're *always* teasing your sister." "*Every* time I give you a chore, you don't want to do it." "You're *always* hitting." If we speak to our children using permanent, through-time language, the child gets the message that he has an undesirable behavior, he has always had this undesirable behavior, and he always will have it. Even if we are right that our child has *always* done something, speaking in this way gives the child an implicit message that he can't change.

In contrast, we can use "Temporary" language when we want the behavior to be temporary: "You were poking your sister *right then.* If you do that, you will need to play in another room *for a while.*" "I know you don't want to do this chore *right now.* You still need to do it, before dinner." "I don't want you to hit Sara. Do you want to play over here so that you have more room?"

Using *Temporary Behavior language* leaves the door open for the child to change. While it is usually not a complete solution in itself, it gives you a much better chance of being successful in using other parenting methods such as redirecting a child's behavior or "time out."

When to Use Language of Permanence

In general, when you *do* want your child to do something more often in the future, talk about it using language that implies permanence; when you *don't* want your child to do something, describe it using language implying that the behavior is temporary. Doing this makes it that much easier for your child to think of misbehaviors as temporary, and other more resourceful qualities as permanent.

Some examples are: "Having fun? I'm glad you kids get along so well together." "Thanks for being quiet. It's nice that you are so quiet in restaurants." Just as in the Behavior vs. Personality examples, we begin with something specific, and then speak of it as going through time. If I say "You *are* so quiet in restaurants," I am speaking about this behavior as going *through time.* This is very different than saying "Well, for *once,* you are quiet! I wish you were like this most of the time." Here I am presupposing that the child is *not* quiet most of the time: the only reason I need to wish he were quiet is because he usually isn't.

Although we have presented "Behavior vs. Self" and "Temporary vs. Permanence" for simplicity, they are most effective when used together: *Behavior* and *Temporary* for misbehavior; *Self* and *Permanent* for behaviors you want to encourage.

Respecting the Child

In this chapter we have assumed that "behaviors you want to encourage" are those that also benefit the child, and "misbehaviors" are those that also make the child unhappy or lead to trouble for her. These methods will not work if someone disregards the child's wishes and needs, and simply tries to mold him or her into a rigid idea of what they think a child *should* be.

This is why we began this chapter by teaching the ability to experience what it's like to be your child. With your additional adult experience *and* your knowledge of what it's like to be this child, you can often come up with useful solutions to problems. With knowledge and respect for the world of our children, we can help them learn responses and behaviors that will help them live happy and satisfying lives.

The foregoing is only a very small sample of how NLP methods and understandings can be used to help children grow into happy, capable, and responsible adults. We expect to publish a full book on parenting titled *Parenting Positively* in 1990.

10 *Asserting Yourself Respectfully*

There is an old joke about an elderly gentleman who went to his doctor, complaining that he had a regular bowel movement every morning at 8:30. His doctor looked a little puzzled and replied, "Many of my older patients would be very glad to have regular bowel movements. How is that a problem for you?" The gentleman replied, "Well, the problem is that I never wake up until 9:30."

Although this story is a joke, it is also an example of what is called context reframing: A behavior that is fine in one context becomes a problem in a different one (and vice-versa). We want to make two points with this story. The first is the speed with which your mind reevaluated the old gentleman's situation when you read about his not waking up before 9:30. As you understand these words, your internal image of his situation changed *instantly;* you *saw* it differently.

The second point is that the joke, and the change in your perceptions, results from a presupposition. The fact that he wakes up after 9:30 *presupposes* that he is still in bed at 8:30, even though nothing was actually *stated* about his being in bed at that time. Presuppositions can be used in similar ways to help people perceive problem situations differently. Although it appears that I am simply "talking" to the clients described in this chapter, what I say is always directed at shifting the presuppositions that create or maintain the problem they want help with.

Getting a Raise

Claire, a PhD. counseling psychologist, worked for a major medical school in a large city, with a part-time private practice on the side. She had started the medical school's PMS clinic and continued to manage the successful operation of this clinic. She found her work satisfying and fulfilling, and had the sense that she was making an important contribution. However, she had not been able to convince her chairman to give her the kind of financial rewards that she saw others around her receiving.

Claire was participating in one of our NLP Practitioner Trainings when she asked for some assistance in improving this situation. "I want to be able to approach superiors, particularly male superiors, about salary raises." Claire made her request with a question in her voice. She clearly felt very uncertain about doing such a thing.

"I've asked for raises before," Claire explained, "I just didn't feel good doing it, and I wasn't successful. This has happened repeatedly with a succession of superiors. *Each time* I have asked for a raise, I have been unsuccessful, and each time I feel a little worse."

As I gathered more information about her difficulty, I learned that Claire started feeling defeated long before she even entered the chairman's office: "Another person with the same training background as I have was hired three years after I started working there, starting at a salary that's $20,000 more than mine. He doesn't carry the load that I carry, yet he even has a lot more benefits—more vacation, more travel allowance, and so on. So the last time that I went in to ask for a raise, the situation felt like a set-up. It's all stacked against me before I even get in there." (Claire made a series of gestures off to her right.)

"So is it that you make pictures in your mind of all these things stacked against you before you go into the chairman's office?"

"Yes," Claire confirmed.

By asking more questions, I learned that Claire had a long row of mental pictures of how things are against her. The more pictures she had in the row, the worse she felt. It made sense that doing this before she walked into the supervisor's office would make Claire feel doomed to failure before she even asked for the raise, and make her presentation hesitant and unconvincing.

Someone who feels doomed to failure will nonverbally act very differently than someone who walks in more optimistically. If someone walks into a supervisor's office expecting to be turned down, it makes it much easier for him to go ahead and turn her down.

The same thing happens in other areas of our lives. Imagine that two different people ask you to go to a movie with them. The first person approaches you apologetically, with her head hanging down a bit, as if she expects you to say no, and perhaps as if she isn't worthy of your saying yes. Does this make you feel more like finding something else to do? Imagine a second person asking you to go to the same movie, but presenting this idea as something that's attractive. This second person has a pleasant, inviting look on her face, and clearly thinks the idea is very desirable. Which person is more likely to make you *want* to go to the movie?

I went on to learn a little more about what Claire thought of as "things stacked against her." The man who had the same training level as Claire at a higher salary was in good rapport with her chairman. He took the chairman out to dinner, shared jokes with the boss, and had the boss over to his house frequently. These were not things that Claire considered appropriate for her to do.

In addition, Claire said the financial officer had been giving false information to her boss. "The last time I asked for a raise, my boss said, 'I would love to give you a big raise; you deserve it. But our financial officer says we don't even have the money to pay our phone bills this month.' Then I went to our head accountant, and he said we have $260,000, just riding along!"

"And what stopped you from going back to the chairman and saying, 'Oh, I just found out we have $260,000. How big is our phone bill, anyway?'" Claire and the training group laughed.

"That happened *just* before I came to this seminar, so I haven't been able to do anything yet."

Claire went on to explain more about how she managed to feel bad when she went in to ask for a raise. "There's so much past history. I've had a long history of being treated like a second-class citizen by all my superiors over the years. When I started working there, I was on a time clock. At the end of the year, they owed me three months of overtime. But they just cut me off from that and said, 'No, we're not giving you that; we're just going to take you off the time clock with no financial reimbursement.'"

Now I knew enough about the examples in Claire's mind that I could begin to help her think of them in a different way, so that she could feel more self-assured.

"Claire, a *lot of things* like that *have happened* in the past. See, you don't have just *one* example, you've got *lots* of them." I said this enthusiastically, as if this was a wonderful thing, to pique her curiosity about *how* it was wonderful. "The question is, How is it possible that you would take all these examples," I said, gesturing to the location where she saw all her examples, "and *think* that all this history was to your *dis*advantage in going into a negotiation, rather than thinking, 'Hey, I've not only got one example, I've got *lots* of data and evidence to support me in what I'm asking for,' and get a feeling of strength and power from that?" Although I asked this as a question, my goal was for Claire to start thinking about all this "negative" past history in a new light. The effect is to suggest that she consider thinking of it as support. As I talked, I observed Claire closely to find out if this fit for her.

Claire began smiling as I was talking. She was thinking about the same examples that had made her feel bad and defeated a moment before, but now she looked strong. Obviously she was changing the *meaning* of these past events in her mind. "That's quite an idea," Claire said with a grin.

"Yes it is, isn't it. Because if they had only treated you unfairly once, they could make excuses, and say, 'Well, that was because of this.' But with all of this data, what could they say?"

"Hmmm.". . . Claire let this new perspective sink in even further. She looked more and more resourceful. "Thank you!"

I went on to explain to the group, "Claire *had* thought that all these examples were a reason to have a bad feeling of hopelessness, instead of recognizing the way in which they actually support her request for a raise and are reasons for having a good feeling when she goes in to ask." Although I was talking to the group, sound does travel in all directions, and my purpose was actually to further solidify this new meaning in *Claire's* experience. I spoke of the problem as being in the *past,* and nonverbally emphasized her new way of thinking.

Claire was chuckling now. "Thank you. I can already see the memo I'll write."

Claire's feeling state looked good. But what would happen if Claire went in feeling confident, asked for a raise, and *still* got turned down? Would she be devastated? Being turned down could happen, and I wanted to be sure Claire had a positive way of dealing with all possibilities. I did this primarily by talking to the group, while observing Claire's nonverbal responses closely to confirm that she was responding positively.

"We want to have Claire prepared for anything and everything, right? When I go into a negotiation, I like to know what my bottom line is, and to have positive alternatives. That way I don't get pressured to agree with an arrangement that isn't good for me. I like to know that no matter how it turns out, I have attractive choices, and that I will be fine."

The first thing I wanted to be sure of was that Claire would use her new-found strength in a way that was positive. "When I go in to ask for something, I like to present the data I have in a really positive way so that I ally myself with the person I'm talking to. In a situation like this I might say, 'I really support the organization, and I really want to continue working here, and I'm guessing these things just hadn't come to your attention before. It's important enough to me, and I know it's important to you to have people working for you who are congruently supporting the organization. I want to continue to give the way I have all these years, and that's why I'm bringing this up. It's important to me to get this resolved in a way that's really fair to you and fair to me.'

"This kind of approach is a lot more likely to get a positive response than if I went in blaming and complaining, 'You should have done something about this a long time ago, blah, blah, blah.' Then I'm much less likely to get what I want. But if I speak to the person's positive intentions, and describe how my request will benefit the organization, then I'm a lot more likely to be successful." Claire was nodding her head.

I said all this to be sure that Claire knew how to present her case in a way that invited agreement, and provide her with options if she didn't. By describing my own experience rather than telling Claire what to do, I made it easy for Claire to take in the parts she found useful and ignore the rest.

Next, I wanted to be sure she had a plan even if she did get turned down again. "However, even when I do a really good job of all that, I still can't guarantee that the person is going to be reasonable. The chairman may still say, 'Well, I don't think so,' not recognizing the value I've contributed, even if I'm right about it. If that happens, I want to have something to do next, so that no matter what he does, I am fine.

"One option is to gather specific information about what she would have to do to get a raise. Claire might go in and say, 'Look, there are some things that seem important to me to get out in the open here. I don't know how much you value what I have been doing. I know how it seems to me, and I'd like you to understand that. If you don't value it as much as I do, I would like to know exactly what I would need to do for you to value it that much? What would I need to do to get that raise?'"

It's possible that although Claire thought she was making a wonderful contribution, her chairman may know some ways in which her performance didn't meet his standards for a raise. I wanted to be sure that Claire knew how to find out what her *chairman's* evidence would be that she deserved a raise. She could then decide if it was worth it to her to try to meet these standards. Claire continued to nod her head as I discussed these options. Clearly she was accustomed to gathering this kind of information.

"So Claire, what if the chairman says, 'Sorry, I don't think it's really worth it to us.' Do you already have other alternatives?"

"Yes. More private practice is one option." Claire then mentioned her other options, including working only half-time for the hospital while expanding her private practice.

"And when you think about these alternatives, do they seem like more attractive options if your boss said 'No'?"

"Yes, they are more attractive."

Most of us occasionally make ourselves feel bad by comparing what we think other people in our life *should do* with what they *are doing.* Since we don't have direct control over what others do, this places us in a powerless position. I am setting things up so that Claire makes a *different* comparison: she will feel more powerful as she thinks about *her own most attractive option,* rather than whether her supervision is doing the right thing.

Next I wanted to find out if there were any missing pieces for Claire, so I asked her to test more completely in her imagination. "Claire, I would like you to imagine beginning that interaction with your boss. How will you set this up? Will you ask for a meeting or something like that?"

"Yes. And I will write up a memo that lists all the value that I provide for the department and my history there, and make a proposal for equity."

"And how comfortable and resourceful will you feel as you are doing that?"

"Better. What still gets in my way is that the financial officer who gave the false information has been very underhanded for years, and I might not know all the information until afterwards."

"And you've seen that as a limitation?" Again I'm treating this as Claire's point of view up to this point in time, not as truth. This will make it easier for Claire to take on a more useful point of view in a moment.

"Yes, because I haven't really known what all the information is at the time that I'm speaking to the chairman. For example, the phone bill thing. I didn't know until afterwards what the financial officer had done."

"Now, how can you utilize *that* to your advantage?—the fact that the financial officer has been underhanded before?" I invited Claire to find her own way to use what had occurred in the past to support her, rather than think of it as a hindrance.

"I think I would go ahead and talk with him about the past, and give him that example about the phone bill. If I say that up front, I think it would be *fine,* because that reduces the financial officer's credibility. If she has said something else, then it becomes more doubtful because of her being underhanded in the past." Claire was now speaking with an inner clarity and authority that looked good.

"Only if Claire thought *she* couldn't talk about these things would she be placing an unnecessary restriction on herself. Then she would have to go in feeling bad. But that's not a restriction for *her,* because *she's* not underhanded." (Claire laughs.) "*She's* putting her cards on the table, and she's willing to talk about *anything.* Right, Claire?"

"You bet! Thank you."

"So now when you think about going in and being willing to put all the cards on the table? . . ."

"That feels good. That *really* feels good."

"And now Claire can't lose; She's got a lot of data. *She* knows what she thinks is fair, and what she wants, and if she is not able to get him to understand that, she's got better alternatives. Why would she even want to stay with the department if they weren't willing to acknowledge her ability and skill the way she deserves? It just becomes a less attractive choice. Knowing she has attractive alternatives for any eventuality gives her the assurance she needs to be persuasive."

"Right," added Claire, confidently.

What I've just done is pull together all the smaller changes in perspective I've been building, to be sure they come together as one complete "package" in Claire's mind.

The Results

Eight months after this session, I spoke to Claire, and she enthusiastically related the following:

"It worked really well. I got the raise without really asking for it! You see, when I was at the training in Colorado, we were in a transition period, because a new chairman was hired. The first month after I got back, there were two chairmen during the transition period. So I thought, 'Now is not the time for me to ask.' I had what I was going to do all planned out. Consciously I had *thought* I'd make an appointment when things settled down, and I felt very comfortable about doing that.

"Then one day when I was talking with the new chairman about something else, I found myself talking about raises. I hadn't planned to. It just came out of my mouth smoothly, and he said, 'Yes, of course you get a raise.' That was my *first* raise; after that I got another one. Then in a very similar circumstance, I was talking with the chairman about something else, and said I wanted to have a promotion to Associate Professor. He said, 'Of course we're going to do something about this. What we've been calling you is ridiculous.' So I'm going to get this promotion soon, and along with that comes a third raise.

"I think it has to do with the change in how I feel inside about that issue I had with male superiors. Before that work you did with me, I felt that I didn't quite deserve as much as male superiors, but all that has shifted. There is something about the energy in me that says 'I am capable' and 'I deserve to be compensated,' and that energy is noticed by other people. I haven't been pushy about it, but I know what I can do and what I deserve. I let my capability come out, and others sense that.

"For example, I've been doing some NLP work to help medical students get over test anxiety so they can do better on their board examinations. Just recently I worked with two students who were so anxious when they took the regional exam that they flunked. They knew the material, but couldn't do well on the test because their anxiety was so extreme. I did one session of NLP work with them to help them get over their test anxiety. When they took their National Boards two days after they'd flunked the regionals, they did well, at the 86th and 89th percentile. This came to the attention of our Educational Director, and he's asked me to write a proposal to do this with all our students. And he said, 'And of course you will receive a raise for doing that.'"

What We Can Learn from this Example

Claire clearly had the competence and ability to support her new sense of what she deserved. If she hadn't, she might have lost her job instead of getting several raises. Sometimes people have asked us, "But how do I know if I am capable and will get the raise, or if I am just going to lose my job?" Practically speaking, this can usually be dealt with more easily by leaving how much we "deserve" out of the discussion. Thinking about "how much I *deserve*" tends to put me in a righteous, superior, position which could make me act haughty and rigid—something that others are not likely to respond well to. I know plenty of people who are extremely capable and probably "deserve" to be making more money than they are making. There have been times when we thought we "deserved" to make more money than we did for something. Even if we were right, it doesn't mean the money is available, or that others will perceive value in the same way that we do.

Rather than trying to figure out "How do much I deserve?" it's much simpler to ask, "What is someone willing to pay me for this?" Then I can simply consider my other alternatives, and decide what is most attractive. This puts me in charge of the situation, rather than being dependent on others.

There are many times when we choose an option that is less lucrative because it satisfies other important criteria that we have—we will be able to learn something interesting from the experience, it will help build something valuable and useful for people over time, etc. Even if I "deserve" more, if someone is not willing to pay more, and it's the best option I can think of, then I can feel good accepting it until I can make a better alternative for myself.

What I did with Claire was actually fairly simple. I pointed out how all the things that had made her feel bad could be thought of in ways that *supported* her request. I also made sure that she could present her request in a positive way that would be most likely to get a favorable response. Finally, I made sure that she had attractive alternatives if she got an unreasonable response, so that no matter what happens she can feel good about her options.

In many ways, this is what we are always doing in our work with people—finding ways to utilize the past to our benefit, adjusting present behavior so that it's most likely to be successful, and building in positive alternatives for all future possibilities.

All of us have times when things seem stacked against us. However, often this is only true from one perspective. Looking at things another way can often allow us to utilize the same events in a positive way.

Often people will tell others to "look at the bright side," but usually this kind of advice is ineffective because it doesn't change our perceptions. It can be annoying to be *told* to look on the bright side, when we can't see it, or it doesn't seem real to us. NLP skills made it possible to respectfully utilize Claire's way of thinking, and her nonverbal feedback, to make this bright side *more real* to Claire than the way she had been looking at it. Once this happened, this new perspective became an automatic part of her thinking and actions.

The Ex-husband and His Wife

Roxanne came to see me, desperate to find a better way to deal with her ex-husband, Ron, and his new wife, Sara. Roxanne and Ron had joint custody of their three children. While the agreement seemed clear on paper, it was anything but clear as it was actually carried out. The two years since Ron had remarried had been filled with anger, sharp words, feuding, and unhappiness on all sides. Roxanne had tried to be extra reasonable every step of the way since the divorce four years ago—so that she would be treated fairly in return. Roxanne's perception was that it wasn't working—and that nothing else was either. Roxanne thought she'd continually gotten the rotten end of each agreement, and was very angry about it.

As she talked, she was clearly very upset about the long history of nothing working, and in particular about a recent incident in which Sara had arbitrarily decreed some restrictions on Roxanne's interactions with the three children. It would be easy to get caught up in the soap-opera quality of this situation. However, as Roxanne talked, I began to think about how I could help Roxanne experience the situation differently.

"I don't want to get angry when Sara or Ron do unreasonable things," she stated.

Because Roxanne was in such an emotional frenzy about what Sara and Ron did, her feelings made it more difficult for her to deal effectively with them. Even if Sara and Ron were the two most unreasonable people in the world, if Roxanne had some way to feel resourceful anyway, and to make sure her own needs and goals were met anyway, she would be much better off.

None of us can fully control what others do, and we all encounter "tough situations" when the deck seems stacked against us. We can get mad, depressed, or upset that "things are against us," or we can find ways to get what we want even when others are unreasonable. It is much more empowering to notice what we can control, and use that to get what we want, than to feel helpless about what we can't control. Whenever possible, I assist people in finding these ways.

I was glad Roxanne was already focused on having more choice about her own emotional response. First I asked her, "What is the useful purpose of getting angry?"

"Well, I need to help the children grow and learn," she answered. "I get angry when Sara and Ron interfere. I suppose the *positive purpose* is making sure it's possible to carry out plans. In other words, being able to function."

"So you have thought about 'carrying out plans' and 'being able to function,' as being the same thing?" I asked. I hoped that as I held up what had been an unexamined assumption of Roxanne's for examination, she would begin to see things differently. I wanted her to notice that it's still possible to function even if a particular plan is interfered with. "Plans" and "being able to function" are two separate things. However, Roxanne didn't respond to this, so I tried something else.

"In what way does not being able to carry out plans enable you to function *better?*" I asked Roxanne. She looked very confused, and I had to repeat the question several times to get her to answer it. Her confusion resulted from my asking her to generate evidence for a belief *opposite* to the one she held. She had been getting uncontrollably angry because she thought Ron and Sara's interference with her plans was a monumental limitation to her. I was asking her to consider how it *helped* her functioning rather than limiting it.

"I suppose it stimulates my creative resources," Roxanne finally answered thoughtfully.

"In what way does this stimulate your creative resources?" I asked, wanting to amplify Roxanne's experience of this new perspective.

"Any time I had a problem and went on, it stimulated my creative resources. I guess that always happens." Roxanne said. She was looking and sounding much more positive than she had a few moments ago.

"So this *always* happens." I said, underscoring her remark.

"Yes. Now I'm feeling a lot better," Roxanne said, with more strength in her voice.

This may *sound* like just playing with words, but it isn't. Roxanne's *experience* was shifting as she took in a new belief. I wanted to further emphasize this new belief by finding other ways in which her creative response would be supported by her values.

"In what way do you think your demonstrating this new response will be of value and a learning for your children? . . . For example, your responding this way will be a model for your kids of how to respond well internally, even when others are unreasonable. That is something that will go with them through time. Even if you aren't able to carry out plans in the moment, over time there will be advantages. Even when there is superficial annoyance, you can have an underlying sense that this is what develops something positive in your children through time." Since Roxanne had been concerned about her children's development, I was helping her build an experience of how she could utilize whatever Ron and Sara did to have a positive impact on her children. Roxanne agreed, and told me she was pleased with this new way of understanding.

The transition Roxanne made seemed to me almost too remarkable and too fast to be believable. Since Roxanne's previous angry response had been so strong and so persistent over a period of years, I wanted to test thoroughly to see if this difficulty was completely resolved, or if more needed to be done. "So now when you think of this, is there anything that could stop you from being resourceful?" I asked.

"I have this bit of doubt, or panic," Roxanne responded thoughtfully. "I have this little nagging doubt: 'What if this time I don't survive?'"

"Oh, so you're going to *die* because someone is unreasonable, huh?" I said. Roxanne had made an extreme statement, so I exaggerated it to help her begin to realize how ridiculous it was.

"Not really," Roxanne laughed, "It's more like the world is ending," she clarified, back to a serious tone of voice.

"So you won't *die,* it's *just* that the *whole world will end?*" Again, I exaggerated what Roxanne said, with a twinkle in my eye and in my voice. I was inviting her to notice the absurdity of what a part of her had taken very seriously. Roxanne smiled.

"So how do you manage to have this panic?" I asked.

"I think it comes from my not taking care of myself adequately." Roxanne revealed. She described her experience of playing basketball. "I say 'excuse me' and step out of the way even when it's my job. All of my life I didn't let myself have any needs. I didn't feel safe standing up for myself. It's been like if somebody wants something from me, I'm supposed to give it to them."

Clearly, we'd uncovered an important second belief that needed transforming before Roxanne could have what she wanted.

When I asked, "Do you believe in being fair?" she responded, "Yes."

Since "fairness" usually includes equality and reciprocity, I now have a belief of Roxanne's that can be used to change the belief that is a problem to her.

"So is that what you think everyone else should believe too?—that if somebody wants something from them, they should give it? Is that what you want your children to believe?"

"No."

By having her apply her standard for herself equally to other people, I was starting to loosen up her belief. This is often helpful when someone has different standards for themselves than for others.

"So what makes you so special that it's OK for you, but not for anybody else?" Since she thought of herself as *un*deserving, I reversed this assumption and acted as if she were getting *special* treatment this way, and it wasn't fair.

Roxanne laughed. "I don't know. Part of me feels outraged about that."

"What if you want something from yourself," I asked. "Are you supposed to give that to your*self?*" Now I'm applying the same belief that "she should give something" in a way that she hasn't applied it before—to herself instead of others.

"I guess so," Roxanne replied.

"What have you wanted from yourself that you're supposed to give yourself?"

"More respect; that it's legitimate for me to exist."

It was clear that Roxanne knew what she needed, but she still wasn't actually giving it to herself. I knew I hadn't yet gotten the shift in Roxanne's experience that I was going for, because I wasn't seeing the nonverbal expression of someone who was loving herself. I realized I needed to change my approach to find something that would make complete sense to Roxanne, and actually shift her experience.

"Actually, giving other people what they want is a pretty good guideline," I said, pausing for impact. "It's just a matter of understanding what it really means. Sometimes people confuse what people *say* they want, or demand in the moment, with what they *really* want—what will really make their lives better over time." Although I was accepting her belief, I was starting to make a major change in the *meaning* of "giving other people what they want."

"You know how when kids are growing up, they want and demand a lot of things in the moment. They want candy, or their own way about something. And you know that if you were to always give them exactly what they ask for, it just wouldn't work out in the long run. They wouldn't grow up to be the kind of person anyone else wanted to be around. And that's not what they *really* want. They wouldn't end up having a quality life, which is what they *really* want.

"An unreasonable adult is no different than an unreasonable kid. You know how people are when they grow up always getting what they asked for. Since they never had to learn how to take other people's needs into account, they end up being the kind of grownups that can't get along with other people, and they have major problems in life."

"Hmmm," Roxanne was following me; this was making sense to her. Her nonverbal expression had shifted, but I could tell that this new belief wasn't securely "locked in" yet.

"In the same way, if you don't take your place in the world, and go for your own needs first, this is what you would be doing to people around you—making them into the kind of people who expect everyone to do everything for them, and don't know how to respect another person. That's not helping someone else. That's the last thing on earth they need if they're *already* having a little trouble taking other people into account."

I first used the example of children, because I know that any mother will probably understand. Then I shifted to adults, and to other people in general, so that Roxanne will respond differently with *anyone* in that category, not just with Sara or Ron.

"So going for your own needs and wants first is really what other people want more than anything else," I summarized. "Otherwise in some way *they* won't have a quality life. It will mean problems for them later on." Roxanne was completely with me this time. Her whole body was responding to this new way of thinking about giving other people what they *really* want. It was going in.

"Where else will this realization make a difference for you?" I asked Roxanne. I didn't really care how she answered my question. My purpose was to get *her* to presuppose her new response, and to apply it more broadly in other situations, to completely lock in her new way of thinking.

The Results

About six weeks later Roxanne reported on how she was doing. "I've had *plenty* of opportunities to test what we did!" she joked. "When Sara or Ron have done something unreasonable, I feel completely different. I kind of laugh about it to myself. It's mostly just amusing. Feeling differently about it has made it *much* easier to deal with the practical matters, and go after what I want for the children.

"Something else interesting has happened," Roxanne went on. "Ever since I was a little girl, I've had a recurring nightmare. I've never remembered exactly what happened in it, but I had a feeling that got worse and worse, until finally I woke up with a terrible feeling all over. After I got divorced, I had a lot more of those dreams. After the session with you, I had what seemed like the same dream, only I had *good* feelings. Somehow it seemed the same, except that I felt resourceful and woke up with good feelings all over." I took Roxanne's changed dream as unconscious confirmation that an important and deep change had occurred.

In the months that followed, Roxanne still had some tough times dealing with Ron and Sara, and some difficult decisions to make. However, she had taken a significant step in building a more solid footing for herself. Thinking about herself differently made Roxanne feel more resourceful, and this feeling made it easier to deal with the difficulties.

The kinds of questions I was asking Roxanne are an important part of the field of NLP. Utilizing language in these specific ways can help us make transformations in our beliefs quickly, and arrive at new perspectives. When we actually see things differently, our problems often melt away. Just as we can quickly and easily change our perspective of the man in the joke at the beginning of this chapter, we can also quickly shift our perspective and our feelings about our own lives. These shifts don't require pain or time. They only require having another way of perceiving events that really makes sense to us.

11   *Resolving Grief*

Four years after Al and Sheri stopped dating, he was still preoccupied with her. Nearly a year after the split, Al had heard Sheri was getting married, so he went to city hall to search through marriage license applications. When he couldn't find her name, he thought to himself, "I still have a chance." Al had dated very little since then. Whenever he passed Sheridan Boulevard, her name, Sheri, still "popped out at him."

We began studying the grief process in 1984, and developed a method for resolving it effectively, based on what people who spontaneously resolved grief well, did without knowing it. Since so many others have benefitted from this method, it seemed likely that Al would too.

First, I asked Al to think of Sheri and tell me how he thought of her. He saw her in a small, still picture slightly to his right. "It's very dark and depressing. I don't like to look at it."

"What do you see in that picture?"

"I see when we broke up. That's the last time I saw her."

People often recall the bad times rather than the good times they had with someone they loved. That can make the yearning less, but it also keeps them distant from the positive feelings they had with the lost person. This prevents them from being able to resolve the loss.

"Find out what happens if you change that picture to one of the very special times you had with Sheri, when things were going well.". . .

"It's less depressing now, but I feel pulled even more strongly. That's what I'd like to have back again—the good times."

110

This is typical of the way people think of someone who is lost to them: small, distant, inaccessible. That's what causes the feeling of emptiness; you can see the lost person, but she is so distant from you that you can't feel the good feelings you once had with her.

Next I asked Al to set that picture aside temporarily. "Now think of someone who is no longer in your life, but when you think of him or her, you feel good—you have a sense of *presence or fullness,* rather than emptiness. How do you think of that person?" Al saw his old high school friend, Fred, to his left, life size, and moving. As he did this, he said, "Boy, that sure feels better!"

I checked to be sure he really felt fully *with* this person. "Do you feel almost as if Fred is here in the room with you? Can you feel what it's like to be with him, even though he's no longer part of your life?"

"Yes, it's almost like he's in the room with me."

I'd just found out from Al how *his* brain codes an experience of someone who is actually 'lost,' but about whom Al has a positive sense of 'presence.' It was in a certain location, life-size, and moving. This will be key information in helping Al resolve the loss of Sheri.

"Would you have any objection to being able to think of Sheri in the same way, so that you could feel the good feelings that you had with her instead of that depressing emptiness?"

"Well, it would be nice to feel those nice feelings again, but wouldn't it get in the way of meeting other women?"

"That's an important consideration. You certainly don't want to just sit at home feeling good about Sheri. Actually, when we're done, you'll feel much *more* like meeting other women. Thinking of Fred this way hasn't stopped you from having other male friends, has it?" Al agreed that it hadn't.

"However, thinking about Sheri the way you have been has kept you hung up on her and gotten in the way of your meeting other women. This process will allow you to regain the good feelings that you had with Sheri, just as you already have them with Fred. Those were *your* good feelings and you deserve to have them in place of the longing and emptiness you've been feeling. More important, later we'll use those good feelings as a guide to what kind of new relationship you want to build with someone else in the future."

"Well, that sounds all right," said Al, agreeing to go ahead, but still a bit doubtful that this could make a difference.

"Good. First I want you to think of one of the most special times you had with Sheri, when things were going well. . . . Then I want you to see her life-size and moving, over here on your left in the same location where you saw Fred. You can think of her in the *same* way that you think of Fred, almost as if she were here in the room with you."

Al began to smile and relax, obviously feeling better. "That feels nice. It's been a long time since I've felt like that. . . . I do feel differently about her now."

"Even though you have lost that relationship with Sheri, you can still have those good feelings with you." Further testing confirmed that Al now felt comfortable thinking and talking about Sheri. His brain now had her categorized differently—not as someone to grieve over, but like Fred, someone to feel good about. NLP allows us to tap into how our brains *code* experiences, and this is what enables us to make such surprisingly rapid changes.

It might be tempting to stop at this point, since Al has learned how to replace his feelings of emptiness with warm feelings of love and caring when he thinks of Sheri.

However, even if Al went on to develop new relationships on his own, he might try to exactly duplicate his experience with Sheri. In the novel *Lolita,* a 40-year-old man is still trying to find an exact replacement for the 13-year-old girl he loved over a quarter-century earlier. You can't replace the *person* you have lost, but you *can* develop a new relationship that has many of the same valued *qualities* that you had with the lost person.

The next step will help Al go even further in preserving the benefits from his past relationship with Sheri. It will make sure Al uses his past experiences to find and develop new loving relationships. This is what people who spontaneously recover quickly from tragic losses have done.

"Now I want you to close your eyes and review all the good experiences you had with Sheri—never mind the bad ones; they don't matter right now. As you do this, I want you to think of the *values* you experienced in that relationship. Different people value different things in a relationship. Some value the warmth and intimacy, while others value a friendship that is less intense, but still a comfortable being-together. Some people value spontaneity and variety, while others value steadiness and dependability. Humor, intelligence, and liveliness are just a few of the other things that people value in a relationship. Some people find that in a relationship they were able to appreciate themselves more, and *that's* part of what they valued. . . .

"As you identify the various values that you experienced with Sheri, I want you to put those into a separate image in a different location. This image might be more symbolic or abstract, but it will preserve the essence of the special experiences you had with Sheri.". . .

"I see a warm, white light that permeates anything it touches," Al commented.

"Great. Now in a third location I want you to imagine what form those values might take in your future. How might you satisfy those same values with another person? This image can be somewhat vague and unclear, because you don't know yet who you will meet and enjoy in the future, but the image will have that warm, white light. Imagining how you can experience those same values with someone else will direct your attention toward searching for other women and discovering what kind of satisfying relationship you can develop with each one you meet.". . .

"I've got it. That makes me feel more hopeful."

"Now take that picture and multiply it, as if it became a deck of cards. As it multiplies, each card may turn out a little bit different, but each one will have that warm, white light, each one still preserving the essence of the kind of relationship you want to develop. . . .

"When you have that stack of pictures, I want you to imagine that you cast them out into your future, so that they scatter throughout your future, some nearer to you, and others farther out. After you scatter them, you may be able to see the warm, white light of each one, twinkling like a small star.". . .

"That's amazing. I can actually see all those little sparkling lights."

"Great. Now I want you to think of Sheri the way you used to, small and dark, and see if you can get the old feeling of loss back.". . .

"I can't really do it. I can sort of see it briefly, but then I think of those sparkling lights in the future."

This process took about twenty minutes. For another demonstration and an outline of the process, see our videotape "Resolving Grief." (1)

The Results for Al

A few weeks later Al called to report several interesting changes. In the week following our work together, at work he found himself talking comfortably to a friend of Sheri's, whom he had previously avoided. He had begun dating again and was enjoying it. Finally, he reported something that was a fascinating demonstration that the changes we had made were thorough. He said that the next time he approached Sheridan Boulevard he was wondering what would happen. As he looked up at the sign the word "Rid" popped out at him instead of "Sheri"!

A few weeks later he used the grief process by himself to change his feelings about two other old girlfriends. We are always pleased when someone learns enough about a process to use it themselves without our assistance.

In the year following, Al continued dating and developed a close relationship with a woman named Julie over a six-month period. He said to me, "This last year has been amazing. I would never have imagined that one short session could have so much impact."

Shortly after this, Al called "in a tailspin" and close to tears. Julie had told him she "just wanted to be friends"—she was involved with someone else. Since then he had been preoccupied and had trouble sleeping. Although Al knew the grief process, he hadn't used it, thinking that would prevent any possibility of getting back together with Julie. I reassured him that not only would the process help him feel better, it would also make him much more resourceful and reasonable if she did show any interest in renewing their relationship. (See the section on "pregrieving" later in this chapter.)

A week later he called in a much better state. The night after he did the grief process with himself he had a pleasant dream for the first time in a month, instead of the anguished and confused ones he had been having. He had talked with Julie on the phone, feeling calm and resourceful, and had arranged a tentative coffee date.

None of us can prevent losses from occurring. Al now has a way to deal with lost relationships in his life in a resourceful way. Each time, he takes with him the value of the relationship he has had as he moves forward to make new connections with others. When we know how to do this, we can use all our experiences to build better and better relationships with others.

Many Forms of Loss Can Be Resolved

Since loss is something that we all experience, we have had opportunities to use this grief process to resolve a wide variety of losses, usually in one session. These include a young mother who gave up her baby for adoption, an older mother who lost an adult son by suicide, and men and women who have lost their loves to horrible diseases or accidents. In almost every case, the client experienced a tremendous relief and reconnection with the lost person, and with the *value* in that relationship.

Although most people think of loss in relation to people, there are many other losses that can be resolved with this method. The loss of a pet, a ring, a home, a job, or an ability—all can be as devastating to some people as the loss of a relationship.

We have used this process with injured athletes who have lost their prized ability to play their favorite sport, and with people who have lost their job, home, or their native country. It has been very gratifying to be able to make such a difference with these people so quickly.

About three months after I assisted a woman grieving over her mother's death, her husband wrote:

"A brief note to let you know how grateful I am for your spending the time helping my wife deal with her grief. We both thank you for your kindness, your time, your warmth and your genuine concern.

"Since your intervention, she has been able to accept her mother's death and has literally put the grief in perspective. She is handling stress a lot better now, and because of that, stress has been taken off our work and our marriage. Again, many thanks. I wish you and yours health and well-being, and better living through NLP."

As a young child, Ruth had a close girl friend with whom she played almost daily as long as she could remember. This closeness had been important to both girls. Then Ruth's friend suddenly moved to another state. "It's as if a part of *myself* left, and I've been missing it ever since," Ruth explained. She had tried a variety of therapeutic methods to try to resolve this loss, without success. Several months after using this grief resolution process, Ruth commented, "After so many years, it's nice to finally have that loss resolved and complete." The warmth and richness in Ruth's voice confirmed the depth of what she was saying.

Only six weeks before I worked with her, Anita had lost the three people who had been closest to her on three successive days. On May 6, her boss was killed in a car accident; on May 7, her mother died; on May 8, her fiance, who had been in Africa experimenting with communication with animals was eaten by a lion! Not surprisingly, Anita complained of emptiness in her life. I asked her which death was most difficult for her to deal with, and then guided her through the resolution process with that one. when we were finished, she looked thoughtful and said, "I could just do the same thing with the others by myself, couldn't I?" Anita reported later that going through this process had made a big difference for her.

Loss of a Cherished Dream

We have found this method to be especially useful when people are grieving over something that they never actually had, except as a hoped-for dream. A woman who finds that she cannot have a child, or a businessman in "mid-life crisis" who realizes that his expectations of success are not likely to be realized, may grieve as deeply as someone who has actually lost a child or a top-level job.

When these dreams are as vivid as the memories of people who have actually lost something, lost dreams will produce the same feelings of emptiness and loss. Using the grief process with their *dream* enables people to experience the dream as an ongoing resource, with the same fullness as if they actually had it.

Use with Abusive Childhood

We have even used this process with people who were abused as children, grieving the loss of a happy childhood that they never experienced. When a parent dies, they lose whatever positive relationship they had with the parent, and they also lose the hope of every having the loving, caring relationship that they wanted.

A number of professionals we have trained in this process are now using it routinely with those who have been physically or sexually abused. It enables these people to recover the loving parent relationships they missed out on while growing up. This provides an experiential foundation for a sense of self-worth and well-being.

One of several organizations now using our grief process in this way is the largest private not-for-profit psychiatric hospital in the country, *Our Lady of Peace* in Louisville, Kentucky. Mary Ellen Zuverink, Ph.D., who trained members of the hospital staff in the grief process, recently told me:

"We have been using the grief pattern in our institution with all sorts of success," she said excitedly. "We're working on the toughest kinds of cases; if it works with these people, it can work with *anybody.*

"One young woman was clinically depressed and suicidal, grieving the loss of her mother. She was an adult child of an alcoholic, had been physically abused by her mother, sexually abused by her brothers, and had had a rotten life generally. After doing the grief process, everything turned around for her. She said afterwards, 'I feel like I've had a heart transplant.' This was about seven months ago, and now she's in great shape. She just visited me, and said that was what had really done it for her. She was in good shape when she left the hospital, and she was in even better shape when she came back to see me."

She went on to give me examples of other patients with multiple problems who were grieving over a major loss. "Once that's taken care of, a lot of other problems simply drop away," she said. "I'm so glad you're doing this work. It's really needed. I feel so fortunate to be able to pass this process on to others."

She also told me that the results from this one process have really opened up the staff's thinking about what is possible. "We've seen the results—how people can change so quickly." Because it is a major psychiatric hospital, many people's lives are being affected.

How Long Does Grieving Take?

Most books on grieving claim that the person "must" go through a series of four or five stages to resolve grief over a period of time. Different authors list slightly different stages, but they usually include denial, anger, and bargaining, before acceptance. Often even this "acceptance" is more of a resignation than the kind of resourceful resolution that we have observed people achieving.

While this is certainly what *has happened* to most people in the past, it has very little to do with what is *possible.* Saying that it *has to be* that way is like the people in the last century who said that flying was impossible because it had never been done. Some people have always grieved quickly and resourcefully. By studying *how* these exceptional people successfully resolved their grief, we discovered the key elements and how to teach others to proceed through those elements quickly. We have found that a lengthy waiting period is simply not necessary—it's only a result of not knowing what to do.

The fact that grieving is handled very differently in different cultures also indicates that the length of grieving is not fixed. The Irish have a "wake," where friends and relatives talk about the deceased and party for three days, and after this celebration the survivors have "recovered." At the other extreme, in some cultures a widow must mourn the death of her husband for a specified period of years, or in some cases, forever.

We have even used this grief resolution method effectively on the same day as the loss, although of course we do not push anyone to do this. No specific time period is needed; what *is* needed is an understanding of the mental structure of grief and loss, so that you know what to do to change it.

How People Think of Loss

The variety of ways that people use to think of someone who is gone is fascinating. Before reading on, you might find it interesting to pause and notice how *you* represent someone you have lost. . . .

Everyone uses some variation of "There, but not *really* there." One way is to see the person, but he is somehow "insubstantial"—transparent, flat, floating off the ground, in a framed snapshot, etc. Perhaps you can see a dent in a bed, or flattened grass in a meadow, but no one is there. You may see yourself with the person far away, so you are only an observer; you aren't with the lost person so that you can enjoy the good feelings you once shared. One man remembered a dead friend by hearing her voice on the telephone, but it sounded "tinny," like an old recording, instead of a real person speaking.

After resolving a loss, we think of the lost person in our minds in almost the same way that we think of others who are still a part of our lives. They are "alive for us" in a sense, even though we know the person is actually dead or gone. What better way could there be to honor those who have been important to us in the past, than to carry on the *value* they've given us, *with* us, . . . and to go on to share it with others?

When There is Trauma as Well as Loss

If someone has died in a particularly unpleasant way—in an accident, or of a terminal disease—it's often necessary to also use the phobia procedure (see chapter 7) along with the grief process. For instance, I recently worked with a man who had lost his wife to cancer about six months earlier. He and his wife had made unusually good use of their remaining time together, doing enjoyable things, reminiscing about the good times they had shared, and renewing their love for each other. However, there was also plenty of unpleasantness, as the cancer progressed and she became sicker and eventually slipped into a coma.

I asked him to review that period in his mind and carefully separate all the good times that he wanted to preserve and cherish, from the unpleasant times that he might as well leave behind. I first used the phobia method on the unpleasant times, and then used the grief procedure with the special times that he wanted to cherish and keep with him. This allowed him to distance himself from the unpleasantness, as he reclaimed the valued experiences he had with his wife.

Pregrieving: Restoring Personal Power

A variation of this method is useful for what we call "pregrieving," a process that prepares people in advance for a coming loss. This is particularly useful for people with aged or ill friends, or for those who are preparing for divorce.

Pregrieving helps people gain a personal resolution about future events, so that they can deal much more responsively and respectfully with someone who is dying or leaving. Without pregrieving, people can be so involved with their grief response that they aren't able to offer support to the dying person. The dying person certainly has enough to deal with, without the extra burden of helping his relatives and friends cope with his death! One of our Master Practitioners uses this method practically every day in his work with AIDS patients and their families and friends.

In the same way, pregrieving can be useful in any other impending loss, such as an approaching divorce. By resolving the loss in advance, you can feel powerful and resourceful, rather than desperate and helpless. This provides a much better emotional basis for dealing with the practical problems of the separation. This resolution can sometimes even be useful in establishing a basis for a possible reconciliation.

As a surprise bonus, we have found that pregrieving is even useful with couples who plan to stay together! It strengthens their relationship, and eliminates any clinging dependency resulting from thinking, "I can't live without you."

For instance, Ron was unhappy with his intense jealousy over his girlfriend. After one of our Master Practitioners used this method with him, his jealousy vanished. He no longer had the sense that his girlfriend was the "only" way he could have certain valuable experiences. As a result, Ron didn't feel so dependent and helpless. Pregrieving revealed to him that these valued experiences were a part of *him*. He could appreciate his girlfriend more fully without desperately clinging to her. Ron was happier because he felt much more complete as a person, and his girlfriend was also happier because he wasn't constantly worrying about her every move.

Louise had been feeling upset about the possibility of losing her boyfriend. Since he hadn't yet made a specific commitment to her, she felt very vulnerable. These feelings were interfering with their relationship. To Louise, it was a "big issue." After doing the pregrieving process with Louise, she sent a note saying:

"I really appreciate that you gave me attention and help. Once it works, everything seems so trivial, regarding the 'big issue.' It's incredible how fast our brains can learn, with the proper help."

We have personally pre-grieved for our children and other relatives and friends. We find that our awareness that they might not be here tomorrow makes the time we have with them now even more special and precious. When Steve's mother died three years ago, he spent a quiet morning alone, reconnecting with the special times he had with her, and then went on with his life. Even death can become a celebration of living.

In addition to resolving grief, and making it easier to cope with the practical problems of loss, this method builds a sense of personal power and healthy independence, establishing an ability to stand solidly on our own feet as we reach out to others.

References

1. "Resolving Grief" videotape (see Appendix II).
2. *Grief into Gratitude* by Steve and Connirae Andreas (forthcoming, 1990.)

> *Not when the sense is dim,*
> *But now from the heart of joy,*
> *I would remember him.*
> —Rev. H.C. Beeching

The Naturally Slender Eating Strategy   **12**

Perhaps you are or have been a dieter, or you have friends or relatives who are continually trying to lose weight and keep it off. Many dieters are in a life-long struggle to lose weight, while other people seem to stay slender with no effort at all.

Factors in Weight Loss

Weight problems can result from a wide variety of causes. One of the key pieces to making weight loss easy is having the Naturally Slender Eating Strategy, presented later in this chapter. If you want to lose weight, and you don't already have this eating strategy, it may be the only thing you need. At the least it will be a very important first step to becoming naturally slender. Some people who want to lose weight already have this strategy; they need some other change to make weight loss possible. In other cases, learning this eating strategy is an important and significant step in the right direction, but other changes are also needed.

For example, people sometimes overeat when they are unhappy or stressed, because it's a simple way to have some dependable pleasure in life. Dealing with the unhappiness or reducing stress will often remove the need to overeat, and many of the methods described in this book can be utilized for this.

Other people eat reasonably well, but don't exercise enough to maintain their desired weight. Finding an enjoyable way to exercise that fits into your lifestyle is often an important factor. Positive motivation, discussed in more detail in chapter 15, can also be helpful.

Some people don't have a good way to respond to sexual advances; being unattractively overweight can be an effective way to avoid such situations. When such a person learns how to respond comfortably to flirting, and how to say "No" firmly when necessary, the need to be overweight vanishes.

These are only a few of the factors we sometimes encounter with weight problems. *Since every person is unique, our approach is always to find out what will make a difference for this person.* Since the Naturally Slender Eating Strategy provides a foundation for appropriate and easy weight loss, we will present this in detail. Later in this chapter you'll find a step-by-step guide for practicing it and for learning it yourself.

Discovering a Strategy for Becoming Naturally Slender

When I was in high school and college, people sometimes commented to me, "You're *lucky* to be so slim. I'm just not that kind of person. I just don't have that body type." They considered "slenderness" or being "overweight" to be a genetic accident over which they had no control, and so did I at that time. I didn't think much more about this until many years later, when I was teaching an NLP strategies seminar in 1979.

Almost by accident, I discovered a strategy or "thought sequence" which makes it possible for many people to become naturally slender. I encountered a woman who wanted to know her strategy for deciding when and what to eat. Clara was more than 100 pounds overweight and was interested in having some control over her weight. Her thought sequence was very short and simple, and made it obvious why she was so overweight: See food → Eat. I was a little doubtful that anyone would *always* eat when they saw food, so I decided to test her. There was some food in the seminar room, and indeed when Clara could see the food, she was compelled to eat it. She did not consider whether she was hungry or full, whether the food tasted good, how it would affect her if she ate it, or anything else.

I began to design an alternative strategy for Clara to give her a better way to select when and what to eat. My goal was to provide her with a way for her to be naturally slender. When I thought about it later, I realized it was my own strategy! It is what has worked for me for years. Over the ten years since then, we have taught many people this strategy for selecting food, and received many reports back that they also lost weight naturally, without effort.

Most research studies people who have *trouble* losing weight, finding out how they respond to a variety of diet plans and therapy methods for weight loss. In contrast, many NLP patterns have been developed by finding out how people who have easily *achieved* a desirable result are able to do what they do. By studying people who are naturally thin and finding out how they do it, it's possible to teach their ability to others.

People who are naturally slender don't feel forced to be thin. They don't feel bad about "missing out on good food," and they don't restrict their diet. Dieters do all those things. Rather than waging a constant battle with food, it is much easier to learn to *think and respond the way naturally slender people do.* Our investigations since then have verified that most other naturally slender people do almost exactly the same thing that I do, and people with weight problems typically do *not.* Here's the method I use.

The Naturally Slender Eating Strategy

1. First, something makes me think of food. This might be seeing that it's time for lunch, hearing someone mention lunch, feeling hunger, or seeing food.

2. I check how my stomach feels now.

3. I ask myself, "What would feel good in my stomach?"

4. I visualize a possible portion of a food: a sandwich, a bowl of soup, a dinner salad, etc.

5. I imagine eating this food. I think of the taste of this food, and then feel the food slipping into my stomach, and get a feeling of how this amount of this food *will feel in my stomach over time if I eat it now.*

6. If I like this feeling better than how I will feel if I eat no food at all, I keep this food item as one possibility. If not, I discard it.

7. Next I visualize another food I might eat.

8. I imagine tasting this second item, and feel how it feels as it goes into my stomach, and stays in my system for some hours to come.

9. I notice how I like this feeling. Do I like it more than my best choice so far? I keep in mind the food item that makes me feel best, to compare to my next choice.

10. Now I repeat steps 7, 8, and 9 as often as I want to, always keeping in mind the kind of food that I imagine would make me feel the best over time if I eat it. I compare each new possibility to that.

11. When I'm satisfied that I have considered enough options, I eat

the food that I imagined would make me feel best over time, so that I'll get to feel that good.

If you are a naturally slender person, you're probably thinking, "Of course. How else would anyone select food?" However, if you have had trouble losing weight, you're probably having other thoughts. You may be wondering, "But what keeps you from eating chocolate, ice cream, and other fattening things!?"

The answer is "Nothing." Occasionally I do eat fattening things, usually in small portions. Absolutely nothing *keeps me* from eating fattening foods. However, I usually don't want to, because when you think about it, most fattening things make people *feel worse over time,* if they eat them. If I imagine eating an entire basket of greasy onion rings, and imagine feeling them in my stomach, slowly digesting throughout the afternoon, I get a heavy, "yucky" feeling that is *not appealing.* If I imagine eating several bowls of ice cream for lunch, feeling that ice cream in my stomach throughout the afternoon gives me a similarly unappealing, tired, unalert feeling.

In contrast, if I imagine eating a nice large bowl of hot vegetable soup, and imagine feeling *that* in my stomach and in my system throughout the afternoon, it makes me feel much better. For me, this experience is far more attractive, so I usually choose it.

Of course, each of us will respond differently to different kinds of food. You may find that for you a turkey sandwich or a shrimp salad are what make you feel really good over time. Remember that what makes you feel good one day will be different from what makes you feel good another day, because your body changes over time as you respond to events: what you ate yesterday, your activities, how much sleep you got recently, how hot or cold you are, etc. Any food will probably be much more appealing if you haven't just eaten it three days in a row.

What Do You Do if You Overeat?

Another difference between naturally slender people and dieters is in what they do when they do overeat, gorging on some kind of fattening food. Everyone overeats sometimes. When dieters overeat, they often think to themselves, "See, I knew I couldn't do it. I guess I'm just a glutton. I'm doomed to be overweight for life, so I may as well get used to it. Since I can't stick to diets anyway, I might as well eat and enjoy food." A strong feeling of depression or worthlessness often helps keep this pattern going.

In contrast, here's an example of what naturally slender people do when they overeat. Recently we had a house party with a full dinner and a variety of desserts. I stuffed myself, eating far more than I usually do. When the party was over, I noticed that I felt *very* full—fuller than I usually do, even when I eat a lot. During that evening and all through the night, I was aware of the discomfort in my stomach. "It's a good thing I'm noticing this," I thought. "I'm not going to feel like eating like that for a long time." *This experience with overeating gave me the feedback I needed to motivate me to eat more moderately in the future.* The next day when I thought about what to eat, I wanted only small quantities of food that had little or no fat or sugar. It wasn't that I thought I *should* eat those things; that's what automatically appealed to me.

What Makes it Work

The Naturally Slender Eating Strategy is based on having *more good feelings*—more pleasure rather than more denial. As you begin to think like a naturally slender person, you no longer need to use "shoulds" and "rules" to try to force yourself to eat in ways that will make you lose weight. People who overeat usually focus *only* on the pleasurable taste of food as they eat. In contrast, this strategy teaches you to think about what will give you the *best feelings over a period of time.* Overeating on ice cream may be pleasurable in the moment. However, if you imagine how your stomach and your whole body would feel to be so bloated for hours after that much sugar and fat, most people begin to notice that this experience *over time* is not very appealing.

This works even if you don't know the calorie count of a food item. If you've had experience eating a food before, your body remembers your response to it. This creates an automatic *inner motivation* to eat well—because overall it's more *pleasurable* to eat this way.

The Difference Between Hunger and Other Feelings

Greta wanted to lose weight, and hadn't found a diet plan that had worked for her. When I told her about the Naturally Slender Eating Strategy, Greta was very interested. She was skeptical that it was possible to lose weight without struggle, but she thought it was worth a try. If it did work, it would be a welcome relief.

I began guiding Greta through the steps you've already read above. "Imagine you're at a restaurant, and you're considering what to have for lunch. Read the first item on the menu. What is it?"

"A burrito," Greta responded.

"Great. First make an image of a burrito. . . . Now imagine actually eating the burrito, and get a feel for how that burrito would feel in your stomach, throughout the afternoon." I watched Greta for nonverbal signs that she was following my directions, and using the part of her brain capable of doing each of these steps. She did fine until we got to the "feeling" step.

"Do you want me to feel whether I'm full or not?" she asked.

"No, it's not just a matter of how *full* you are," I answered. "It's the *kind* of feeling you get in your stomach. If you eat a burrito with lots of cheese and sour cream on it, your stomach will feel very different than if you eat the same amount of steamed vegetables."

Greta looked confused. "I don't have any idea what you mean," she said. "I don't think I've noticed different kinds of feelings before. I know the difference between feeling good, and feeling bad, or being uncomfortable. If I'm feeling uncomfortable, then I eat."

Quite a few people who overeat are like Greta. They've never learned to make distinctions between different kinds of feelings. Often they haven't learned to tell the difference between the kind of empty feeling that means, "I'm lonely, I want to be with people," and the feeling of hunger, which is a signal to eat. I spent a little time helping Greta learn to make distinctions between her different emotional feelings.

"If all your emotional feelings are lumped together as either 'good feelings,' or 'bad feelings,' then when you feel bad you won't know what to do to feel better. You won't know when to eat, when to invite a friend to go to the movies, or when to do all the other things that satisfy different needs," I said. "You can begin to learn the difference by paying attention to *feedback,* noticing what *actions* make you feel better. If you have an uncomfortable feeling, and visiting a friend makes you feel better, you can begin to recognize *that* kind of discomfort as a message to be with someone. If you have an uncomfortable feeling and after eating something you *still* have the uncomfortable feeling, then probably the feeling wasn't hunger. It's a signal that you want something else. Maybe you're angry about something, and you need to resolve it. Maybe you're bored, and you want to do something more interesting or exciting."

This was making a lot of sense to Greta, who was beginning to sort out when a feeling was hunger and when it was something else. However, she still had doubts. "I've never done this before, so I don't have any experience. If I don't know how different foods feel in my stomach, how am I going to learn this way of eating?" Greta asked.

"Right now, while you're learning the strategy, you can just guess how each food will feel in your stomach over time. It doesn't matter if your guesses are right or wrong, as long as you use the feedback you get after eating to revise your guesses. After you actually eat what you selected, notice how you do feel. Each time you eat you will get more accurate about the kind of feeling each specific food provides."

I explained to Greta how over the years I have become more and more accurate in my predictions. When I was younger, I overate more often, or ate foods that didn't make me feel good afterwards. These experiences were exactly what I needed to get more information about how certain foods would feel in the future. Occasionally I even "sort of" knew that a food would make me feel uncomfortable, but my "sort of" knowledge wasn't very real or compelling. By actually going ahead and overeating on that food, and noticing how my body felt, I got a compelling experience of discomfort that I thought of the next time I considered overeating that food. We all learn from experience. Any time you are wrong in your guess, you can be glad you had that experience so that you can become more accurate in the future.

We spent a little more time rehearsing the process so that it became more and more automatic for Greta. I watched carefully for the nonverbal cues (see Appendix I) that indicated Greta was actually going through the steps appropriately.

About 18 months later, Greta reported that the new eating strategy had worked for her. She had lost weight easily, without struggle. Although she had gone back to overeating twice for a short period of time, she stopped that by intentionally eating smaller amounts for several days, to allow her stomach to shrink. Then it was easier for her to notice how different foods felt in her stomach again.

What is a Natural Weight?

When someone uses the Naturally Slender Eating Strategy, he gravitates toward his or her own "naturally slender" weight. This weight varies somewhat from person to person, depending upon other factors such as genetic background, activity level, and thinking style. Those of us with certain genetic backgrounds and certain thinking styles will be somewhat heavier or thinner than others.

The idea that each of us has a "set point" weight that our body returns to is common in writing about weight control. Our guess is that this "set point" itself is changed when a person changes to a new eating strategy. Certainly people shift to a new and lower "natural" weight.

Accommodating Food Allergies

For various reasons, some individuals—those with food allergies, or physical conditions like diabetes that require a restricted diet—may also need to use other criteria to select or avoid foods. However, as long as the harmful effects are not too severe, and occur within a few hours, this eating strategy will still work well. If a person has an allergy to corn, for example, and that person imagines how they will feel over time if they eat corn, they will notice the allergic sensations, find them unpleasant, and go on to select something else. This strategy can actually help those with allergies or sensitivities avoid inappropriate foods without internal conflict. (Also see chapter 5, "Eliminating Allergic Responses.")

Regaining Body Feelings

Greg asked me for help in learning the Naturally Slender Eating Strategy, because others who were pleased with their results had told Greg he ought to learn it, too. As I guided Greg through the strategy, he quickly told me that he simply couldn't do it, because he had no body feelings below his chin.

Intensely unpleasant experiences from Greg's childhood had made him "decide" when very young that it just wasn't worth having any body feelings. These emotional experiences from the past needed to be taken care of before Greg could learn to feel safe about having body feelings again. I used methods described in chapters 4 and 7 to deal with his traumatic childhood. This provided him with many additional benefits that were even more important to him than losing weight.

Steps to the Naturally Slender Eating Strategy

If you want to acquire this ability to make better food choices for yourself, you can learn it by going through the following steps. Rehearsing what works can enable you to become naturally slender. If you go through these steps thoroughly and carefully, you will find yourself responding to food the way other naturally slender people do.

1. Find a time and place where you can relax comfortably without interruption for about twenty minutes.

2. Think of how you know it's time to consider eating. Is it when you see food? Do you hear someone say "It's time to eat"? Do you look at the clock and notice it's lunch time? Do you feel hungry? You might imagine that you are sitting down for lunch and see food on the table, or that you are looking through your refrigerator, or looking at a menu.

3. Now notice the feeling in your stomach. Notice the *quality* of the feeling you have right now. It's not just being full or hungry that you are checking for, but the way your stomach feels overall. Your stomach will

feel different depending on what you last ate, whether you've been tense or relaxed, etc.

4. Ask yourself, "What would feel good in my stomach now?" You don't need to say this out loud; just hear this question inside your head.

5. Now think of one available food item, one possibility that you could eat. You might imagine a turkey sandwich, a candy bar, a bowl of vegetable soup, a dinner salad, etc.

6. Next imagine eating a portion of the food you thought of. If you thought of the turkey sandwich, you'll get a quick taste of turkey sandwich, and then notice what it feels like as it slides into your stomach. You can get a sense of how the sandwich will feel in your stomach, and how your entire body will feel throughout the next few hours if you eat it.

7. Now compare this feeling with the feeling you had in your stomach before you imagined eating anything. Which feeling do you like better? Will you feel better over time if you eat the turkey sandwich than if you eat nothing? If the answer is a "Yes," keep the turkey sandwich in mind as one alternative you may want to select. If the answer is "No," discard this possibility. Notice that you are deciding based on what will give you greater pleasure over a period of time. There is no point in eating something that would make you feel worse for the rest of the day.

8. Now visualize another possible food item. Perhaps you consider eating a candy bar.

9. Now you're going to find out if you *really* want to eat the candy bar or not. Imagine eating the candy bar, and feel it going into your stomach. Notice the feeling of having the candy bar in your stomach through the next few hours. How does this make you feel?

10. Compare your feeling from Step 9 to your best feeling so far (Step 7). How does the feeling compare to how you would feel if you ate the turkey sandwich? Notice which feeling is more pleasurable to you. Which choice makes you feel better? Keep in mind the item that gives you the best feeling over time.

11. Do this same process (Steps 8, 9, and 10) with several more food possibilities. Each time, keep in mind the food item that makes you feel the best over a period of time.

12. When you are satisfied that you have considered enough possible foods in this way for this process to begin to seem natural to you, notice which food item made you feel the best. Now imagine that you go ahead and eat that food item, and feel the satisfaction of eating what makes you feel good over time.

Additional Rehearsal

Now you've got the basic method. To make sure you continue to automatically use this method, imagine going through the same steps in several other situations. Imagine you're out to dinner at one of your favorite restaurants. Go through the same steps for selecting what to eat in this situation. Then imagine you're at a party, and go through the same steps there. Imagine you're having breakfast at home, and repeat the process. When these steps begin to seem natural to you, this is a sign that the process is becoming automatic, and that you will continue to do this in the future, just as automatically as the way you previously selected food.

Now think about whether there are any particular situations in which you have often overeaten in the past. Some people typically overeat at parties, others only when they are alone. Others only overeat some kinds of food: ice cream, chocolates, pizza, Chinese food, etc. Rehearse again in any situation in which you used to overeat, to make sure that the new strategy is locked in there, too.

Knowing When to Stop Eating

The same strategy allows you to decide when to stop eating. Each time you're about to take a bite, you can very quickly sense how that bite will feel in your stomach over time. Of course you stop as soon as the next bite would make you feel less comfortable than you are now. This gives you a natural way to stop when you're full. As this process becomes a habit, it happens very rapidly and without your having to think about it.

Some people have a rule about eating everything on their plate. Many people eat everything on their plate "so it won't go to waste," but it does go to *waist!* If you have this rule, you may want to always *take small portions,* so you can be comfortable going back for more until you've had just the right amount. Another way to deal with this situation is to buy very small plates. This may sound silly, but it can actually help people eat less. It's a lot harder to overload a small plate than a large one, so people are less likely to eat something "just because it's on their plate." Of course you can always go back for more, even with small plates, but then it's a conscious decision to eat more, not just habitual.

Noticing the Results

After you've learned the Naturally Slender Eating Strategy, notice how it works for you. For most people, this method does *not* result in the kind of dramatic weight loss that frequently doesn't last. Instead, it results in a gradual loss of weight that is maintained over time.

As we mentioned before, often there are many different aspects to weight loss. Having each of these factors in place is what allows someone to be naturally slender. If the Naturally Slender Eating Strategy is the only skill you were missing, learning it will enable you to lose weight easily. If there are additional steps you need to take to comfortably maintain your desired weight, these may be easier for you to notice.

Other NLP Methods for Weight Loss

The Swish pattern, presented in chapters 17 and 18, can build the self-esteem and direction to make weight loss easier. Developing positive motivation (chapter 15) or building a compelling future (chapter 19) are essential factors for others. Sometimes being overweight has a positive purpose (secondary gain), such as wanting independence from parents who are preoccupied with weight control. when this is the case, Six Step Reframing (chapter 8) offers new positive alternatives. You will find a specific example of another woman's journey toward having her desired weight in chapter 16.

Sometimes only one intervention will lead to weight loss. However, if several of the factors that make weight maintenance easy are missing, success results from patiently learning one ability after another until *all* the necessary skills are in place.

I never resist temptation, because I have found that things that are bad for me do not tempt me.

—George Bernard Shaw

13

Resolving Internal Conflict

Joe was an advanced divinity student who worked part-time at a convenience store in the evening. He felt a compulsion to look at "skin" magazines whenever no one else was around, and he couldn't stop himself from doing it. Joe was worried his boss would catch him wasting time looking at the magazines. He was even more worried that news about this would get back to the divinity school. Although Joe had been in many kinds of therapy, nothing had worked to change this. He began to wonder if he was possessed by the devil, and worried that he might completely lose control.

When someone like Joe feels driven to do something he doesn't consciously want to do, we assume that an "unconscious part" makes him do it. When we say "unconscious," we simply mean that Joe isn't aware or conscious of it. We also assume that it is a part of *him*, not some demon or alien being that drives him.

We also make another very important assumption: that all parts of a person have positive *intentions* or *purposes*—no matter how harmful or destructive the behavior is. The importance of this assumption will become clear as we proceed with Joe.

When I first asked Joe what looking at the magazines did for him, he said he didn't know. They gave him a little bit of a thrill, but he also had other ways of getting sexual satisfaction. He was married and happy with his sex life. Joe didn't think there was *anything* useful in looking at the magazines—a bad part made him do it, and he couldn't stop himself.

The way Joe talked about his problem made it obvious that the part was very strong and very alienated from him. Joe did not think of this compulsion as part of himself at all.

Consciously, Joe didn't know anything about this part except that it made him look at the skin magazines, so simply asking *him* questions about the part would get nowhere. The only way to gather information about how Joe's compulsive behavior is useful to him is by going to a less conscious (unconscious) level. One way to do this is to access this part through visualization.

"Joe, I want you to begin to visualize the part that makes you go for the skin magazines. First tell me, in which of your two hands do you want to put that part."

"My right hand. It's over here."

"OK. Now, as you hold out your right hand, that part of you can begin to form.(speaking slowly and softly) It's been a powerful and important part of you. It's been so powerful that you haven't been aware of its useful purpose consciously. And now as that part begins to take shape, tell me what you see.". . .

As I begin this process of discovery, I am apparently speaking to Joe. However, I am also communicating to the part of him that makes him look at skin magazines. Joe has alienated this part by struggling against it and thinking badly about it. As I speak to Joe, I'm beginning to establish rapport with this part by respecting its power and by presupposing that it has positive intentions.

"I see myself looking at some magazines," responded Joe.

"Good, and really look at the details of that part. Notice the expression on his face, how he moves, etc.". . . (Joe's posture and expression shifts markedly as he does this, because he is behaviorally taking on what he experiences as he is driven to look at the magazines.) "And when you can see that part of you really clearly, I want you to ask it what it does for you that's positive when it makes you look at skin magazines. . . . What does it reply?"

"The figure doesn't say anything; I'm not getting any message at all."

Obviously I need to do even more to establish rapport with the part, so that it will be willing to communicate with Joe. Again, although I am apparently speaking to Joe, my communication is intended primarily for the part.

"OK. I want you to continue to watch that part, as we give that part of you time to really sort out what it does for you that is useful by making you look at those magazines. It might review different times and places in which it has made you do this, as it begins to fully recognize its important positive function for you. . . ."

"And as your part does that, I want to tell you about another person who was a compulsive eater. And I'm sure it's not going to be exactly the same for you, because every part has its own purpose and way of doing things. I'd like to give this part of you an example of what I mean when I ask about its positive function. One person who was a compulsive eater asked her part what it did for her, and it turned out that she had come from a military background, and had been raised in a very rigid way, with lots of 'shoulds' and rights and wrongs. The part of her that made her eat was a part that didn't want her to just follow rules. It wanted her to be able to break away and do things in her own way and stand on her own feet." As soon as I said this, Joe responded *very* strongly nonverbally. He jerked, his posture straightened up, and his face became pinker.

"That's it!" Joe said emphatically. "This is a part that doesn't want me to follow rules! It wants me to be my own person and be myself. I'm too concerned with what other people think. My parents always wanted me to do the good and the right thing. . . . The part is nodding his head as I say this! He says that's right."

"Great. And you can thank your part for giving you the confirmation it just offered you. And thank it for being there, interested in assisting you in being your own person. That seems like a very worthwhile thing to have a part of you doing. Do you recognize that as something positive?"

Whenever you get cooperative communication from a part, it's very important to thank it immediately. Even if Joe isn't yet ready to thank the part by saying this, I'm letting the part know that *I* thank it and appreciate its communication.

"Well, I don't like what it *does*."

"Of course not. You don't like the behavior *at all.* But do you want to have a part of you that wants you to be your own person?"

"Well, yes."

"Good. Let your part know that you fully agree with its *purpose* for you, either by silently telling it, or in any other way that's appropriate.". . .

As Joe thanks the part internally, I see his face and body relax slightly, and a slight smile plays across his face. This lets me know that Joe has thanked the part, and the part has responded positively. This is a very important step in healing the conflict that has divided Joe. Next I need to help Joe become clear about the positive intention of the other, more conscious, part of himself.

"And now, keeping this part in your right hand, shift your gaze to your other hand. How would you describe the part that goes here—the opposite of the part that made you look at skin magazines? This is the part of you that wants absolutely nothing to do with skin magazines. It may have something to do with following rules, with doing the right thing, or something like that.

"Yes," Joe answered firmly. "This part is the one that wanted to please my parents and everyone else."

"Give this part time to form clearly there in your left hand—a part that wanted you to do the right thing, please your parents, and so on. . . . When you can see it clearly, ask this part what it does for you that's positive and useful."

"It gets me to do the *right thing,*" Joe stated in a powerful, commanding voice.

Even though I asked for the part's useful *purpose,* Joe responded with *behavior* "to do the right thing," so I need to ask again. "Ask it what it wants for you that's *positive* when it does that."

"It wants other people to like me."

"So this is a part that wants you to have good relationships with other people? Is that what this part wants for you?" I have intentionally changed the way Joe has stated the purpose, because I want the positive intention to be one that puts him in the role of being an "actor," rather than being "acted upon." Rather than having others like him, I restated the question as *him* having good relationships. Since I've changed the way the positive intention is stated, I watch and listen carefully to observe whether he congruently agrees with my restatement. When Joe agreed, I went on:

"It's certainly useful to have a part around to do that for you. Now, thank *this* part for what it does for you.". . .

As Joe thanks this part, again there is a slight relaxation that lets me know he is feeling more appreciative of this part, too. At this point Joe has clearly sorted out the two parts of him that are in conflict about his behavior of looking at the skin magazines. More important, he knows the *intentions* of both parts and he agrees with both these positive intentions.

Joe's internal conflict is a familiar one. Many people have one part that is sensitive to relationships with other people, and another part that wants "to be my own person." However, there is conflict *only* if we think of these goals as in opposition to each other. In fact, there are ways in which these two goals can be mutually supportive of each other. This is what I now begin to make *real* for Joe and his internal parts. The first step is for me to be sure that the two parts recognize and appreciate each other's intentions.

"Joe, does the part of you that wants you to be your own person already have a sense of the ways in which the other part can be useful to it? . . . Being your own person in a vacuum isn't all that meaningful, but noticing and responding to others can make it possible to be your own person in a way that's more fulfilling to you.". . . Joe was looking at his right hand and nodding.

"And the part of you that wants good relationships, may not have noticed until now the way in which being your own person is an essential ingredient to having good relationships.". . .

Joe nodded again, this time looking at his left hand. "So does this make sense to both of your parts?"

"Yes," Joe responded congruently.

"Now, Joe, I want you to watch as your two parts turn toward each other and express appreciation for the positive intention of the other part. You may hear them speaking to each other, or you may see some kind of nonverbal salute or bow in sincere appreciation.". . .

"One of them held out his hands palm up to 'give me ten,' and the other part joined right in."

Since Joe and his two parts all agree at the level of intention, the next step is to bring them all together into a whole, so they can work together smoothly. One way to do this is with a method called "The Visual Squash."

The first step integrates the two parts. "Now, Joe, I want you to gradually shift your gaze to the middle, between your two hands, so that you can see both parts at once, one in each hand. Then allow both your hands to slowly come together, only as fast as these two parts can blend together, keeping the important useful purposes of each, joining together in such a way that each *benefits* from the other, and loses nothing. You may be surprised by exactly how they change and merge when your hands come together, so I want you to take all the time you need for these parts to integrate at their own rate of speed.". . .

Joe's hands began to move together very slowly. After about 40 seconds, Joe's hands contacted each other. As his hands joined, Joe showed dramatic physiological changes: he trembled, his face flushed repeatedly, he sweated quite a bit, etc. This kind of strong physiological response often occurs when two parts that have been very separate from each other come together. This nonverbal response was a good indication that a complete integration was going on at the physical level, as well as at the psychological level. I suggested that he continue for as long as he liked, simply allowing the integration to complete itself. . . .

After three or four minutes, when the changes Joe was experiencing had subsided, I asked him to do the next step: taking his new integrated part back into himself to completely join with him.

"Now keep your hands together and slowly bring this new part, containing all that was of value in both of your other parts, toward your chest. When your hands touch your chest, this blended part can join fully with you, becoming a part of your thoughts, feelings, and behaviors, now and on into the future."

As Joe's hands moved slowly toward his chest, he began to smile. As his hands touched his chest, he took a deep breath. As he exhaled, his face softened, his whole body relaxed and settled, and his eyes became moist.

"I feel at peace, and complete. There's no struggle now."

Now Joe feels wonderful; his conflict is healed, and it is likely that he won't feel compulsed to look at the skin magazines any more. His compulsive behavior was the result of two parts of himself being in conflict.

By going one step further I can be almost certain that he will not backslide. We can make sure he has something *else* to do in place of looking at the skin magazines. When Joe gains choices that are clearly *more* satisfying to his new integrated part, he will be set. This final step was for Joe to go through a process of generating alternative positive behaviors that would improve his relationships with others and at the same time be an expression of his individuality. (See chapter 8 for examples and discussion of this process.)

Several months later, Joe said he was relieved to no longer be particularly interested in skin magazines. "I occasionally pick one up, but I'm not driven to any more. It's no big deal. I don't *have* to look at them, and I don't have to avoid them either." Joe's report let me know the conflict was healed in a way that would last through time. If Joe had reported he *couldn't* look at skin magazines now, that lack of choice would have been an indication that the parts weren't fully integrated and more work was needed.

When to Use this Method

This method of sorting out the opposite sides in a conflict, identifying their positive intentions, and then blending and integrating them, was originally developed by Bandler and Grinder in 1975. It can be used in any situation of internal conflict or ambivalence. Most of us don't have a compulsion to look at skin magazines as Joe did. However, even the most "together" people have some behaviors or responses they don't like, some parts that conflict with each other.

Most people try to solve conflicts as Joe did, by using force or "willpower" to try to overcome an objectionable behavior. Allying yourself with the positive purposes of both sides resolves the conflict more easily. Then it is only a matter of finding alternative behaviors that satisfy both purposes more effectively.

Firmness or Leniency

Judy, mother of two preschoolers, repeatedly found herself in a dilemma. Her children were running wild, and both Judy and her husband were becoming more and more frustrated. Judy knew the children needed more discipline so that they could get along better with other children and adults, and she found herself being quite strict at times. However, another part of her was lenient because she wanted to be sure the children felt loved, and loved her. Since the children didn't get consistent guidelines from their mother, they began to act less and less cooperatively. Using this method, Judy identified these two parts of herself and integrated them, allowing Judy to become the consistently firm *and* loving mother she wanted to be, and to feel good about it.

Shy or in the Spotlight

Liza had a part of her that liked to be the center of attention, and another part that was shy and reticent. When someone complimented her in a group, she didn't know how to respond. She felt awkward and embarrassed because each of her parts wanted to respond in opposite ways. Liza learned that the part wanting attention really wanted her to feel good about *herself.* The part that was shy wanted her to have good relationships with others, and didn't want to be seen as "better than others." This method helped Liza integrate her two parts so that she became comfortable with public attention. After this, Liza no longer felt as much desire for attention, *and* she could enjoy receiving it gracefully when she got it.

Overworking or Collapsing

Luanne had been complaining of stress, and had a variety of physical symptoms. Like many of us, she tended to overwork, in spite of messages from her body that she needed rest. She had one part that wanted her to take care of her body, and another part that wanted her to accomplish things. Since these two parts were separate from each other, she went back and forth between overworking and physically collapsing. Obviously, both goals are important. Integrating these two parts allowed her to consider both her physical well-being and her desire to accomplish *at the same time.* Luanne wrote later, saying she felt more relaxed *while* she worked. She found herself taking short rest times earlier, because she knew fully that taking care of herself wasn't in *conflict* with accomplishment. Taking care of herself is what makes it possible for her to be healthier, so she can accomplish more.

All of us have some kind of internal separation and conflict, though some are certainly less severe than others. Perhaps one part wants to be loved, and another part wants to succeed. One part might want to be taken care of, while another wants to be independent. Perhaps one part wants to be spontaneous, and another part wants to live by planning and routine. Those suffering from bulimia typically have one part that wants to eat, and another that wants to be slender. Whatever the internal separation, this method can heal the split, so that we can more easily and spontaneously act in ways that fit with who we want to be as a whole person, honoring all parts of ourselves.

I would like all of us to live as fully as we can. The only time I really feel awful is when people have not lived a life that expressed themselves. They lived with all their "shoulds" and "oughts" and their blaming and placating and all the rest of it, and I think, "How sad."
—Virginia Satir

14 *Recovering from Shame and Guilt*

Rita had a problem with shame and was embarrassed to discuss it. She wanted to change her feelings so she wouldn't be plagued with shame, but she also wanted assurance that she wouldn't have to tell me any more about it before she agreed to work with me.

Most of us have some experience of shame in our past, and like Rita, don't like to discuss it with others. That's what shame is all about. Shame is a response to violating someone else's standards. When we feel shame, we are usually afraid of rejection or abandonment due to this transgression of real or imagined external standards. For some people, seemingly trivial behaviors like farting in public (or even writing about it!) might cause shame. "Putting your foot in your mouth" by saying something unintended might bring about mild shame. Or the transgressions might be far more serious. Some therapists consider shame to be the root of many personal difficulties, especially the "codependent" behavior observed in the families of alcoholics and other drug abusers.

Ideally, shame alerts us that we have offended other people, and that if we want to continue being friends with them, we may need to change our behavior. However, for many people the agonizing feelings of shame just make them feel like an unworthy person.

Fortunately, I didn't need to know what Rita's shame was about in order to work with her. "What do you need to think of in order to feel shame? You don't need to tell *me* about it; just notice for yourself." Rita's gaze shifted down and to her left, as she looked at a spot about two feet in front of her. Her face darkened as she glanced down at that spot.

The Experience of Shame

I asked Rita more questions so I could learn more about how she was seeing "shame." Rita's face contorted and became tenser as she looked at her image. When Rita was most ashamed, she imagined herself sitting at a table, with others seated all around her looking straight at her disapprovingly. The other people were all much bigger than she was, and rather than moving as they would in real life, she saw them as if they were almost completely still—frozen in one spot, staring disapprovingly at her. The picture was dark and dim.

This is typical of people when they feel ashamed. Almost all experiences of shame involve seeing "big" others staring disapprovingly straight at us. The picture is usually dark and still. If you temporarily try this out, you can probably experience shame, too.

Healing Shame

Knowing this internal structure for creating shame makes it possible to do something about it. As a first step in helping Rita heal the shame, I asked her to think of a time when she violated someone else's standards, but rather than feeling shame, she had a more resourceful response. When Rita thought of this situation, she looked to a different location, higher and to her right. She saw herself from the outside, but she could also step into the image and go through the experience again. Other people were moving, and were the same size as she was. She also noticed that she had a thin, transparent, protective shield all around her body.

Now that I know how Rita thinks about a more resourceful experience of not meeting someone else's standards, I can use this information to transform her experience of shame.

I asked Rita to look back at the experience that made her feel shame. "You can see those people staring at you. What happens when you shrink them down in size? Make them the same size as you are." Rita liked this new picture *much* better. She felt much more powerful when the other people were the same size.

Now Rita was ready to recode her experience of shame—making it the same in her mind as the way she had coded her resource experience. "Take that picture, and move it to the same spot where you saw the resourceful experience of not being ashamed."

"It got brighter, and turned into a movie, too," Rita said, looking and sounding still more resourceful. The "others" in her picture were no longer staring straight at Rita, but interacting more naturally, sometimes looking at her, and sometimes looking at each other, or looking away. When I reminded Rita to add her thin transparent protective shield, she had the sense of being able to see the situation that had previously caused her shame, yet feel comfortable and resourceful.

Now Rita felt resourceful, but this isn't enough. She might cheerfully violate others' standards, and possibly suffer severe consequences as a result. Since shame involves violating someone's standards, it's important to assist Rita in *deciding* what standards *she* wants to live up to, and which standards are outdated or belong to other people. When Rita saw others as so much larger than herself she could not *evaluate* standards; she was just over-whelmed by bad feelings. Now that Rita feels resourceful, she is in a better position to consider the standards she violated in this situation.

"Rita, as you observe that experience now, notice *what* standard you violated, and *who* thinks it's important. Is it a standard *you* want to have for yourself, also? Or is it one that other people have, or you have had in the past, but you don't want for yourself now?" Rita said the standard was not one she wanted for herself.

"So what standard *do* you want for yourself?". . . Rita identified one, without telling me what it was. Next I checked to be sure her new standard was reciprocal, like "the golden rule." "Is the standard you want to live by also a standard that you would be happy to have others around you live by?" Again Rita nodded. Nonverbally Rita was giving me cues that her new standard would be respectful of others.

"Notice what *you* want to do in this situation, given that you recognize other people's standards, and you know you have different standards that you want to live by. You might just want to notice this difference, and not be bothered by their standards. You might want to do something to maintain a good relationship with them, even though they have different standards. Or you may not want to have anything to do with them. You have many alternatives, and of course you can try one alternative, and later change your mind."

Rita nodded. "Yeah. I think I want to work in a different situation. I don't want to work with those people any more—their standards are dumb, and I don't want to be around them."

Previously Rita had felt inferior to these other people—her feelings of shame were in the grip of their standards, even though Rita didn't agree with them. Now Rita was acting a bit "superior" or "snotty." If she goes back to these people and acts superior, she may make *them* feel ashamed or angry and suffer the consequences. Since I don't want to create a worse problem than her shame, I want to assist her in arriving at a response that is more balanced and more useful to her.

"I'm wondering what happens if you think of those people with a sense of compassion, Rita. How does your experience shift when you let them have their own standards—even if those standards seem a bit absurd to you, and you know you like your own standards much better for yourself? We all have our limitations, and you can let them have theirs, even as you have a sense of compassion toward them, and respect for them as people. What is that like?"

As I was talking, Rita began to look softer, kinder, and more solid. With this perspective, Rita may still choose not to work with these people. However, she can leave them with a sense of respect for them as people, rather than rejecting them with a feeling of superiority.

What we have done so far solved the specific situation that Rita was thinking about, in which she didn't agree with other people's standard. However, this solution would be inappropriate when she *does* agree with the standard she violated. When she agrees with the standard, we want this realization to motivate her to apologize or make amends in some way, so that she can continue valued relationships.

I next asked Rita to think of a situation in which she violated someone else's standard that she *did* agree with. When she had chosen an example, I said, "First I want you to appreciate the fact that you noticed this, so you can do something about it. If you hadn't noticed, you might have continued to act in ways that damaged your friendship with these people." Rita looked slightly surprised, but then smiled, saying, "That is true, isn't it?"

We made sure Rita saw her memory of this experience in the same location as her original resource experience—higher and to the right, with other people the same size as her and interacting naturally rather than staring at her. The transparent shield again allowed Rita to comfortably view this situation.

"Now I'd like you to decide what *you want to do* to meet your own standards. Do you want to apologize, or make amends in some way? What can you do to let these people know you share this standard and will do your best to uphold it in the future?". . .

Rita looked thoughtful. . . . "I can think of several things I could do, and I think I'll be most convincing if I do them all."

Rita's expression and tone of voice made it clear that she was already committed to doing these things, and planning how to do them, so I didn't need to assist her in that.

"No one on earth meets *all* their standards *all* of the time. If nothing else, there are times when two standards are in conflict and we have to make a tough choice between them. However, you can think of being a person who *notices* when you violate your standards, and adjusts your behavior for the future, as a much more important standard to meet than any *particular* standard.". . . Rita still looked very thoughtful, so I asked her if she had any questions or concerns.

"No, I'm just thinking that I don't ever have to feel ashamed. Either I shrug something off as not important to me, or I do something to correct the situation. It seems so easy.

"I know where this feeling of shame comes from," Rita revealed. "When I was growing up, my grandmother always hovered over me, shaking her finger at me, and telling me I should be ashamed about lots of things."

"And I'm sure that must have been very unpleasant for you. And there were probably some of her standards that you didn't agree with, and others that you did agree with. Wouldn't it be wonderful if you could do what we just did with all those experiences of shame as you were growing up?" Rita agreed whole-heartedly.

The many experiences Rita was referring to would have taken months to deal with if we had to resolve them one at a time. Instead, I decided to use a process similar to the "decision destroyer" (described in Chapter 4), to transform Rita's past experiences all at once. When I asked Rita where her past was located, Rita gestured off to her left, in a straight line, where many people have their past memories stored (see Chapter 19 on timelines).

"Close your eyes, Rita, and take this experience of having your own perspective and having a new way to respond to not meeting someone else's standard along with you as you go back in time. Go way back, to before any of those experiences with your grandmother, taking this powerful resource with you. . . .

"And you can let yourself drop down into your early childhood with this resource. Then let yourself move forward through time, noticing how the experiences that *were* shame, now shift because of this new perspective and ability you have. . . . Come all the way up to the present, and when you arrive in the present, see yourself moving on into the future responding differently with this new resource." Rita arrived at the present with a smile, pleased with the results.

Behavior vs. Self

Even though Rita had often been troubled by shame, she thought about shame in relation to specific things she had *done* at specific times and places, rather than as something about her self, her *being*. She did not think of herself as a "shameful person," but as someone who sometimes did shameful things.

In contrast, Jane also experienced shame, but in a more general form. For Jane, shame was more of a comment on her *being,* and her self-worth, not just her behavior. Whereas Rita would say, "I'm ashamed of what I did," Jane would say, "I'm ashamed of *myself.*" She talked of shame as having to do with "my core." I respected Jane's courage in bringing this issue up in a seminar, and deciding to resolve it. "Normally I wouldn't think about or talk about these things," Jane said, "because the people I'm around don't do that. But I recently recognized that I have this issue, and here I feel safe to look openly at this, to just lay it on the table and take care of it."

When I asked how she brought on her sense of shame, Jane said she literally saw herself as grotesquely ugly and deformed, naked, with a circle of larger "other people" staring directly at her disapprovingly. Like Rita, Jane's shame followed the usual pattern of *large others staring straight at her.* It was wonderful that Jane had brought this image to consciousness, because now she could do something about it. This was certainly something *worth* changing. When I asked her what would happen if she stepped into this picture, Jane said her shame would become unbearable.

Jane's image of herself nude is a generic example of shame: all her faults are exposed to others. It's like an extreme of those dreams most of us have had, of being in public and discovering we aren't dressed, or we still have our pajamas on. Being naked with others looking on disapprovingly seems to be a classic experience of shame.

Jane, too, wanted to have more choice about shame. "It's hard for me to think of a time when I'm not ashamed," she said. "It's like at some level I'm always seeing that picture of myself deformed and naked. I can only think of one time in my whole life when I didn't feel shame." Jane's resource experience of "not shame" was in a different location, and very similar to Rita's; Jane also had her "personal shield."

I asked Jane to look again at her image of shame. "First let your image of yourself change, so you are no longer deformed, and you can see yourself as you really *are*," I invited. "You can also put clothes on if you want to, because you really *do* wear clothes, and as you look at that image of you, you can notice how your inner beauty shines out.". . . As I gave Jane time to make these adjustments, her expression became more pleased and resourceful. Now she was ready to make the image of herself larger, with the other people staying the same size. After this, I had her shift the picture to the location for "not shame," and to add her "personal shield.". . .

Next I asked Jane to sort out her own standards, just as I did with Rita. "In our culture, people have a wide variety of standards that can work. Your standards are different from mine, and both yours and mine are going to be somewhat different from any other person's. From this position, you can begin to think about what standards you want to have for yourself. Knowing that you can act on your chosen standards, you can also modify your standards as you learn more about the results of your actions over time. You can notice when other people have different standards from you, and this can help you decide what *you* want in each situation. When others think it's their job to impose their standards on you, you can notice that that's just another part of *their* standards—what *they* think is best to do. . . . And decide what standards *you* want for yourself. . . .

"And when someone else's standards are different from yours, you can still respect them, feeling comfortable in the knowledge of your own standards. . . .

"And when you do something that violates your own standards, you can simply decide what you want to do to apologize or make amends, without any need to feel shame. Everyone makes mistakes, and when you realize that you have made one, you can be glad this awareness gives you a chance to correct it. If you didn't notice when you made a mistake, you wouldn't have an opportunity to correct it, and you'd risk losing the friendship of people who are important to you."

I made sure Jane generalized this new perspective about her own standards into other areas in her life. She looked visibly relieved to be thinking of herself in a new way.

A month later, Jane said her "deep embarrassment" about herself had diminished. "When I think about the things I used to be *very* embarrassed about, I don't feel as embarrassed or as threatened now. I'm not as red-faced—I'm more OK. I think I still have more steps to take to feel completely worthwhile, but I don't think my next steps have to do with shame—it's other issues."

The Impact of Shame

Shame has been described as "the secret emotion" or "the hidden emotion." It is a minor inconvenience for some of us, but can be devastating for others.

When people feel shame, usually they also feel *ashamed about* feeling shame, so they're not inclined to talk about it. This is why Rita, Jane, and many others who do something about it have our respect.

Creating the "safe environment" Jane talked about can make it easier to move toward resolution. One way to help create this safe environment for anyone dealing with shame is to recognize that no one is to blame. Shame is the result of someone repeatedly giving us the message, "You're bad," often without telling us *exactly what* they didn't like, and usually without giving us a clear idea of what we could do instead, or how to do it. Parents, teachers, and other "authorities," do this only because *they* don't have any better choices. We all do our best. When we know better, we do better.

In a sense, someone who feels shame does so because he was a capable and quick learner in an environment where shame was being taught. *Now* that same ability to learn quickly and deeply is useful in learning to have a *different* sense of self.

In severe shame, it's as if the person has only one standard for themselves. "I should please others"—*any* others! Putting too much emphasis on pleasing others can result in submitting to a variety of abuses without complaint.

In transforming shame, it is essential to recognize the difference between someone else's standards and our own, and to be very careful to decide on useful standards for ourselves. As we do this, we are building a sense of self, or what is often called self-esteem or integrity: "This is who I am; this is what I believe is important." In a very real sense, we begin to exist as individuals only when we can stand on our own in this way. Until then we are mirror images of someone else—anyone else—and dependent on them for a sense of our identity. Woody Allen's chameleon character "Selig," in the movie of the same name, is a good example of a person with no identity, no soul of his own.

Both Rita and Jane were able to shift very quickly from experiencing shame to a much more resourceful response in which they identified their own standards. If someone has never really thought about their own preferences, it may be important to take more time to explicitly think about their standards. If someone is ambivalent or in conflict between two standards, methods described in chapter 13 can help sort out and resolve this conflict.

Frequently the feeling of shame is linked to other difficulties the person also wants to change. For example, it's often useful to deal with traumatic past experiences, using methods described in chapters 4 and 7.

Although it's usually easier to deal with shame if you have the assistance of someone trained in this method, the outline below is presented for those of you who are interested in using this method on your own.

The Shame Resolution Process

1. Identify what you think of when you feel ashamed. When do you feel shame? What do you feel shame about? It may take you a few moments to become aware of what you have to see or say to yourself to experience shame. Almost everyone has a picture, although they often aren't aware of it at first. It can help to ask, "If I knew what it was, what would the picture be," and see what comes to mind.

Most people see others as *much* larger than themselves, frozen, staring directly at them. Usually the others have disapproving looks, or are saying something disapproving, and often the image is dark.

2. Think of a time when you violated a standard, but you didn't feel ashamed. Instead, you dealt with the situation in a manner you consider appropriate. We'll call this your "Resource" experience.

3. Notice the "coding" differences between "Shame" and your "Resource" experiences. Do you see these experiences in different locations in your personal space, and/or at different distances from you? Most people do.

Notice how large you and any other people are in both your "Shame" and your "Resource" experiences. Be sure to use a resource experience where you and the other people are the same size.

Notice whether each experience is a movie or a still picture, color or black and white, etc. Notice whether you have some type of transparent shield in your resource experience. Any other differences are also important to notice.

4. Transform "Shame" into a "Resource" experience.

a. First make sure the you in the picture looks the way you actually look. If there were any physical distortions, as with Jane, let these shift into "the real you with your inner beauty coming out."

b. Now either make yourself larger (or the other people smaller), until you are the same size.

c. Change the location of your "Shame" picture—move it to the location of your "Resource" experience. Often other coding differences will spontaneously change when you do this.

d. Make any other coding changes to make what used to be "Shame" into a "Resource" experience. This may mean turning the experience into a movie, adding color, or making other shifts.

e. If you had a personal "shield," make sure it's in place. If you didn't have one, you may want to add it. Imagine a transparent shield surrounding your body, so that you can still be fully responsive to others, yet have a sense of being protected.

5. Test. Do you now have the same resourceful feelings about both of your experiences? If not, check for other differences in codings, and change them in order to complete the transformation of "Shame" into a "Resource."

6. Evaluate Standards. First ask yourself, "What standard did I violate in the experience where I used to have shame?" "Is this a standard I want to keep for myself, or is it someone else's standard?" "If I don't want this standard, what standard do I want for myself?" "Is this standard one I would be happy to have others in my life also use?" (The golden rule question.)

7. Programming Your Future. Given the standard others have, and the standard you want for yourself, first decide what you want to do and then imagine yourself acting accordingly in future situations in which this difference in standards might come up.

8. Generalize Your New Learnings.

a. First go through Steps 1 through 7 with another experience of shame, using the same resource experience. Most people find themselves going through essentially the same shifts in the second experience, so it goes even more quickly and easily. Doing this makes sure that your brain thoroughly understands how to deal with experiences in which you violated others' standards.

b. Now that you have transformed two experiences individually, you are probably ready to take these learnings and spread them throughout your entire past. You can accomplish this by reading through the next paragraph and then closing your eyes to do the process.

Think back to your earliest experience of shame. Let's say you were four years old. Now imagine that you take your new ability to deal with shame with you as you jump back to a time *before* you were four years old. Next you will travel rapidly forward through time, *taking this new ability with you.* As you move rapidly forward through time, let all your old experiences of shame shift as you move up through time into the present. As you are moving forward through time, you may have some sense of how your old experiences shift. After you arrive in the present, you can look back on your past to see how it is different. Then you can imagine yourself moving on into the future with these new abilities, sensing how your future will also be different with this new skill.

Guilt

In our research on guilt and shame, we have noticed that although guilt is similar to shame, there are some important differences. The experience of shame often doesn't have much information about what a person did wrong, or how it harmed others. Guilt, however, always includes some representation of how what you did has harmed others, often including how they will be harmed in the future. Guilt is a feeling response to violating *your own* standards, while shame involves violating the standards of others.

When we work with shame, and we ask "Is this standard one that you want for yourself," sometimes the person says "Yes. Even though it's someone else's standard, I also want it for myself." As the person realizes they have violated their *own* standard, they may begin to feel guilt instead of shame.

Overall, dealing with guilt is similar to shame in that we first shift it to a more resourceful experience of being able to comfortably evaluate the situation. Then we ask the person to examine the standard to find out if it needs to be updated, revised, or redefined. Finally we explore what the person wants to do to resolve the situation.

Pablo was feeling guilty about something he had said to a close associate, and it had been bothering him for some time. Before asking him to think about this guilt, I said, "Pablo, I know there have been times when you did something that didn't fit your standards, but rather than feel guilty about it you simply started thinking about what you could do to make it right. Most likely it was just a small thing you did wrong. I'd like you to identify one of those."

When Pablo had found one of those experiences, I went on, "Now I'd like you to compare this experience—let's call it 'deciding what to do'— with your experience of guilt, and notice how those two experiences are different."

As Pablo focused on the differences, he noticed that his guilt was a very close, flat, still picture—about a foot away—and about twenty degrees to his right, while his "deciding" experience was a 3-D movie that was farther away and about thirty degrees to his left.

When I asked Pablo to take his guilt experience and move it over to the location for "deciding," it automatically transformed into a 3-D movie of possible alternative things he could do to rectify the situation. When he did this, his whole body relaxed, and he felt much better. With the incident in this position, Pablo could easily go on to consider several alternatives, and decide what he thought was the best thing to do.

Before he did that, I asked him to review the standard that he had violated, to be absolutely sure that it was appropriate, and not in need of any revision or modification. After some thought, Pablo said, "I'm glad you asked me to do that, because I don't do that very often, and I need to keep that in mind. At other times in my life it's been really helpful to carefully reexamine my standards. But in this case I don't want to change anything. It's definitely a standard I want to follow." Pablo then went on to consider alternatives, and decide what he wanted to do. Then it was only a matter of actually imagining doing this in the future, so he would be sure to do it at the appropriate time.

With both guilt and shame we first establish a more resourceful state. Then we examine the standards to see if they need revision, making sure the person knows what values he wants to follow. Finally we search for future actions the person can use to live out the desired standards, and rehearse actually doing them in the future.

Sorting Out Standards

Although people's values seem to vary widely, when you ask them what they *really* want, there is actually a great similarity. Everyone wants to live a satisfying life in which they are free to do what they enjoy doing—sometimes alone, and sometimes in relationship with others.

Sorting out our standards, or what we value, is something most of us continue to do over a lifetime, as we learn, and as our situations change. The process described here transforms both shame and guilt into a careful examination of standards and choices. This frees us from being tyrannized by unexamined external standards, and empowers us with our own preferences and decisions. Updating our internal experience to fit more with the choices available to us can allow us to recognize how we *are* completely fine, and to move forward out of a recognition of our worthiness. If you would like to review your own standards, the outline below may be useful to you.

Standards

Standards of behavior are efficient guidelines for deciding what to do. Like the rules that parents give children, or the office procedures in a business, they make it quick and easy to make most decisions.

Problems occur either when we violate our standards, or when our standards need adjusting. Here are some typical kinds of problems that occur.

Single Standard Problems

1. A standard may be *too general and universal.* "Always be honest" (even if it harms someone).

Solution: Get more specific. When and where will honesty be best? Is it ever *not* best? (I asked one client to "footnote" the ten commandments with specific exceptions.) Every good idea has times when it doesn't apply.

2. A standard may be *out of date.* For instance, it may be appropriate for a small girl's limited mind and world, but not for a grown woman's.

Solution: Update and revise the standard.

3. A standard is too "*all or none.*" It is just as bad to scratch someone's finger accidentally as it is to murder them.

Solution: Make explicit comparisons to make the standard into an continuum of greater or lesser importance.

4. The person's standard is appropriate, but they have not learned effective behavior or motivation to be able to achieve it. Most poor spellers *want* to be able to spell well, but don't know *how* to. In contrast, someone may know *how* to do something but lack the ability to motivate themselves to *want* to.

We sometimes tell people, "If you did something 'even though you knew better' you actually *didn't* 'know better' in the sense of being able to motivate yourself and/or do the behavior you wanted to do. In a sense, only *part* of you *knew better.*"

In the days before antibiotics, I knew a child of ten who needed to soak a badly infected finger in hot water. He knew that he would not be able to keep doing this if he were alone, so he followed his mother around all day long, so that she could remind him when he forgot.

Solution: Teach whatever is missing so that the person both wants to and knows how to carry out the standard.

5. The standard is appropriate, but the person didn't foresee that a particular behavior would violate it. We can never predict *all* the conse-

quences of our actions with certainty, so we all make this mistake sometimes.

Solution: "You realize that it's impossible to *always* notice ahead of time that an action will violate standards." If the person simply made a stupid mistake, it can be useful to say, "Everyone makes mistakes; it's impossible not to, no matter how desirable perfection might seem. Usually your mistakes don't harm anyone else. You can probably think of hundreds of times when you drifted across the yellow line on a highway, but no one was there, so it made no difference. Sometimes, however, the same small mistake makes a big difference. When it does, you can do everything in your power to make sure it doesn't happen again, and do what you can to undo or compensate for any harm you've done."

However, if someone does this frequently, he may not be able to plan ahead well.

Solution: Teach how to make more detailed internal movies of the future consequences of actions, so he has a way to plan ahead better.

6. Although it is less common now, some people are troubled by *thinking* about violating a standard: "The thought is as bad as the deed."

Solution: You can point out that there are very important differences between thinking and doing, for example:

"You may think it's the same to do it as to think about it, but it's certainly different to that other person who would *only* be harmed if you actually did it. He not only hasn't suffered from it, but doesn't even know you're thinking about doing it! The more considerate of others you are, the more this difference is obvious."

"If you think it's as bad to think it as it is to do it, you obviously haven't done it, because I've done it and there *is* a difference."

"Socrates said that the good people do only in fantasy what the bad people do in reality."

"God gave us the ability to *think* about doing things so that we could consciously decide to *do* only the things we can see will have good consequences and *not* do the things that we foresee will harm ourselves or others. Thinking about bad things is actually a way to *help* you sort out alternatives, and be confident about which is best."

"Since you haven't actually done it, there must be a stronger part of you that knows better and is guiding your behavior."

Two (or more) Standards

Often when we violate a standard and feel guilty, we are actually *following* another more important standard that we may not be very aware of. It can be useful to ask ourselves, "What standard was I *following* when I violated another standard?" This is another way of saying "What is the positive purpose I had in violating that standard?" As we realize that we were actually *following* a more important standard, it can give us a sense of success and integrity—in contrast to the failure of guilt or shame—that is a good basis for considering what to do in the future.

Solution: Sort out standards and their outcomes, and prioritize or integrate them (see chapter 13). Then run internal movies of acting the way you want to act in the future, so that what you want to do is "programmed" into your thinking and behavior.

For example, being neat may be an important standard for Joan, but caring for her children may be even more important to her. When Joan knows this is how she prioritizes her standards, she can feel *good* about leaving the dinner dishes when her daughter is upset and needs her assistance, instead of feeling ashamed about being messy.

Meta-Standards

Someone who is rigidly perfectionistic will feel guilty often. Sometimes rigid perfectionism results from believing "Everything I do has to be perfect." Or "My guru knows the right way to do *everything*." You can think of this as a *meta-standard:* a standard *about* all standards.

The first useful step is to recognize if you have this kind of perfectionism about yourself. Shifting to a more useful appreciation of mistakes as a vehicle for learning may take additional steps over time. Having a meta-standard about using feedback can make this shift easier. We often offer the following perspective:

"One of the highest standards you can have is that you are the kind of person who *notices* when your behavior doesn't match your standards. When this occurs, you can either adjust your behavior to match, or reexamine and adjust your standards when they're out-of-date or inappropriate. If you didn't do that, your standards would be completely arbitrary and meaningless. Being a person who adjusts and learns from mistakes is much more important than doing everything perfectly the first time."

It's useful to have standards that direct us toward the experiences we want to have in our lives. When we notice that we have violated a standard, we can simply examine our standards and behavior, take steps to adjust them, and make amends for any harm we may have done. In this way we can lead an ethical and moral life without having to experience guilt or shame.

Positive Motivation   **15**

Brian was attending one of our NLP Practitioner Certification Trainings. When we began teaching about motivation, he was particularly attentive, since motivation had been a problem for him as long as he could remember. Once he began doing something, he usually did well, but he always agonized over getting started. Getting himself to mow the lawn usually took much longer than mowing the lawn itself. Brian's desk was a complete mess because he'd never been able to motivate himself to clean it.

Getting into the kitchen to wash the dishes after dinner sometimes took Brian hours—his wife Joyce could attest to that. It wasn't one of the things that had made their relationship smoother in their twelve years together. Brian and his wife had an agreement that most nights she did the cooking and he did the dishes. This was agreeable to both of them, except that Brian tended to put off the dishwashing—sometimes until the next morning, or later. His wife was really annoyed when she found the dirty dishes still in the kitchen the following evening when she got home from work and was ready to cook dinner.

Many people had accused Brian of being a procrastinator, and he had to admit it was true. He didn't enjoy putting things off; he just didn't know what to do about it. Brian found himself berating himself about this quality, along with most of the people who were close to him. However, this hadn't done any good. He always *tried* to do better. He *wanted* to make things smoother in his relationship with his wife. It just never seemed to work out that way.

Using specifically targeted questions, I found out how Brian motivated himself to do the dishes. Once I had this information, Brian's problem made sense. Brian began by looking at all the dirty dishes, and then thought to himself in a stern voice, "You *SHOULD* do the dishes." After this, Brian immediately had a rebellious feeling of not wanting to. This was enough to keep Brian out of the kitchen for a while. However, soon Brian started imagining how his wife would be really mad if the kitchen was still dirty. Again he told himself, "You *SHOULD* do the dishes," and again felt that he didn't want to. What finally got Brian to do the dishes was imagining his wife so furious that she was ready to leave him. At this point the internal voice said urgently, "Oh no, not that!" and Brian finally felt motivated to do the dishes. This feeling of uncomfortable urgency stayed with Brian until he cleaned up the dishes. Brian then felt relieved until the next time.

This may seem like a lot of drama over a simple task such as doing the dishes, and it is. However, we've discovered that many people go through something similar. What makes this particularly important is that *Brian motivated himself to do everything in his life in exactly the same way.*

For instance, when Brian wakes up, he first imagines the things to be done before leaving for work, and tells himself "You *SHOULD* get up now." He immediately feels that he doesn't want to get up, and stays in bed longer. Then he begins making pictures in his mind of the disasters that might happen if he doesn't get up. He sees himself arriving late to work, and his boss and co-workers very annoyed. When Brian finally makes these pictures disastrous enough, the internal voice says, *"Oh no, not that!"* Only then does he finally feel the urgency to get up and get ready for work. Brian goes through the same sequence with other tasks: yard work, taking his car in for a check-up, assignments at work, etc. He experiences the same drama whenever he needs to do anything that isn't inherently enjoyable. In shorthand, Brian's strategy is:

Visual →	Auditory →	Kinesthetic
See task	Say "You should do it"	Feel bad

Then Brian keeps cycling through making a picture of the disasters that could happen if he doesn't do the task, talking to himself, and feeling bad.

Visual →	Auditory →	Kinesthetic
See disaster if I don't do task	Say "You should do task."	Feel bad

Only when the visual picture of disaster gets bad enough does the voice make him feel bad *enough* to do the task.

Not only was Brian's way of motivating himself slow and cumbersome, it used bad feelings to get him moving. Every time he attempted to motivate himself he felt bad, and only when he felt *really* bad was he successful in becoming motivated! When you think about how often we all motivate ourselves to do things each day, you can realize how often Brian felt bad.

Brian definitely wanted assistance in learning better motivation. "I put things off all the time, and I feel miserable doing it," he said. "I'm tense and nervous a lot of the time. The only time I really relax is when I'm on vacation and there's *nothing* I *have* to do." I agreed with Brian; a new motivation strategy would make a major difference for him.

We have studied many people who are able to motivate themselves easily to get things done, even when the task isn't fun in itself. One interesting thing about these "excellent self-motivators" is that they use *positive* feelings to motivate themselves instead of the unpleasant urgency Brian used. They *enjoy* getting things done, rather than feeling the misery that many people like Brian experience. After gathering a little more information from Brian, I taught him one of these "excellent self-motivator" strategies.

One key to making Brian's strategy work well for him was to change the internal voice that made him feel bad. Brian told himself, "You *SHOULD* do the dishes," or "You *SHOULD* clean your desk," in a voice that sounded a little like an army sergeant. For most of us, if we hear someone telling us, "You *HAVE TO* do dishes," or "You *SHOULD* clean up," we immediately feel that we don't want to. Try this out and find out how you feel. Listen to a stern voice telling you "You *SHOULD* do something." Does this make you feel more like doing it, or less?

Teaching a New Strategy

I began by asking Brian, in an inviting tone of voice, to do the following: "Listen to an internal voice saying, enticingly 'It will be really nice when the dishes are all clean!' I don't know what tone of voice makes *you* really want to do something, but you can hear it in a voice that sounds really enticing to you.". . .

I watched Brian carefully, using his eye movements (see Appendix I) and nonverbal physiological changes to let me know that he was following along. Brian looked completely different as he listened to this new voice— much more relaxed and pleased.

"Next you can *see* what the kitchen will look like when it's *completely clean.* The dishes are all done, and the kitchen almost glows with cleanliness." I gestured upwards, so that Brian could easily use the part of his mind that is able to make pictures.

"And next you can feel how good you'll feel when you are completely done with that job.". . . Again I'm watching Brian closely to confirm that he is actually doing what I ask, and responding with pleasure. "And you can take this feeling of satisfaction with you as you begin doing the dishes, knowing that you can feel good about each dish you wash in the same way, because every dish brings you even closer to that clean kitchen."

Brian's New Motivation Strategy

Auditory	→	Visual	→	Kinesthetic	→	DO IT!
"It will be nice when it's done!"		See kitchen clean		Feel Satisfaction		

Next I went through this same kind of rehearsal in several other areas of Brian's life, guiding him in using this new strategy to get out of bed, and then to complete a task at work. I did this to be sure Brian's new positive motivation would generalize, becoming a part of his unconscious thinking process whenever he wanted to do something.

Many people are astonished that a few minutes of rehearsal can install a new pattern in spite of perhaps 30 years' experience with an old pattern. The key is that we're not trying to erase the old pattern. We're simply teaching a new alternative that is more effective. If you have ever driven to work for some time, and then discovered a shortcut, you know that it didn't take you long to automatically take it.

Afterward, Brian said, "That went well in my imagination, but what if it doesn't stick? What if I don't do things anyway?"

"Well, I'm sure that you can recall all the misery you've experienced in the past, and you can imagine what kind of disasters will happen if you don't respond fully to the new strategy you have, can't you?" I said. "That part of you that motivated you by making you feel bad will do so again, and I suggest that it make you feel even worse. Of course if you do respond immediately to your new strategy, there will be no need for those disastrous bad feelings." Here I was utilizing Brian's old strategy of avoiding disasters to get him to fully take on the new strategy. As I talked, Brian looked back at me with a twinkle in his eye, increasingly motivated to use the new strategy.

Later Brian reported that he had become very motivated to get things done. "My wife can't believe that I'm doing the dishes right away," he said. "I completely cleaned my desk for the first time in years. And I'm enjoying it! In fact, I'm enjoying getting things done so much that I think the next step for me is going to be learning to prioritize and decide what's really worth doing. I'm a little concerned I might do too much."

Following Brian's lead, I assisted him in deciding how he could prioritize possible tasks he wanted to accomplish, and how he would know when it was time to be motivated to take a break.

Jennifer

Jennifer also complained of having difficulty motivating herself. Unlike Brian, she didn't have a voice telling her she should do something. Instead, when Jennifer tried to motivate herself to do the laundry, she thought of what it was like to do the laundry. Then, of course, she felt that she didn't want to. After all, fiddling with dirty clothes isn't very appealing. This same method did work wonderfully to get Jennifer motivated to go dancing, or anything else that was fun. She just thought of what it is like to *be dancing,* felt good doing it, and was motivated to do it. However, Jennifer usually put off doing anything that wasn't fun.

Many tasks in life simply aren't fun to do. Even though we don't enjoy *doing* them, we want to *have them done.* If we try to motivate ourselves by thinking of what it's like to do these tasks, we won't feel motivated at all. We'll feel like we *don't* want to do them. What's *motivating* about these tasks is seeing them *completed;* because that's what we *want.* If we visualize the clean kitchen, the mowed lawn, or the finished work, we're much more likely to be motivated, because then we're thinking of what we want.

Assisting Jennifer in thinking of the finished task made her motivation strategy work for her. Jennifer didn't have to have an entirely new sequence, she only needed to change *what* she visualized. Rather than imagining *doing* the task, she needed to see it *done.* Again I rehearsed her as I had with Brian. "See the laundry all done, with your clothes put away the way you want them to be. Now feel the satisfaction of having it all done."

As Jennifer did this she smiled and said, "That works. I want to do it right now. But how about other things? I am a therapist, and I need to turn in regular reports on my sessions with clients. I have a lot of trouble getting interested in doing those reports. They're not at all fun to write. Will this work for that?"

"Definitely. Let's rehearse with your reports. How do you know it's time to be motivated to write your report? Is it right after the session is finished?"

"Yes." Jennifer agreed. "If I did the reports right away, it would be a lot easier. I let them stack up and do them at the end of the week when they're due. Then it's hard to remember what to write down."

"OK. Imagine that you have just finished a session—you've just said goodbye to a client. Now you see the client report all finished, and feel good because it's completely done."

"That doesn't work, because I don't really care about those client reports," Jennifer interrupted. "I think they're dumb, and they don't do any good, so I don't feel motivated when I think of having finished the report."

"OK. If they really don't do *any good at all,* maybe you would be better off if you just didn't do them."

"Oh, but then I would lose my job. It's a requirement."

"Oh, so there *is* something good about doing the reports. Doing the reports helps you keep your job. I don't know all the ways in which that's valuable to you. Perhaps it's a matter of income, the satisfaction of helping people, doing something worthwhile in the world, or whatever."

"Yes, those things are all certainly part of it."

"So instead of just seeing the report finished, it might be useful to see—next to it or around it—what's really valuable to you about doing it—having your job and all that it provides you. Do you have an image of that?"

"Yes. That works a lot better."

"Good. And seeing that, you can feel the satisfaction of completion." (Jennifer grins.) "You can also keep that in mind and carry this feeling with you as you begin writing the report, feeling more and more satisfied with every word you write, until you are all done." When I went on to ask Jennifer to rehearse doing this in several other areas in her life, the results continued to satisfy her.

Jennifer had gotten what she wanted, but I thought she could probably use something else that she hadn't asked for. As I mentioned before, her strategy had only two steps (V → K). Since she doesn't have an auditory step, she will not pause to talk to herself about any other factors that may be involved. Typically people with this kind of strategy will often act "spontaneously" or "impulsively" on partial information, and later regret it.

First I needed to check to discover if she experienced this kind of problem. Since many people are compliant and tend to agree with whatever you say, I deliberately phrased my question to be the *opposite* of what I expected, so that she would have to correct me.

"Jennifer, you're probably the kind of person who carefully considers all the ramifications of doing something, and never regrets getting involved with a person or a project. Is that right?"

Jennifer looked startled and said emphatically, "No, that's not true at all! I'm the opposite of that. I *often* regret getting into things; that's one of my major problems."

First I needed to regain rapport with her by explaining: "I thought that might be the case. I only asked in reverse to be sure that I wouldn't be 'leading' you. Since that is a problem for you, there is something very effective we can do about it. I'd like you to try this method to see how well it works for you.

First, think of one of those situations in which you got motivated, but later regretted it. . . . Now see what it was that motivated you then, and feel the excitement of wanting to do it just as you did at the time.". . .

Jennifer looked doubtful as she said, "Well, OK, but that's what got me into trouble later."

"I know, that why we're going to add something. Right after that good feeling of being motivated, have an internal voice ask you: *'Is there anything else that might be useful to consider before I go ahead?'* In this case, you know what went wrong later, so you know what else you could have considered at the time you were motivated. One way you can consider that is to add it into the picture you make and see whether or not it still motivates you. There may be many things to consider, or only a few, and they may be likely or unlikely. Some may be inconsequential, while others may be very important. Even when something is well worth doing, it may be *more* important to do something else first. If you pause for a moment to question if there is anything else like this to be considered, it can protect you from later regret and disappointment.". . .

"That certainly would have made it different. When I think about the other factors that were in that situation, I'm not motivated at all."

I then asked Jennifer to rehearse this sequence with several other past situations, so that she could discover more about the kinds of important considerations she had been ignoring. Then I had her rehearse in several likely future situations, including her laundry and report-writing.

After this, Jennifer found her reports and other tasks much easier to do, and she seldom regretted what she was motivated to do.

The Four Most Common Ineffective Motivational Styles:

In our work with many people, we've noticed four typical motivational styles when things "go wrong" in motivation. You may recognize one or more of these as familiar; they aren't mutually exclusive. Some people do all four, until they discover a better way.

1. The Negative Motivator. Like Brian, many people can only motivate themselves by thinking of the disasters that will happen if they *don't* do something. They think of getting fired if they don't show up at work on time. They think of their family abandoning them if they aren't nice. They think of their car completely falling apart if they don't take care of it. However, thinking of negatives is unpleasant, and usually doesn't get people motivated quickly.

A negative or "disaster" motivational style *can* be very effective for some people and for some tasks. In some situations it's useful to think of what's worth avoiding. Lawyers often think of what could go wrong, and then write careful legal agreements to deal with possible problems. One lumberjack with an unusually good safety record used an "away from disaster" motivational strategy to continually remind himself of the things that could go wrong if he wasn't really careful. If he hadn't thought about what to avoid, he might not have been as careful. Some things in life are well worth avoiding, particularly in dangerous contexts.

However, if someone motivates himself *only* by thinking of what to avoid, even when he gets things done, he is likely to experience lots of stress and bad feelings. Another problem with negative motivation is aptly described by the old phrase "Out of the frying pan and into the fire." By focusing on what you're avoiding, you may not notice that you're headed for something worse. Reacting to negatives doesn't leave you much time to consider the positive things you *do* want in your life.

For many people who have been negative motivators, it has been very useful to add some positive motivation. This is what we did with Brian, who now thinks of how satisfying it will be to have things completed. Brian now thinks of what he *wants,* instead of what he *doesn't want.* We recommend at least including what someone does want along with thinking of the disasters to be avoided.

If someone's negative motivation style has been working effectively to get things done, we are always very careful in any changes or additions we suggest. For example, Howard was a successful banker, who motivated himself by thinking of avoiding losing money at every turn. Since Howard valued his success and did not request a change in his motivation, we did not propose one. If we had suggested any change in Howard's motivational style, we would have needed to be *very* careful to preserve his effectiveness as a banker.

2. The "Dictator" Motivational Style was also apparent in Brian's approach to motivation. The Dictator motivates herself by giving orders in a stern, unpleasant tone of voice. Sometimes these are identifiable as the voices of parents or other authority figures from our past. Someone using this approach frequently uses words like *"HAVE TO,"* *"SHOULD"* or *"MUST."* As with Brian, most people respond by *not* wanting to do something, followed by procrastination.

Someone who has been using this style can usually become more easily motivated by changing to *invitations* rather than *orders.* Shifting to a pleasant, enticing voice tone makes a big difference, as does changing the wording. *"HAVE TO's,"* *"SHOULD's"* and *"MUST's"* can often be replaced with phrases such as "It will be *nice* to," "It will be *useful* to," "I *want* to."

3. The "Imagine Doing It" Motivational Style. Many people think of what it is like to *do* a task, instead of seeing it *done.* Like Jennifer, these people can usually motivate themselves easily to do enjoyable things, but not "chores." Motivation is very difficult for anything that isn't inherently fun, and this lack of motivation often becomes a major obstacle to success and effectiveness.

The solution is to think of the *completed task* instead of the experience of doing the task. Occasionally you need to go a step farther and think of *what's valuable to you about having the task completed.* If there really isn't anything of value about completing a task, it's probably not worth doing. If there *is* something of value in completing a task, you can visualize that value to make motivation easier.

4. The Overwhelm Motivational Style. Some people begin by imagining the entire task as one large, looming, undifferentiated mass of work, and naturally feel overwhelmed. If we see an entire house to clean as one big job, it can be overwhelming. If we think of writing a dissertation or a book as one big task to be accomplished *now,* it can seem impossible. When someone feels overwhelmed, they usually feel incapable of even beginning a task, and tend to put it off.

Often a good first step is to move the picture of the task farther away and make it smaller. This gets the task "down to size." Next you can do something we call "chunking down." You may remember the old joke: "How do you eat an elephant?" The answer is, "One bite at a time!"

You can begin by seeing the whole task completed, and then notice what series of smaller steps will lead to completing the entire task. For example, I can see the housecleaning completed, and then see a series of the smaller steps that will lead to completion: dusting, windows, floors, one room at a time, etc. I can see each of these steps completed, so that I can be motivated to do each step, one at a time. Now instead of having one overwhelming task, I have a series of smaller tasks, each of which seems do-able. If any step still seems overwhelming, I can subdivide it into even smaller steps. If I can't see how to do that, I can ask someone, read a book or magazine or do something else to gather information about how to do it. Gathering information then becomes the first step I see in moving toward my goal.

Learning a New Motivational Style

For some people, just understanding what they do that doesn't work, and what kind of motivational style would work more effectively, is enough to result in change. However, most people need to go through a carefully-guided sequence of rehearsing a new motivational strategy in order for it to become automatic. Typically, a half-dozen rehearsals are enough to learn a new sequence. Jennifer and Brian each gained a new motivational sequence that was as automatic and unconscious as their old sequence had been. After doing the guided rehearsal with us, they didn't need to "try" to motivate themselves in the new way or "work at it." They simply found themselves doing it automatically.

This is one of the ways that NLP is different from just offering advice or preaching. One can say, "Just think positively. Think of the benefits and you'll be more motivated," and occasionally such general advice will work. What makes NLP much more effective is that we know how to give very specific instructions to rehearse a new strategy so that it becomes automatic. We know how to guide someone to use the appropriate part of their mind for each step, and we also use nonverbal indicators to track whether the person is actually making the change or not. We also know how to immediately offer suggestions if the person misunderstands, or encounters obstacles or objections.

Making a New Motivational Style Work in Your Life

Occasionally when someone learns a new motivational strategy, they discover other shifts they want to make so that the motivational strategy will work even better for them. Brian, for example, discovered that because he was now so motivated, he needed to find a way to carefully prioritize what he really wanted to do, to be sure he got adequate rest.

Louise, another procrastinator, found herself reluctant to learn a new motivational strategy. After we created an environment in which Louise felt safe to explore her objections, she discovered that she feared she might fail. As a procrastinator, she had never really tested her abilities. She could always say, "I could have done it. It's just that I never really tried." She was afraid that if she were motivated to do more, she might discover that she wasn't as capable as she hoped. We used another method (see Chapter

8) to help Louise honor and respect this part of her in such a way that she could go ahead and learn the new motivation strategy.

If someone makes poor decisions, this may not be a big problem if he also has difficulty motivating himself to carry them out. However, when he learns to motivate himself better, he may start acting on his poor decisions and get into trouble. In this case, it's important to also improve his decision strategy. (See the next chapter.)

The importance of positive motivation has been widely recognized, but the ways people have used to try to change it have been hit-or-miss at best. NLP now provides a systematic approach that can be tailored to each individual's specific needs.

16

Making Decisions

Decisions, decisions! We are constantly making them—some major, some minor; what shirt to wear, when to have a haircut, which salad dressing to eat, what TV newscast to watch, what car to buy. Some decisions we agonize over. Others are made so rapidly we might not even think of them as decisions. That's because our way of making decisions is so automatic that the process is out of consciousness—it operates without our thinking about it.

When we were first learning about brain programs, we were attending a seminar with Richard Bandler. Richard asked each of us to find out how someone else at the seminar made decisions.

I paired up with a woman named Holly, and asked her how she decided what to order from a menu. This is an easy situation to use to identify someone's way of making decisions. First Holly looked at the menu, which is a good way to find out what your choices are in a restaurant. Next she asked herself internally, "What are other people having?" Another internal voice then said in an annoyed tone, "No! Think for yourself!" Then Holly felt bad. These two internal voices continued to argue, making Holly feel worse and worse. When she finally felt bad enough, another voice said "Oh, pick anything. It's better than this!" Holly then made a *random* choice from the menu. She literally just pointed at something and ordered it!

However, even after Holly had ordered, she wasn't done. Her two internal voices continued their argument back and forth, saying things like, "You probably made the wrong decision." "Well, at least I picked for myself!"... and on and on.

When Holly saw her decision program outlined on paper, she said, "That's amazing! I've made *all* my decisions that way! I decided to get married that way, and when to have kids, and where to live—everything!"

You may already realize what this indicates about Holly's life. For Holly, all decisions—even small ones—were painful. I noticed the pained expression on Holly's face, and realized she had looked that way since arriving at the seminar that morning. It all fit.

Later that day I learned something else that fit. Holly had been in therapy for more than a year with a therapist who was also at the seminar. Throughout this therapy, Holly had continually complained to her therapist that she was dissatisfied with everything in her life. The therapist had dutifully helped her to "explore her feelings of dissatisfaction" and "to express them to get them out of her system," as so many therapists have been trained to do.

He laughed ruefully when I told him about Holly's decision program. It was instantly obvious to him that she could have expressed her feelings for the rest of her life without benefit. What she needed was a new way to make decisions that were satisfying.

Holly's decision program led her to make choices randomly. When she felt bad enough, she picked *anything*. If you select lunch randomly, probably the worst result is a little indigestion. But if you pick a husband or wife randomly, there are major consequences. Your chance of finding happiness is pretty small. Her decisions had nothing to do with what she liked or didn't like, resulting in widespread dissatisfaction. Holly never considered how something looked, felt, sounded, or tasted.

In the exercise, Holly had already elicited my decision program, so I helped her learn that one. It goes as follows:

Read		See		"Taste"		Get		Pick		
item on	→	picture	→	item	→	feeling of	→	best	→	ORDER
menu		of item				evaluation		option		

Holly learned this new program quickly. As I rehearsed her through this sequence, I made sure she looked in the appropriate eye-direction for each step, so that I knew she was actually using the part of her brain that can do that task best (see Appendix I). To help her generalize this new decision program, I rehearsed her through using the same basic program for several different types of decisions—selecting cloth for a blind person (by feel) and selecting a dress to buy (by appearance).

Holly was learning a way to make decisions by considering each option, evaluating it, and selecting the first option that satisfied her enough. It's a simple process, but radically different than what Holly had been doing. Later in the day, I observed her making decisions quickly and comfortably. When Richard Bandler asked her if she wanted to come up to the front of the room, she instantly said "Yes," without pausing and wrinkling her forehead as she previously had.

There are a number of effective decision programs, and Holly could have benefitted from any one of them. Holly learned something very important for her that day, and I learned something equally important from her. Many of my mentors both in and out of graduate school had taught that helping people express their feelings was always the first step toward healing most psychological problems. I'm sure that *sometimes* it works that way. For the person who doesn't know how to express feelings, learning to do that has a very positive impact. However, for Holly, the simple "unemotional" act of learning a new way to make decisions was much more respectful, caring, and effective. Nothing could have been more healing or more satisfying to her than learning a skill that will be useful every day of her life.

Whenever people accuse NLP of being "cold" and "technological" because they think "it doesn't deal with feelings," I think of Holly, and of many others whose lives have been deeply touched by NLP, and who have experienced a personal transformation that had previously eluded them.

Creativity

Ralph could only afford one session with me, so I felt some urgency in achieving fast results. Many clients present a specific problem, such as a phobia, a weight problem, or a problem with jealousy. Ralph's complaint was much more general and vague, the kind of situation some might call an "existential crisis." Ralph explained, "I'm dissatisfied with what I'm doing, and I don't know what I want to do with my life. I'm not really doing anything now. I make some pots, but that's not really what I want to do. I used to teach, but I don't want to do that, either; I'm not comfortable teaching."

Ralph listed several other job options, explaining why each wasn't right for him. He thought of himself as a hippie, objecting to most jobs on moral grounds. "The ways to make money involve doing what I don't want to do," he explained. "I don't want to be in an uptight role. I want to do things that require money, but I don't want to get the kind of job it takes to make it. I know there must be alternatives, but no one has let me know what they are."

Examining the Problem

Ralph considered his problem to be primarily a matter of values and maintaining his integrity—living up to who he wanted to be. However, as Ralph talked, I observed him carefully for nonverbal clues about the structure of his difficulty. It seemed possible that Ralph's problem had less to do with his values, than with a brain program that prevented him from easily finding a satisfying career. I noticed that each time Ralph talked about a possible job, he went through the same sequence of eye movements (see Appendix I), which indicated how he was considering possible jobs and deciding that he didn't like them. Ralph's brain program went like this:

Visualize a remembered possibility	→	Talk to myself about this option	→	Feel how much I like/dislike this option

In many ways this is a good decision-making sequence, but it has one very significant drawback. Since he used *remembered* images, Ralph could only consider ideas or possibilities that he had actually observed, or that someone else had told him about. At no time did Ralph use the part of his brain that creatively visualizes *new* possibilities by adjusting or recombining remembered images.

I tested to find out if Ralph went through the same brain program when he made other decisions. Indeed, he decided what kind of pots to make or what food to order at a restaurant in exactly the same way. When Ralph made pots, he had an easy time deciding what to make *if he had already seen a pot that he liked and wanted to make.* Ralph had trouble with indecision only if he hadn't seen anything he wanted to make.

Clearly, Ralph's difficulty in deciding what to do with his life was similar, but on a larger scale. It was a natural consequence of how he made decisions. He could only think of possibilities that he'd seen before. Since none of the options he had seen or heard matched his values, Ralph was stuck. He had no way to "make up" new possibilities that could be more satisfying to him.

Offering a Solution

Once I knew this, I used NLP methods to enable Ralph to draw on his creative abilities in his decision-making. Since he was a potter, I used designing pots to teach him how to make a simple decision in a new way. As I guided Ralph through this process, I used hand gestures to indicate where to look, so that he would be using the portion of his brain appropriate to each step of the decision process.

"Imagine that you are deciding what kind of pot to make. First see one possibility." (Ralph automatically looked up left as he always had.) "Now change that picture in any way." As I said this, I gestured up to his *right* so that Ralph would look in that direction and begin to use his ability to visualize creatively. "It doesn't matter if you like it better or not—just make it *different* in any way. It might be bigger, or a different shape, or taller or shorter. Nod when you have made a change in that pot you are seeing. . . ." When he nodded, I said, "Now say something to yourself about the pot,". . . (Ralph nodded.) "And now get a feel for how much you like this possibility."

Eye Direction:

up left	up right	down left	down right
Visual Memory →	Visual Construct →	Auditory →	Kinesthetic
Seeing one remembered option.	Changing the picture in any way.	Commenting on the option.	Getting a feel for how much he likes it.

"Now see a second possibility—another pot you could make. . . Now see it differently; change that image in any way. . . . Now talk to yourself about the pot. . . . Now get a feeling of how much you like this possibility. . . ." I continued gesturing to make sure Ralph's eyes moved to the appropriate direction for each type of processing. After he had considered five pots, I asked Ralph to select the one he liked best of those five. "Imagine actually going ahead to make the pot you like best."

To help Ralph begin to generalize this ability, I next had him decide what to make for dinner in the same way. Then I went on to ask him to make several other minor decisions in different areas in his life. After rehearsing this new "brain program" with Ralph for about fifteen minutes, I tested by asking him a question that required him to make a simple decision. Watching his automatic eye movements, I observed that he continued to use the new program spontaneously. Several months later, Ralph wrote me saying he was now living in another state, and was pleased with the course his life had taken.

Ralph's old brain program for decision-making is a typical one. Many of us think only of the choices we have seen or tried before, instead of considering things in new ways, using the creative ability we all have. Using this ability can enrich our lives, as it did for Ralph.

Many people believe that "being creative" is a personality "trait" that is difficult to develop. And indeed, developing creativity is virtually impossible if we never use the part of our brain that puts experiences together in new ways. NLP offers a direct and practical way to train ourselves to automatically use parts of our brain that we haven't yet used fully.

Weight loss

Since making decisions affects everything we do, it can be an important factor in a wide variety of problems that may seem very different at first. When Alice asked me to work with her, she did not ask for help in making decisions. That was far from her mind. What concerned her were 25 pounds of unattractive fat. Alice had tried everything she could think of to lose weight, including many kinds of therapy with many different therapists. She had even tried several NLP practitioners, who had used some standard approaches that are often effective with weight problems.

Alice told me her story with a sense of resignation to her "fate." "At first I was optimistic," she said. "I thought it ought to be easy to lose a little weight. But after so many different therapists who were supposed to be excellent, I began to wonder. Maybe I should forget about losing weight and just get used to being fat."

Alice was obviously discouraged about her problem and didn't expect to get results. The idea of working with a "tough" problem was an exciting challenge, so I eagerly began gathering information. Alice wanted to lose 25 pounds and keep it off. *Keeping* it off was the key. Occasionally she'd managed to lose a few pounds but had always put them back on immediately.

From working with weight loss often, I know that the same "problem" can have very different causes in different people. Some people overeat when they get in uncomfortable emotional states, because eating is the easiest way for them to feel better. Most of us have done this occasionally. Other people don't eat too much, but the *kind* of food they eat causes them to put on weight. They need an automatic way to select food that leads to weight loss (see Chapter 12). For others, motivation to exercise is the key.

I learned first that Alice didn't overeat in the morning or at work during the day, only at home in the evenings. Then I began to zero in on the key to her difficulty, using specific questions to elicit information most of us aren't usually aware of. I wanted to discover the brain program that resulted in her problem.

I learned that when Alice returned home from work, she walked into the apartment where she lived alone, looked around, and if she saw *nothing* to do, she felt bad. Once she had this bad feeling, she immediately thought of food, which made her feel good. This sent Alice off to the refrigerator to get something to eat—almost anything would do—so that she could have more of this good feeling. However, as she ate she also started talking to herself about how she shouldn't be eating. This made her feel bad, which again made her think of food so that she could feel good. A diagram of her brain program might look like this:

| See nothing to do | → | Feel bad | → | See food | → | Feel good | → | EAT |

It was becoming clear how Alice stayed overweight. Eating was the only way she had to deal with seeing nothing to do. She didn't overeat in the morning because she had to do things to get to work. She was a nurse at a hospital where her day was scheduled with plenty to do. Because of her busy schedule, Alice's brain program for "seeing nothing to do" was never triggered until she went home.

Alice went through this same thought sequence each time she came home and saw nothing to do. Even though she wanted to lose weight, food was the one thing she thought of that gave her good feelings.

I asked Alice what happened when she arrived home, and did see something to do. She responded, "If I see something to do, like my sewing machine with a dress on it to be finished, I just complete the project; then I *don't* eat."

What wasn't so obvious was how to change her program in a useful way. I puzzled over a solution that would work for Alice. Any time we change someone's brain program, we are very careful to preserve any benefits of the old program as we add more. I could have given Alice a new program that would make her feel good when she looked around and saw nothing to do, but this could lead to her becoming a "vegetable" in the evening. She might come home and just sit around feeling good.

As I looked more closely at Alice's brain program, I realized that it is actually a decision-making program. Its purpose was to give Alice a way to decide what to do when she saw nothing to do. The problem with the program was that the only choice she considered was eating. If we *think* we have only one choice, it's no choice at all—it's more like an order. If you have only one choice, you take it, and Alice did.

Alice desperately needed a way to generate possible choices other than food. In addition, Alice's decision program began by having bad feelings right after seeing nothing to do. Few of us feel creative when we feel bad. Starting with bad feelings makes it almost impossible for Alice to think of other possibilities. I knew I needed to give her a brain program that kept her in a resourceful state as she generated choices.

Here's the new brain program I mapped out for Alice:

See nothing to do	→	Ask "What would I enjoy doing?"	→	See one possibility	→	Imagine doing this possibility	→	Get a feeling for how much I like this option

Just as with Holly and Ralph, I rehearsed Alice through each step of this new program, making sure that she looked in the appropriate direction for each step.

After Alice had thought of five different things she might enjoy doing, I asked her to pick the one she liked best. Since this was an "off-hours" decision-making program, I had Alice think of what she would *enjoy* doing. If she had needed a new decision-making program for work, I might have had her ask something like, "What will be the most *effective* or *useful* thing to do now?"

Altogether it took about two hours to gather all the information I needed from Alice, and only about 20 minutes to provide her with the new decision program and make sure it was automatic.

Sometimes people wonder, "Won't I have to *think about* doing it the new way?" Most of the changes made with NLP result in an automatic shift in feelings or actions. We all demonstrate over and over that we're capable of acting automatically. If Alice could eat automatically, over and over, she can use the new brain program just as automatically. It's only a matter of giving her brain a new program that works better.

Eight months after this session with Alice, I called for a report. Alice said she had lost weight effortlessly, and had kept it off. Now that she had a way to think of and evaluate *many* options, eating was seldom her best choice. Several years later I received a letter from Alice confirming that she was pleased to still be at her desired weight.

As she lost weight, Alice gained something far more important than slimness. She now had a more effective way to make decisions.

Whenever changing someone's decision strategy, it's important to carefully consider all the ramifications. Alice's new ability to decide will make her a more creative person generally, not just keep her from overeating. She asked only for help with her weight; not to be more creative. Even though most people would be pleased with this additional benefit, every ability has its drawbacks, and as the person responsible, I need to consider them carefully. Alice had been satisfied in a job in which she followed a schedule set by others. When she is better able to *generate* choices, she could become dissatisfied with such a job. This dissatisfaction could result in her quitting or being fired. If she had been married I would have had to consider how her husband would be able to relate to a more imaginative wife. Would he welcome it, or would this unbalance their relationship in some way I could assist them in dealing with? It seemed clear that in Alice's case the benefits far outweighed any possible disadvantages.

Keys to Good Decision-Making

With Holly, we needed to provide an entirely new program for decision-making. Her old program had no steps that were relevant to making a decision. With Ralph, we kept his basic decision-making program, adding a step that would allow him to generate new ideas and be creative.

There is no one "right" decision-making brain program for everyone. What's important is the question, "Are you making satisfying decisions reasonably quickly, usually without regret or undue complaints from others?" If you are making satisfying decisions now, then your brain program for decision-making is probably fine for you.

Here are some elements that most people want in their decision-making program:

1. Access to Creative Options: Ralph is an example of adding this. He needed to access the creative part of his visual imagination to help him generate new possibilities to choose from. As with Ralph, you can build this into your decision-making program.

2. Using All Your Criteria at Once: Janice discovered something interesting about her decision-making brain program. She had difficulty buying clothes. When Janice walked into a store, an internal voice said sternly, "You *should* buy something on sale." Janice then looked at the sale dresses, felt bad, and thought to herself, "I don't want to buy something on sale." Then she looked at the regular-price dresses and felt good. Immediately, the first voice again spoke up preachily, "You should buy something on sale!" and Janice again felt bad. This inner conflict continued until she created in her mind a bright, vivid picture of herself dancing in the desert in the sun, wearing the clothes she liked (from the regular-priced rack). This picture was so bright and attractive that it took all her attention away from the voice that wanted to buy things on sale, and she purchased the more expensive items she liked.

All of this had been automatic for Janice, and out of her conscious awareness. She laughed when she found out what she had been doing. "I never thought about it," she said, "but I never buy any winter clothes. My ex-husband used to buy all my winter clothes, and I haven't bought any winter clothes since I got divorced 3 years ago!" This made sense, since winter clothes wouldn't look or feel good on someone dancing in a hot desert.

What Janice needed was a way to consider all of her criteria at the same time. The voice that urged Janice to buy sale clothes probably wanted to save money. The voice that wanted to buy more expensive clothes may have wanted quality. Rather than going back and forth between these two values, Janice could have resolved her conflict using the integration method described in Chapter 13. Then she would have *one* voice that identified all her values as she walked in the store: "What clothing will best satisfy *both* my desire to have good quality *and* a good buy?" or "What is the best quality for the money?" Janice could then evaluate each item of clothing for *both* values at once, and rank each item. She could then select something that best meets all her criteria.

If you find yourself going back and forth between different values; "This one is more attractive but this one is more practical," you may benefit from having a decision-making program that allows you to consider *all* of your values at once.

3. Using All Sensory Modalities: Beth said she was unhappy with the way she made decisions. She made decisions quickly, but sometimes regretted them. For instance, when shopping for a coat, she tried on several coats until she found one that felt really comfortable, and immediately bought it. She never looked at the coat in the mirror, or thought about how it looked on her. She bought on feel alone. However, after purchasing the comfortable coat, Beth would *see* an attractive coat in a store window, regret her choice, and think, "Oh, I wish I'd bought an attractive coat like that!"

What Beth needed was a decision-making program that automatically considered both the *comfort* (feel) and the look of the coats *before* she bought.

Depending upon the decision you are making, one sensory system may be more important than others. For instance, if I am selecting a record, it makes sense to pay more attention to its sound than to the picture on the cover. However, for many decisions, *all* of our sensory systems are important. If you select someone to date only on the basis of how that person looks, you may pick an attractive person, but not notice in advance that the person has a horrible tone of voice—until you have to listen to them talk for an entire evening. For this kind of decision, you probably want to consider *all* your data—how you've seen them move; the sound of their voice and what they talk about; your feelings when you're with them, and what it feels like to be touched by them. Considering *all* sensory systems before deciding can be built into your automatic way of making decisions.

4. Future Consequences: Many people do not consider the longer-term consequences of their decisions. For instance, people with weight problems typically think of the immediate pleasure of eating, but not of the future unpleasantness of being overweight. Adding an experience of the future into the decision process can result in a profound change in the way a person makes decisions, as we describe in Chapter 19.

For an example of doing this, see the excellent videotaped client session, "Making Futures Real," with Leslie Cameron-Bandler (see Appendix II).

Probably no other brain program has more impact on our lives than decision-making, because it's involved in almost everything we do. Whenever someone has a difficulty, one of the first things we ask ourselves is, "What kind of decision-making could have created this situation?" Then we find out how this person makes decisions. If the problem results from poor decision-making, offering a better way to make decisions will solve the person's complaint *and* also many other problems in his life. This is what we call a *generative* use of NLP, offering ways to get much more than people know how to ask for.

Dealing with Disaster   **17**

Kate had worked for us about two years when she came in one morning, her eyes bulging, her skin abnormally white. She definitely did not look her best. She stopped me upstairs in the kitchen where I was getting breakfast for our boys, on her way downstairs to the office. "Did you hear about what happened?!" With an unusual urgency in her voice, she recounted the details of the accident the night before. "I saw the whole thing! A car went out of control right in front of me last night. If I hadn't slammed on my brakes, it would have run right into *me*. Two people were killed, and two are in intensive care."

Kate had watched a car go out of control, veer inches in front of her, crash into a van, flip over and land on its roof. She stopped her car immediately and got out, both wanting to help and not wanting to face what she might see. Kate apprehensively carried a blanket over to the van, where she saw a man sitting on the ground, obviously hurt, with blood on his face and arm. As she watched, the man slumped back onto the ground, his eyes rolling upward, showing white. Kate panicked, thinking he might have died. "I couldn't handle the possibility that he had just died, so I walked away." Kate only waited long enough to make her accident report, and then left in a state of shock.

The first time I listened to her story about the accident I thought, "It's understandable that she's very shaken. She watched the fatal accident, and knows it could easily have been her." Seeing something like that usually makes people think about their mortality. However, each time she came in to work over the next few days, she had something new to report about the accident, always with the same urgency in her voice and disturbed look on her face. "Have you heard what they found out now about the person in intensive care?" The accident seemed to be consuming all her waking attention.

Kate, too, became concerned about her response to the accident, and wanted to change it. She told me that since the accident, she had been very nervous any time she was in a car. Her nervousness was even worse at night and when others were driving. She kept imagining accidents were going to happen, and panicking. Kate had to drive past the scene of the accident every day on her way home from work. Even after arriving safely at her house, she repeatedly went over the details of the accident in her mind, keeping herself in a state of anxiety.

Although the accident scene had been unpleasant, that wasn't what was bothering Kate. What deeply concerned her was that she had been unable to help when the man slumped over. She had wanted to help, but couldn't. That was when she "lost it."

Kate told me that the feeling she got when she panicked at the accident reminded her of the feeling she used to get as a child when her mother woke her up in the middle of the night and shook her violently. Kate said she always felt out of control, and mentally "left" when her mother did that. It seemed likely that this abusive history had contributed to her intense reaction to the accident.

Creating Panic

I asked Kate to go back and remember the accident just before her panic, in order to find out exactly what made her respond so strongly. We discovered that when she saw the man lying there, she focused on his bloody face, and "zoomed in." The more she zoomed in close on his face, the more she felt out of control and frozen. As Kate did this with me in her imagination, her whole body became tight and immobile. Zooming in clearly worked to produce panic in Kate. When I asked Kate to "unzoom" the face and move it further away, she felt better. Her whole body relaxed and began to move again.

A New Self-image

Knowing how Kate mentally created her feeling of helplessness and being out of control provided the information I needed in order to change it. The first step was to assist Kate in creating what would become literally, a new self-image: the Kate who could deal with the same situation resourcefully.

"Imagine the Kate who could deal with that kind of situation really well. She's probably not ecstatic about accidents, but if one happens, it's not a problem for her. *She has the resources* to *deal with it effectively.* You don't need to know what those resources are; you can just tell by looking at that image of Kate that *she has lots of choices and abilities.* You can know that by the expression on her face, the way she moves, breathes, and gestures, the sound of her voice, etc."

Kate tried to develop this image, but I could tell she wasn't succeeding to her satisfaction. She looked anything but charmed with this "more resourceful" Kate she was supposed to be seeing. "Do you see the Kate who can handle this type of situation yet?"

"Well, I can see that Kate, but it's not realistic. I'm not her."

"What makes her not realistic?" Sometimes when someone says this, it's because they're seeing themselves in black-and-white, and the picture needs to be in color to become real and convincing. Or they may see it as transparent, and it needs to look solid to be real. I expected something like this, but Kate responded with a different concern.

"*That* Kate can handle the situation, but I can't because I don't know how to do first aid or CPR, and I really don't know anything medically about what should be done. Maybe I need to take medical classes to feel better."

It seemed unnecessary for Kate to go around feeling panicked and out of control just because she isn't an M.D. Many people have little medical knowledge, and yet can function well at accident scenes doing whatever they can do without panicking. Kate seemed to be thinking of this as an either/or situation: either she had to be completely medically competent so that she could feel in control, or she had to feel totally out of control. Kate's objection told me exactly what to do next.

"Kate, rather than seeing the you who could do CPR, I want you to see the you who may not know any more about medicine than you do sitting here now, but she has the resources to deal with a difficult situation as best she can, given what she knows. Perhaps this is the Kate who can walk into an emergency and decide on the spot how she can be most helpful. Panic is irrelevant to her, because she knows how to quickly and calmly assess what she *can* do, and not try to do anything she knows she can't do. What this Kate knows is not medicine, it's how to use whatever information and skills she has to act in the best way possible. She may make mistakes once in a while—as all of us do—but she also has the resources to learn from them, and use these learnings next time." As I talked, Kate's face began to relax. She looked more and more pleased with, and attracted to, the capable Kate of the future that she was seeing in her mind's eye. This was the kind of nonverbal response I wanted to see.

Changing Her Automatic Response

At this point, I knew what made Kate panic: the memory of zooming in on the man's face. I also had helped Kate create an image of her capable self. However, being *able* to see herself as resourceful is not enough. This image must flash in her mind compellingly *at the right time*—whenever she thinks of the accident, or when she actually encounters an accident in the real world.

The next step is to connect these two images in her mind, so that every time Kate thinks of the man's face, it will automatically transform into the image of seeing herself with the resources to deal with this kind of situation. This is what will allow Kate to immediately *feel* resourceful when she needs to.

NLP teaches many ways to connect images in our minds, and each of us is unique in what works best for us. I already knew that "zooming in" was impactful for Kate, so I decided to use that to connect the two images.

I first tested my guess, to find out if Kate felt more attracted to the capable Kate of the future if she brought the image closer and zoomed in on it. When she tried this, she smiled and said, "Yes." Then I asked her to clear her visual screen in preparation for linking the two images.

"Now see the unconscious man up close and zoomed in. As soon as you can see that, also see a very small image of the capable Kate, way out on the horizon. . . . Now let the image of the capable Kate zoom in close very rapidly at the same time as the image of the man in the accident quickly "unzooms" and moves off so far away that you can't see it any more."

Here we ran into another minor obstacle. After trying this, Kate frowned slightly. She stopped and said, "I'm not sure I'm really seeing these images," concerned that she might not be doing it right.

"What I'd like you to do is just *pretend* that you are doing it. Many people don't *really* see these things consciously, they just do it *as if* it's real. I'm not very conscious of most of my internal pictures, but if I *pretend* that I really see these things, it works just as well for me as it does for someone who says he actually sees images in his mind. As long as you pretend well, it works fine."

This seemed to satisfy her. Kate closed her eyes and exchanged the images quickly by zooming one out as the other one zoomed in. This time her nonverbal responses indicated that she was really doing it. As she began, her body was motionless and frozen; a moment or two later she relaxed and smiled in the same way she had previously when she was seeing the image of the capable Kate.

"Now blank your internal screen and do the same thing five more times. Each time begin with the man's face up close and the image of capable Kate far way. You can let these images exchange even faster each time you do it.". . .

The Results

When Kate was done, I carefully tested to find out if her new response was automatic. First I asked Kate to make the image of the man so I could observe her response. Instead of feeling panic, she felt capable and resourceful. She also found that she felt the same capable feelings if she thought about any other part of the accident scene, or if she imagined driving a car.

However, Kate wasn't convinced that anything would really be different. I, too, would have found this rapid, dramatic change in her response difficult to believe, if I hadn't successfully used the same method with many other people. I pointed out that driving home would be a much better test, since any driving had bothered her since the accident, and she would also have to drive past the accident scene. She agreed this would be a good test. This work with Kate took almost an hour.

The next day Kate came to work quite pleased. She had been comfortable driving home, and going by the scene of the accident, and she hadn't been preoccupied with driving or accidents during the evening. About a month later she saw a bike accident in which the rider cut his head with the rim of his sunglasses and was bleeding. Kate immediately responded by helping him resourcefully and calmly. About two months later she witnessed another accident involving a car and a bicyclist, an older man whose face was bleeding. Again Kate was very resourceful and calm in helping assist him and the car driver into calming down and handling the situation. It's now about three years since our work together, and Kate remains comfortable and resourceful with respect to driving and accidents.

The Method

The procedure I used with Kate is called the "Swish" pattern (also see Chapter 18), because it's often helpful to make a "swishing" sound as the person exchanges the two images. The swish pattern was developed by Richard Bandler (1, 2). People have been talking for years about the importance of a good self-image in mental health and in the ability to cope and change. However, no one has previously been able to provide a specific and direct way to make the self-image more resourceful, and utilize its power to help people change.

When to Use the Swish

We have used this method to help people with a very wide range of unwanted behaviors and responses. It has been particularly useful with unwanted habits such as overeating, smoking, and nailbiting. A demonstration with a woman who had a long-standing nailbiting habit is available on videotape (3), and a demonstration with a smoker is available on audiotape (4).

Couples and Families

Although the Swish pattern is an individual method, we have often used it to help families and couples build the kind of family life they want. All of us occasionally respond to a friend or family member with feelings or actions we know are not useful. Even when other family members are acting inconsiderately or unlovingly, and even if a situation may be "their fault," by gaining more resourcefulness *ourselves,* we can often respond in more useful ways.

For example, one woman got outraged when her daughter spoke to her using a certain "snotty" tone of voice. The daughter probably was indeed being obnoxious. (We all have this ability from time to time.) However, the mother recognized that no matter *what* her daughter did, the *mother* wanted to have ways of feeling better and getting what she wanted. Using this method with the mother improved her relationship with her daughter without doing anything directly to shift the daughter's behavior. This session is available on videotape (3), and demonstrates how you can link sounds or voices instead of images, to get the same results. When our unresourceful feelings result from things we hear or say to ourselves, this same method is more effective using sounds rather than images.

Sometimes *several* members in a family or couple want more choice in their responses. One couple basically got along well, but wanted to improve their relationship in the area of several long-standing difficulties. The wife complained that her husband sometimes "distanced himself" from her, and she criticized him for this. We discovered that in her mind, when she thought of him in these situations, she literally saw him moving away— although he actually stayed in the same location in the "real world." The husband experienced his wife's critical comments as "piercing." He imagined her criticism as an instantaneous "laser bolt" that zapped him in the chest, and he felt powerless to respond. By identifying these inner images, and connecting them to a resourceful self-image, they were both able to have completely different, and much more loving responses to each other in similar future situations.

Discovering internal pictures that create problems continues to fascinate us. While at first they seemed a bit strange or bizarre, they make sense out of our resulting feelings and behavior. We have noticed these same kinds of images (or sounds) in ourselves, when *we* feel or act less than fully resourceful. Knowing how to discover these experiences, and knowing how to link them to an image of our more resourceful self, can make an enormous difference in our lives.

References

1. *Using Your Brain—for a CHANGE,* by Richard Bandler, Chapter 9.
2. *Change Your Mind—and Keep the Change,* by Steve and Connirae Andreas, Chapter 3.
3. "The Swish Pattern" videotape (see Appendix II).
4. "Introducing NLP" audiotape (see Appendix II).

Problems will always be with us. The problem is not the problem; the problem is in the way people cope. This is what destroys people, not the problem. Then when we learn to cope differently, we deal with the problems differently, and they become different.

—Virginia Satir

18

Intimacy, Safety, and Violence

Mack, in his early 30's, had been an alcoholic for four years, now dry for ten years. He rode a big Harley-Davidson motorcycle, black leather jacket and all, and always acted completely cool and in control. One of his favorite expressions was "Rip your face off." Mack's complaint was that he often felt bad, and wanted to do something about it. When I asked him what made him feel bad, he said, "Well, like if I see a certain person's face, then 'Ughh,' I feel bad."

I began asking questions to find out the exact images or sounds in Mack's thinking that produced his bad feelings. "How do you get the bad feeling?"

"Because of what's attached to the last experience with that person." Mack gestured up and to his left, indicating that there is a remembered picture out of his awareness, that the bad feeling is "attached to." Since he's not aware of the picture, he has no control over it; he just notices that he suddenly feels bad. I continue questioning him to bring this picture more into his awareness.

"And how do you know about that right now?" I asked.

"I lived it. I look at the person's face and I go, 'Oh, shit!'" (Mack says this with a mixture of disgust and anger.)

"So let's say that this person walked into this room right now and you see this person's face. How do you get to the 'Oh, shit!'?"

184

Mack gestures up and to his left again. "I just remember the last incident with the person. I didn't like what she did, and I didn't like what I did."

"So it's that memory that makes you feel bad. Can you see how you picture it?"

"Yeah, I can see that incident."

Now we have something useful to work with. By changing his response to the memory itself, we can change his bad feelings.

"Mack, now let's experiment a little with that picture. First move it away from you." (Mack relaxes.) "Does that change your response to it?"

"Well, yeah, it's a lot less intense."

"Now bring it in closer."

Mack's head and shoulders move back and he tenses up. "That makes it worse."

"Now try making it bigger." (Again Mack's head moves back and he tenses up.) "That makes it worse, too, doesn't it?"

"Yeah."

Finding a Key: Three-dimensionality.

"Is the picture two-dimensional or three?"

"No, it's flat, it's like a slide."

"Try making it three-dimensional."

Previously Mack's body showed more or less of the same "Oh, shit!" response. Now, however, he shows a different *kind* of response. His body becomes softer, his shoulders relax, and he breathes out softly. "How does that change it for you?"

Mack's voice becomes very soft. "It becomes *real.* It becomes softer; it becomes more like a person rather than just a picture."

"How does that change your response? *You* look a lot softer, too."

"Well, the picture is a lot softer. My feelings went 'Ohhh,' instead of 'Rrrf!' It was a lot different; there wasn't as much feeling of violence."

"Imagine that this person came into the room now and you see them and then remember what happened before in 3-D. Run a little scenario. What would that be like?"

Mack looks thoughtful and contemplative. Again his body softens and relaxes. "It's different; it's *real* different," Mack said softly. "It's not like I want to run up and say 'Oh, it's OK,' and it's not like 'Here's your ass, go home!' either. It is a lot softer. It's not such a black-and-white response."

"Right. When you make the picture 3-D, *you* also become more three-dimensional; you're softer and have more depth. Try this out in another situation where you think it might be useful to have that three-dimensionality."

"Hmmm." Mack remains still, thinking for about fifteen seconds, and then smiles and begins talking in a soft low voice. "Yeah. I was thinking of when I was talking with Amy earlier about what she needed. If it's not flat, then it's a whole lot easier to see other stuff, a lot more possibilities."

"So you agree this would be a useful change for you, right?"

"Well I'm not sure. If I did that all the time, then I can't keep everybody out there," Mack said, making a "stop" gesture with his left hand and arm.

"If you don't have certain resources for dealing with people, then you have to keep them at a distance because they're too tough to deal with. But if we build in some resources, then you can let them in and deal with them. Then it doesn't have to be an either/or situation. You will still have the option of keeping someone at a distance when that's appropriate. We never remove any choices, we only add new ones. And we won't make any changes until you are satisfied in advance that you want them."

"Well that sounds all right. I can go for that."

Creating a New Resourceful Self

"Now close your eyes, and take a little time to develop an image of the you that you want to be in dealing with that person from your past. I'll offer some suggestions from which you can pick whatever seems appropriate for you. You might want to see the Mack who has the ability to respond to others as three-dimensional people, and who at the same time can get much more of what he wants for himself *and* for those other people. You might want to see him with the ability to respond to both positives and negatives at the same time. That Mack doesn't just see people as good or bad, but can recognize the positive *and* negative qualities of everyone, and all the variations.". . .

Mack moves his left hand from left to right several times as he nods his head. "Shades of color."

"Yes. And that will make it easy for that Mack in front of you to have a more measured response, both as he gets to know someone he likes, or when someone intrudes and he needs to get some distance. . . . And that will also give that Mack the ability to understand other people more completely, so that it will be easier to deal with them. . . . Another thing you might want him to have is the ability to decide when he wants to be close, and when he wants some distance, and to act on it. He can be close, and appreciate closeness, (Mack smiles broadly.) and he can also decide when he doesn't want that, (Mack nods) and all the degrees of closeness in between those possibilities.". . .

Mack opens his eyes. "OK. It seems like the only thing I don't have in this is a 'safety' thing—something that keeps me safe." Mack gestures with both hands to form a shield in front of his chest.

"Safe from what? Physically safe?"

"Naw, I don't have any problems with that. You're taking away the safety I've built in—"

"You still have all the other behaviors you've used for many years. We can't take those away, and I don't want to anyway. I'm only suggesting that you use your old skills in a new way."

"I just don't see those as acceptable behaviors any longer."

"OK. You have a sense of what safety means to you, even though you can't put it into words, right?" Mack agrees. "Close your eyes again, and let yourself get a sense of that feeling. You know unconsciously what safety means to you, and you can let that unconscious knowledge transfer itself into that image of that Mack who can be safe in other ways. And you don't even need to know exactly how he's able to be safe, or what kinds of choices he has. You only need to be able to recognize when you look at him that he has the ability to have that kind of safety—as safe as a human being can be. And my guess is that he'll be far safer than the old Mack was, because he'll be safe in a more solid and real way. . . . How does he look up there?"

Mack opens his eyes, looks up, thinks for a while, and then smiles. "Enough." He slaps his thigh for emphasis.

"When you look at him, do you *know* that he's safe?"

"Yeah, and a lot of other things, too," Mack added with a nod and a smile.

"Do you like that you?" Mack nodded quickly. "Check him out really carefully. Is it all right with you if you become like him?" Mack looks carefully at his image as I continue talking. "Because if you have any objections whatsoever, we want to modify that image. Is this a person who is going to be able to deal with the various situations you're going to be in, in a resourceful way, someone who is able to learn from his mistakes and go on from there?". . .

"Got it. Got it. It's all there." Again he slaps his thigh for emphasis.

Linking the New Self-image to the Old Problem

Now that Mack has an image of himself with the resources he wants, I am ready to link this "solution" to his "problem" experience. Since I know *three-dimensionality* and the *closeness* of images are important to Mack, I use these.

"I want you to close your eyes again and take a good look at that image, so that your unconscious can memorize it carefully, . . . and then set it aside briefly, safely in your memory. . . . Now go back to that picture we started with, of the person with whom you had a bad experience. See it close and two-dimensional. . . . Now, far away and two-dimensional, I want you to see the image of yourself that you just memorized. . . .

"Now have those images quickly exchange places. As the picture of that other person recedes into the distance, it will become three-dimensional. At the same time, that picture of yourself will come close and become three-dimensional." As Mack does this, his head and shoulders go back a little and he smiles.

"Good. Now blank your mind briefly, and then do the same thing again about five more times. Blank your mental screen after each one, and let each one happen a little faster." Each time Mack does this, he smiles and takes a breath.

"Now there was this one person who used to make you feel bad, right?"

As Mack thinks about the person, he smiles, then laughs. "Yeah, there *was.*"

Mack has just responded resourcefully to the same image that used to make him feel bad, confirming that he now has a new and automatic response.

"Now think of some other people you've had difficulty with in the past, to find out if this new response has already generalized."

As Mack thinks of someone else, he breaks into a smile again. "No problem!"

"Now imagine that one of these people did something obnoxious in the future." Again Mack breaks into a broad smile and laughs. This session took about twenty minutes.

Mack's Experience Afterwards

In the weeks after this session, Mack noticed himself changing in ways that pleased him. He even sold his motorcycle, which had been a prized possession, "because I don't need it anymore." He also realized he still needed a more complete experience of personal/emotional safety. In Mack's childhood, disagreements had always resulted in physical abuse and the end of a relationship; he had *no* personal experience in which an intimate relationship had survived a serious disagreement. Since he knew from other people that it was possible, Mack purposely created a number of disturbances in his marriage, to verify that their love could survive it. For Mack, doing this gave him the full experience of personal safety he needed to complete the work. Mack told us later, "Now I am comfortable moving through the world in a new way." We were glad Mack found his own way to take the next significant step.

It is now a year and a half later, and Mack now counsels people with drug and alcohol problems. In a recent conversation, Mack spoke about another incident which demonstrated his new attitude.

"Something happened recently that let me know I'm not the same person I used to be. A guy came into my office all 'coked' up. He was on the edge of losing control the whole time. The court had sentenced him to 26 hours of therapy and level II education, but he hadn't been told yet. I had to read this paper telling him his sentence, and when he heard that, he 'lost it.' He came at me with his fists doubled up."

"My first response was 'You're a dead man.' Then I thought, 'What I want is to get control of my space.' It wasn't a life or death situation anymore. I took the guy down onto the floor to protect myself, in a very gentle way."

"Is that different than the way you would have done it before?" I asked.

"Oh yeah!" Mack responded quickly, "Before he would have been out the window! Well, not really, but he would have gotten hurt on the way to the floor. Years ago almost the same thing happened to me. A guy pulled a knife on me. He got *hurt* on the way down."

Creating or Defusing Violence

We have presented this example in considerable detail, because of its importance in understanding the problems that people often have with intimacy, safety, and violence. Governments and leaders recognized many years ago that the only way to get decent loving human beings to go out and kill other people is to somehow make the enemy inhuman. National propaganda campaigns during wartime always depict the enemy as a flat cartoon, or as a sub-human animal rather than as a person.

The same thing happens at an individual level. When Mack saw someone else as a flat cardboard figure, it was easy for him to "rip his face off," as he put it. When he saw others as three-dimensional human beings, Mack's own response became deeper and more human. Violence became much less likely, both because he felt differently and because he had alternative choices.

Some people are violent because they were taught that violence is an appropriate response in certain situations; it's simply a learned behavior. However, most people become violent when they run out of alternatives. Think of some time when you were violent, or feeling close to it. Did you *choose* violence out of a variety of alternatives? Or did you feel out of choices, frustrated that nothing else you tried had been effective?

People become violent when they run out of choices and feel frustrated and impotent. When we, as a society, run out of choices in dealing with violence, we resort to more punishment, control and prisons. These all increase the offender's sense of impotence, which in turn leads to more violence. The solution to the problem of violence is not more violence, but to teach alternative positive ways of thinking and behaving. On an individual level, learning to see others as three-dimensional, gaining personal resources to feel emotionally safe, and knowing how to manage closeness and distance, can make an important difference, as they did for Mack.

Personal   **19**
Timelines

Every language has some way to express time—the awareness of past, present, or future. In some cultures, time is thought of as a series of cycles: birth, death, rebirth, etc. In English, time is often thought of as a "line," and many of us learned history out of books that had diagrams of events occurring in a line across the page.

It has been recognized for some time that some people are more "past-oriented," some "future-oriented," and others "present-oriented." These time orientations can be the basis for exceptional skills, and can also create serious problems in people's lives. For example, you may know someone who is always preoccupied with the past. You may know someone who never plans for the future, or someone who is always planning and seldom able to enjoy the present. We thought to ourselves, "Wouldn't it be remarkable if we could find out how people's internal maps orient them in time, and if we could find a way to directly *change* that?" At the time we didn't realize how *many* more applications our explorations would have.

The Discovery of Personal "Timelines"

One of our most interesting discoveries was that each of us has our own personal *internal* way of coding time. Unconsciously, we each have ways to recognize something as a part of our personal past, present, or future. Even more intriguing was our discovery that the way we code time has a major impact on who we are and how we respond—what is often called our "personality."

191

For Cathy, whom you'll read about in this chapter, understanding and changing her internal time coding was the key to many other changes she had wanted for herself. Changing Judy's timeline helped her get over her husband's affair. For Ruth, adding a future allowed her to develop compelling goals and feel motivated to work to achieve them. As you read the examples in this chapter, you can also begin to understand how *you* code time. You may get a sense of how your own way works well for you, or how you might want to improve it. You'll get a sense of how time codings offer a key that unlocks certain "secrets" of our personalities.

Finding Your Time Codings

How do you tell the difference between the past and the future? This is not a matter of philosophy but a very practical matter. When I plan my day or the next week, I need to have some way of knowing that I haven't already *done* the tasks I'm thinking of. My brain needs a way of knowing that they are in the *future*, not the *past*. Occasionally, of course, we get these codings confused. Have you ever thought about talking to someone or writing a letter, and later been convinced that you had already done it? You'll understand how that happens later in the chapter.

I'd like you to actually try the following mind-experiment before reading on. Think of waking up yesterday, and think of waking up tomorrow. Think of both of these experiences *at the same time.* How can you tell the difference between them? How do you know one is past and the other is future?

Nearly everyone imagines or senses these events in two different locations in personal space. If you think in pictures, one picture may be to your left, while the other is to your right. One might be higher or lower that the other, it might be closer or farther away, or one might be in front of you and the other behind you. Even if you don't consciously see anything, can you sense that it's as if waking up yesterday and waking up tomorrow are in two different spots? . . .

Now try adding waking up one week ago, and one week in the future. Now you'll be imagining four different events that occurred at different times. You probably don't clearly remember waking up a week ago, and that doesn't matter at all. You know you did wake up a week ago, and you know you probably will wake up a week from now. You can just sense *where* you think of these events.

As you notice *where* you sense these events, you are beginning to understand what we mean by "coding time." Location is one of the ways your mind codes events. By imagining these events in different locations, your brain knows whether each one is in the past, the present, or the future. You can go on to imagine waking up five years ago, and five years in the future, and find out where these times are for you.

Sometimes discovering your own time codings is much easier if someone trained assists you in doing this. Another person can notice your nonverbal indicators of location, such as where you look and gesture. However, you can also learn a lot on your own.

Now that you know the location of five years ago, one year ago, yesterday, right now, tomorrow, a week in the future, a year in the future, and five years in the future, you are ready to notice more. You can let all the other events from your past and your future "fill in" on your timeline. Again, it's often much easier to just get a "sense" that you are thinking of your entire past—the series of events that make up your experience—rather than to consciously see them all. The same goes for your future. You can get a sense that your entire future goes off in a particular direction, even if you don't know exactly what is out there.

Many people imagine their past in a pathway off to their left, the present in front of them, and their future in a pathway off to their right. Some people have this reversed right to left. Others have the past in a pathway or "tunnel" straight behind them, and the future going out straight in front. There are an infinite number of ways to organize time, and there is *no right way*. While many people have more or less straight lines, others have something more like a tunnel, or an arc, or even a helix. Although each way of organizing time has predictable advantages and disadvantages, some ways provide more problems than solutions. Often changing the way you code time can provide a solution to difficulties, make certain tasks easier, or make desired experiences become more natural.

Now you may be ready to notice other aspects of your time coding. How large are the events in your past? Is an event the same size in the long-ago past as it is in the recent past? If you're not sure, guess. Do you see your past in color, or in black and white? Do you sense that you have a series of slides, or do you have movies? Do you see yourself in the past, or do you see what you saw at the time? If you could see it consciously, would it be clearly focused or fuzzy?

Now notice these same things about your future. How large is it? Is it in color? Slides or movies? Do you see yourself? Is it clear or fuzzy?

Now notice the ways in which your past and your future are different. In addition to having the past in a different location, it may be clearer. Many people see the future as fuzzier, or their future may include many branches. These are ways to indicate uncertainty about what will happen.

Now that you've noticed something about your own timeline, it will be easier to follow along with other people's experience of changing time codings. Since the way you code time has such an important impact on who you are, you may find some of the changes described here interesting and useful for yourself.

Using the Discovery: Building a Future Timeline

Ruth had a tendency to never plan. She lived for the present. While she generally enjoyed life, Ruth sometimes felt that her life had no direction. "I don't have goals, and sometimes I think I would be better off if I did," Ruth confided. "Usually I enjoy life, but lately I've been feeling depressed, and I don't know where to turn. It seems like I can't look forward to anything."

I quickly explored Ruth's timeline. As I had guessed, Ruth had a long "past" timeline, going off straight to her left. Her present was right in front of her, but she had almost no future at all. When she described her future, Ruth said, "It seems small and gray, and it stops about six inches to my right. It doesn't really have anything in it."

Ruth's lack of a future literally gave her no direction, no way to plan, and nothing to look forward to. As long as her present was enjoyable, this didn't matter too much. However, when her present was depressing, it became a major problem. The obvious solution was to assist Ruth in building a future for herself.

"Ruth, most people have an internal map of the future, just as you have a map of the past. Of course your future map needs to be much more flexible or vague, because none of us knows for sure what will happen in the future. Having a future map provides us with what you want—a direction in life, something to look forward to. You want to have a sense of what's important to you, and where you are going."

Before proceeding, I wanted to find out if Ruth had any objection to having a future, particularly because she had said, "I *can't* look forward to anything." It turned out that Ruth did have an objection that she hadn't been aware of consciously. When Ruth was 12, her mother was killed in a car wreck. Ruth was devastated; her whole future had been destroyed, and she concluded then and there that she should never count on anything again. "Looking back on it, I can see that I just wiped out my internal future then, and never wanted to build one again. I really did start living for the present. I didn't know I was doing that then—I just did the best I could."

"And that makes a lot of sense, especially to a 12-year-old, because you knew the present was something you could count on," I agreed, validating the positive purpose of what Ruth had unconsciously done. "So what kind of a future can you build now that you really *can* count on? What kind of a future can you build that can't be taken away from you no matter what happens, and that *will* give you the sense of direction that you want?"

I went on to suggest how Ruth could accomplish this in a way that wouldn't set her up to be devastated again. "I'm guessing you'll want some way of knowing you can live and plan for the future, without knowing exactly what the future will be. You can just see a pathway, a direction, to let you know you *have* a future, without knowing exactly what will happen. You don't want to imagine anything too specific on your future timeline, like 'I'm going to get married next year,' because you don't know if that will happen. However, you *can* put your *values* in your future, a representation of the *kinds of experiences you want to move towards in your life.* So whatever you want more of, you can put it on your future timeline. This might include having close relationships with people, or finding a way to make your own contribution in the world. It can include health and well-being, or many, many other things. You can have the sense that no matter what happens, you can find a way to have these things."

In addition to placing values on her timeline, Ruth felt more secure when she had built in many alternate pathways or forks in her future. This gave her the sense that there would always be a route for her to take, even when another route got blocked off.

Six months later, Ruth was pleased with her direction in life and was feeling much better overall. "I still have my down days, but I'm not depressed like I was." Everyone has "down" days; seeing them in the context of a flow of future events leading to something positive makes them much easier to deal with. She had also decided to go back to school to get training in a technical field that interested her. "Now I'm working for the future. That's something I wouldn't have done before."

Putting the Past in the Past, and Developing a Future

Some people benefit from a fairly complete timeline shift. For Cathy, a timeline change became the key that allowed many other changes she wanted to fall into place.

Cathy approached me in a seminar, asking me to work with her timeline. Since she had been in a basic timeline training with us, she already knew that her timeline was organized the *opposite* of the usual way.

Most people look to the left when seeing visual memories, and to their right when constructing internal pictures of things they haven't seen before. This has to do with brain organization (See Appendix 1). Although some people are reversed, people usually see their past on the *same* side that they look to see visual memories. Since we have to make up the future, a person's future timeline is usually on the same side that he sees constructed pictures.

Cathy, however, did the opposite. She saw her *past* on the side where she *constructed* pictures, and her *future* on the side she looked to for visual *memory.* This meant she was using the part of her brain that specializes in *memory* to imagine her *future,* while she was using the part of her brain that *constructs* things to organize her personal *past.*

Without really knowing what might come of it, Cathy thought perhaps she would benefit from having her timeline the way most people do. I guessed she was right, since most people have been more satisfied with their future timeline in the same location as their visual constructed images.

First, I checked to be sure where Cathy's timeline was. Indeed, it was the opposite of most people's. Next, I found the qualities of her current timeline. Her past was clumped together pretty much in front of her, but went slightly off to her right, while she sensed her future was off to her left. "There's not much to it. I don't really have a future," Cathy revealed.

I had seen this before, so it wasn't a surprise. People who have their future where they see visual *memory* either don't have much of a future, or their future seems very *fixed*—more like most people's pasts.

I am always very careful when changing someone's timeline, because the way each of us sorts out our past memories is a basis for our sense of what is real. I wanted to be sure to preserve any advantage from Cathy's current way of sorting out time. "Part of my purpose is for *you* to really notice what your timeline is like now. If you still prefer this way after we experiment with having it a different way, you can just put it back the way it is now. Or, you can pick certain contexts where you want to have time organized in a new way, and keep your old way for other contexts."

Although people's timelines have a pervasive impact on their lives, we have discovered by experimenting that they are surprisingly easy to change. Basically you just ask someone to experiment with imagining it differently, and find out how that changes their experience—particularly with respect to problems they have had. Since people's skills are also often a consequence of the timeline they have, it's extremely important to preserve the skills and advantages they now enjoy when making any changes.

Next I asked Cathy to try switching her timeline from left to right, and to notice what happened. At first she was concerned that her future was strange. "It's funny. It isn't a line anymore—it almost oozes out in lots of different directions." I told her that was probably an excellent choice. Her unconscious had automatically found a good way to let her know that the future isn't fixed, and is full of many possibilities and options. In fact, this is the way many people successfully organize their future.

Hearing that her "oozing" future was probably useful, Cathy relaxed, and looked at her future a little more. "Suddenly my future is very colorful. That's very interesting!"

I was glad to hear about this automatic change in Cathy's experience. A colorful, bright future is literally much more attractive to people, and usually works better than a dim, dark one.

Since Cathy's future timeline had been short before, I wanted to make sure it went farther into the future. "Notice how far your future goes now, and if it is spreading.". . .

"It went farther out as soon as I moved it to the other side; it's growing out more now," Cathy commented.

"Good, and you can continue to let it grow unconsciously in an appropriate and useful way."

Next I asked her to check her past timeline. Cathy said, "I get the sense it's experimenting with itself. It's undulating, and moving around, trying to find a place to be."

At this point, Cathy liked her future much better, and her past seemed to be experimenting. I suggested that she continue letting her past shift around, so she could gather more data about what would work best.

At this time, Cathy wasn't aware of any objections to her new time arrangement, but later that evening she became aware of one. "I felt nauseous, and like something wasn't quite right about my past. It was as if my past wanted to go back to where it had been, so I checked inside and asked for the positive purpose of its wanting to go back." Asking for positive unconscious purposes is a widely useful NLP method for dealing with objections, which Cathy was familiar with through her previous NLP training (See chapter 8, Positive Intentions).

This internal question revealed to Cathy why her timeline had been organized in such an unusual fashion, with the past where most people have their future. Since she was born, Cathy had gone through a long series of serious health problems. She had had many illnesses doctors couldn't diagnose, and some illnesses that are often "terminal," including a bout with cancer.

"That was my lifelong history, so I thought of myself as a sick person. Every illness or accident I ever had (that I remember) was on the right side of my body, and it had been important to keep the illnesses and the past together on the right. Unconsciously it seemed like if I put my future on the same side with my illnesses, that meant I would be sick in the future, and I didn't want that." Cathy went on, "Last night I realized it was time to recognize that I am a healthy person now—that all those illnesses are in the past. As soon as I realized that, my new timeline settled in, and I felt much better." Now that her objection was taken care of, Cathy was pleased with her new timeline.

The Results for Cathy

Three months later, I called Cathy to ask about the results of this timeline change.

"I've been thinking about writing you a letter. That was one of the most incredible pieces of work anyone has ever done with me. It's reached into every part of my life. It was really global. I've been talking to a lot of people about it because it made such a difference."

Later, Cathy sent a letter with more detail:

"Since I started studying NLP, I had done a lot of work around health issues because of the cancer and many other childhood illnesses. That helped, but it seemed like 'a piece was missing.' I was also trying to clarify career issues that had reached a crisis point, and also some relationship issues. In retrospect, I'm sure I was having difficulty with all those because I could see no future. Now, everything is very clear—literally. I see paths, choices, goals, and I have been resolving things. The past seems so much farther away and in an appropriate place.

"Other things are different, too. Before I used to *avoid things* I didn't want. That kept me pretty negative. For instance I have been in a job I haven't liked, and was always thinking about how to get out of it. Now I'm thinking about what I *want* to do. It's much more positive. My relationships are the same way. I used to think about what to avoid, and now I'm moving toward what I want. "I'd say that some part of me stopped or died when I got cancer. I'd guess that's when my future ended. The doctor told me about the diagnosis by throwing the pathology report in my lap, and then proceeded to describe his ideas for treatment, which involved removing the right side of my face.

"I'm also aware of how it's changed the way I code things in my mind. Before, I was living in the past in many ways. Things that had happened years ago seemed like just yesterday. It was like the past was right on top of me. Also, my positive and negative experiences weren't sorted out.

"I tried shifting my timeline before on my own, but it shifted back almost immediately. That's where you came in. Now I have a future that fans out in different directions, and it's positive. That change put the past where it belonged, in the past. Now I feel like my mind is organized in a way that makes sense. My whole timeline is longer now, so I can tell the difference between the past, the present, and the future.

"The timeline change was the key. I'd already done a trauma fix around the cancer, and some other pieces. A lot of things were finished by that piece of work."

I was glad for the dramatic and pervasive nature of Cathy's changes. I was also aware that having done so much previous change work with other NLP methods, she was "ripe" for this profound change. If she hadn't done this previous work, I would have needed to use several other methods to help her deal with her traumatic past *before* I helped her change her timeline.

If someone had made Cathy's timeline shift permanently before she had sorted out that she was now a healthy person, they might have caused her to become ill again by putting illness in her future. This is an example of why timeline change work needs to be done with care and sensitivity. Problems like this can be recognized and respectfully handled by people well-trained in NLP.

Timeline Reversals

Usually when someone has their timeline reversed from their eye accessing cues, as Cathy did, it creates certain predictable restrictions and limitations in their experience. For example, their future is either undeveloped, or it seems fixed. When someone has this, we have them carefully "try out" letting their timeline shift to the opposite orientation, to find out how they like it, carefully checking for objections. Timeline reversals can also relate to learning disabilities, discussed later in this chapter. So far, I've found only one person who wanted to keep a reversed timeline. Since I encountered an ecological objection that I didn't find a way to deal with, I left his timeline as it was.

Will I Benefit from Changing My Timeline?

You may wonder how you can know if a change in your timeline will help you get more of what you want out of life. Some people are completely satisfied with the way they currently organize time. Many others find benefits in either subtle or major shifts. What follows are clues that can point the way toward useful timeline shifts. The only way to know for sure is to experiment by trying on a different way of coding time, to find out if you like it better.

A Change in the Future

The following are signs that you may benefit from a change in the way you code your future:

1. Having trouble planning for the future. Is your short-term or long-term planning ineffective? Do events sneak up on you and find you unprepared?

2. Lacking goals or direction. Do you think of yourself as only living for the moment? Do you have little idea of the direction you are going? Some people are happy with this orientation, while others want to add more responsiveness to the future.

3. Do others complain about your lack of planning, or your lack of direction and goals? Sometimes someone without a future doesn't notice the difficulty it causes, but others do.

4. Do you have difficulty motivating yourself? In chapter 15, Positive Motivation, we describe several keys to motivating yourself more effectively. These work much better if you also have an attractive future timeline.

5. Have you been depressed? Sometimes depression is a result of literally having nothing to look forward to.

6. Do you have difficulty maintaining the lifestyle you know would benefit you over time? For example, exercising regularly, losing weight, stopping smoking, etc. People with drug or alcohol problems can often benefit from having a more compelling future timeline.

How to Change Your Future

If you want to consider changing how you code your future, here's what you can do.

First notice how your future is coded now. Where do you see it? For most people, the future is arranged in a line or pathway going in a particular direction. Is it big, bright, colorful? Or is it dim, dark, small, behind you, etc.?

If your future is very small, short, or is located somewhere where you can't see it very well, you won't be very responsive to your future wants and needs. People with this kind of future often have difficulty with weight loss, maintaining good health and exercise habits, or with planning ahead or setting and reaching goals.

If you want to become more future-oriented, changing how you think of the future may be an important step for you, as it was for Ruth. Here are the steps:

1. First, let yourself know you are only experimenting. You are trying out another way to see your future. If you or any part of you has any objection to the new way, you will put your timeline back the way it was.

2. Now begin to try out a variety of ways to see your future, and find out which is best for you. If your future was behind you, let it swing out

to the side and around until it angles out in front of you. Let it move around a little, angling higher and lower, until it seems like it's in the "right place." In general, *the more your future is big, bright, and right in front of you, the more "future-oriented" you will be.*

Be sensitive to any objections that you, or any part of you has to seeing your future in a more visible location. For instance, do you visualize possible disasters to avoid in your future? If so, its important to transform these into something more positive, so you can feel good seeing what you want to move *toward,* in contrast to seeing what you want to *avoid.*

Are you envisioning your future as bright and colorful, so that you can look forward to it? People who complain of a "dim future" literally have very little to look forward to. When people say "My future looks bright," they are literally reporting on their internal experience. If you brighten up your future on the inside, it will become much more attractive—as long as you are seeing what you *want,* in contrast to what you don't want.

If your future timeline was short, let it grow out farther, to give you the sense of a longer future. You may want to imagine a network of branches, to let you know you have many options. You may want to imagine the general direction you are going, and place some representation of your values on this line, rather than specific events.

Values can be represented literally or symbolically. If you want to have warm, close, relationships in your future, you can see people being intimate on your future timeline. Or you can see a warm glow, a white light, or any other more abstract image that signifies close relationships to you.

If your timeline was small, let it enlarge, so you can experience the impact of the future more strongly as you look at it now. This change increases motivation to achieve goals.

You may also want to make it more colorful, more three-dimensional, or to add sparkling points of light. Allow yourself to experiment to find out what works best for you.

3. When you are done experimenting, notice what timeline arrangement you like best. With your chosen timeline in place, imagine going through a day with it. Does this allow you to be more the person you want to be? If it does, imagine going to bed and waking up the next day with this new timeline automatically there, and notice how it works for you.

If you discover you don't like this new timeline as well as your old one, be sure to let it shift back to the way it was before you return to your reading or other activities.

In all the foregoing, we have focused on building a future for someone who doesn't have much of one. However, it is also possible to be *too* future-oriented. Some people are *so* preoccupied with the future that it keeps them from enjoying the present. If you can't enjoy the future you're planning for when it finally arrives, there isn't much point in planning for it! Yet some excellent planners never get to enjoy the future when it becomes the present.

If a person is too future-oriented, it can be very useful to teach them how to make their future less preoccupying, at least in some contexts. This might include moving the future off to the side, making it smaller, less colorful, etc. It can also be useful to separate the past and future so that there is more room for the present. (See "Creating a Present," below.)

A Change in the Past

Many people have benefitted greatly from changes in their pasts. Here are some indicators to find out if you could benefit, too.

1. Are you preoccupied with the past? Do you spend time ruminating about the past when you'd rather be doing something else?

2. Do you frequently find yourself overwhelmed by unpleasant memories?

3. Do others often say things to you like, "That's the past and that's over. Let's get on with things now."

4. Do you have little or no memory of past events? When someone asks you about the past, is it a struggle to think back to what happened?

5. Do you only repeat things you've done before, and want more choice about adding richness and variety to your life?

6. Do you make the same mistakes over and over again, rather than learning from them?

A positive response to any of the above *could* be signs that you will benefit from shifting the way you code your past.

Changing Your Past

If you think you are too preoccupied with the past, check *where* and *how* you imagine your past now. Is it right in front of you? Is it bigger, brighter, and more colorful, compared to your future? Most people who are preoccupied with the past have it located in a place where it's so prominent *that's almost all they can see.* The following steps guide you in discovering what past timeline arrangement might work better for you.

1. First let yourself know that any shifts you make are only temporary. This allows you to experiment freely with different ways of organizing time. You can always put your timeline back exactly the way it was before you began if you don't like any of the new choices.

2. If your past is right in front of you, try moving it off to one side

or the other. Which side feels most comfortable for you? For most people, moving it off to the left feels best. However for some, visualizing it off to the right works better. This has to do with the way our brains are organized (See Appendix I).

3. Notice how it feels to have the past farther out to the side instead of right in front of you. If your past is large, you may want to experiment with making it a little smaller. Do you like that better? Imagine going through a day with your past in this new location. Now is it easier for you to notice what there is to do in the present, and easier for you to notice your future goals? If it seems useful, you can move your future at the same time, placing it more in front of you.

4. You may want to think of your past timeline as flexible—almost as if it were on a hinge, so that it can move farther to the side or behind you when you are doing something where the past is irrelevant, and more in front of you when you want to remember things from the past easily.

5. The last step is for you to decide whether you think the new arrangement of your past works better for you or not. *There is no "right" timeline arrangement,* and *every* arrangement will have advantages and disadvantages. *Each of us can find an arrangement that's best for us,* and learn to adapt it to different circumstances.

If you have any reluctance to trying out a new timeline arrangement, simply put your timeline back the way it was when you started. If this is the case, you may want to find someone trained in timeline work to assist you in dealing with objections and exploring alternative timeline arrangements that will suit all your goals. *If you aren't certain you like the new arrangement better, be sure to put your timeline back the way it was.*

If you do decide to adopt a new timeline arrangement, you can let your unconscious know that your timeline can continue to adjust and adapt on its own, so that it works even better for you, as you go through the day. You can internally say, "If any part of me discovers an objection to this new arrangement, please give me a strong signal that will let me know that some further adjustment is necessary.

6. Ask yourself, "Are there any times when I want my old timeline?" Perhaps you sometimes enjoy reminiscing with old high school friends. By asking "When will that old timeline arrangement still be the best for me?" you can keep it for contexts where it's more useful.

Do You Have Trouble Remembering the Past?

Some people have trouble remembering the past, or don't have the sense that the past is a positive resource they can easily draw upon. To explore whether a timeline shift will make a useful difference, you can follow Steps 1-6 above, substituting the following for Steps 2 and 3:

2. Probably your past is located where you can't see it at all, or way off to the side where it's hard to see. Your past may be behind you, far away, or so spread out that it's easy to ignore. For example, yesterday may be 10 feet away, with last week a block away, etc.

3. Experiment with moving your past to another location where you can see it more easily. Bring it more to the front, make it closer or bigger, etc. If you have any reluctance to trying this, leave your timeline alone, and wait until you can find someone trained in these methods to assist you. Some people have their pasts "behind them" because unpleasant things happened in the past, and they feel much better if they don't have to look at or think about those past events. If this is the case, you need to have a way of dealing with these unpleasant memories (See chapter 7) *before* moving your past where you can see it. Transforming these unpleasant experiences into resources for you first makes it much easier to access your entire past.

If it is comfortable to move your past timeline, move it to some location where you can see it. If it was behind you, let it swing around like an arm until it becomes visible. You may want to leave it to the side—out of your central vision, yet where you can easily notice it. If your past was so spread out that you couldn't see it, you may want to try bringing it all in closer. Preserving the same sequence, allow all your experiences to move closer together. However, if your past was all clumped together, you can experiment with spreading it out a bit. You can experiment in other ways, as well.

After doing this, continue with Steps 4 and 5 above. You will probably still want to have your past in its old configuration in certain situations, or when you do certain activities. Try out the old and new configurations in your major life contexts—work, play, close relationships, sports, etc.—to find out which works better. Remember that if you change your mind, you can always put it back the way it was.

Building More of a Present

Adam was always thinking about either the past or the future, but never seemed to enjoy what was happening *now*. He was very intelligent and capable, and wanted to be sure to retain these abilities, but thought his life would have an important added dimension if he could enjoy the present more.

In exploring Adam's timeline, we noticed that Adam's past and future were arranged in a V, much like most people's. However, rather than having the past go out from his left side, and the future going out from his right side, the way most people's do, Adam's past and future came together in a point right in front of him. The past connected directly with the future, so he essentially had no present.

I asked Adam to experiment with moving his timeline apart, so that the past and future were separated by his body, allowing some room for the present. As Adam did this, his body began to move a bit more than it had been, and his skin color became a bit redder.

"This is interesting," he commented. "I feel more aware of my body when my timeline is apart like that."

"Yes. Now you have room for *you* in the *present,* as a part of your timeline. It's not just past and future." Adam liked this new arrangement, and I made sure he still had equally good access to his past and future, so that he would be able to process information as easily as he had with his previous timeline.

Before this change, Adam had no way to enjoy the present—he was always thinking about what *had* happened, or what *would* happen. Separating your past and future timelines can give you more of a present to enjoy. It can also be useful to experience your timeline as flexible, so that when you want to focus on the present more fully, it's as if both your past and your future can swing around behind you, out of the way.

Getting "Go For It!"

Positive motivation has many aspects to it, some of which we describe in chapter 15. The way a person's timeline is arranged can also have a powerful impact.

Some people have their timelines arranged with their past in a pathway straight behind them, and their future in a path straight in front of them. If yours is not organized this way, you may want to at least try this to find out what it's like. This kind of timeline arrangement can result in a lot of "go for it" motivation, because you're so focused on the immediate future you're headed for. You're right there on your timeline moving into the future. If your future, immediately in front of you, is also big and bright and moving, this can be *very* motivating. It is a tremendously useful arrangement when you want to concentrate on getting something done NOW. If this timeline arrangement seems unusual to you, we suggest you explore it a bit. Are there certain situations where this timeline arrangement would add to your ability to be motivated, and to concentrate and ignore distractions?

Like anything else, there can be drawbacks to this arrangement. People who have this organization may also be strongly motivated to eat that cake, have a beer, or take that drug, because of the immediate pleasure. If you *always* imagine the past behind and the future straight in front of you, it may be much more difficult to avoid repeating past mistakes. After all, what you did before is *behind you,* where you can't see it. In addition, your long-range future may be on the far side of your immediate future, so you can't see it either. With this "go for it" timeline arrangement, both past mistakes and long-range future consequences are sometimes ignored.

One way to deal with this obstacle is to make the more distant future bigger, brighter and more colorful than the immediate future. With your attention focused on more distant events, when you consider that cake, beer, or drug, you'll be much more aware of the future consequences. Noticing the future excess weight, hangover, or withdrawal will easily motivate you to decline opportunities to make your life worse. You'll be more inclined to have "go for it" for activities that will make your life better overall.

If your future is typically directly in front of you, and your past behind you, we suggest that you try out some variation of the "V" timeline arrangement we described earlier. Let your past angle off to your left, and your future shift to being at an *angle* off in front of you to your right, so that you can look at both past and future at once. A few people will find the reverse of this arrangement to be more appropriate. If you find it hard to move your timeline, you can leave your timeline in place and turn your *body* until your timeline runs from left to right. Notice when and where this might be useful. This arrangement allows you to have a lot of information available to you at once. This can be very useful in planning, decision-making, and in maintaining consistency over a period of time.

Ideally we can each notice *when* and *where* different timeline arrangements are useful for us, and develop the flexibility to adapt our sense of time to fit these different situations.

Confusing the Past and Future

Ray, a lawyer who was attending a seminar, asked for a timeline change. "My past and future both go straight in front of me, almost on the same line for about six weeks into the past and into the future, and then they branch out to the left and right like a Y. I'd like you to help me sort out the past and future better. Sometimes I get confused about what has happened. I'd also like to be more motivated."

It turned out that Ray's current timeline arrangement had an important advantage for him, which we needed to preserve. "I want to notice the mistakes I've made so I can avoid making them over again," Ray informed me. With his recent past right in front of him, Ray easily noticed his past mistakes. He then coded those experiences by making them darker, and then literally flipped these pictures of making mistakes over onto his future timeline. This was very easy to do because his immediate future timeline was right next to his recent past timeline.

Working with Ray, we quickly found a way for him to sort out his past and future more clearly, while preserving his way of noticing and avoiding past mistakes. In fact, the new arrangement allowed him to accomplish this positive purpose much more effectively.

"Ray, now you've got a Y timeline. Try letting the fork of the Y come closer and closer to you until you have a V, with your past going out from your left shoulder, and your future out from your right. . . ." (Ray nodded.) "Now you can mark out your past mistakes in some way, perhaps by putting a bright border around them, so that they are identified as opportunities for learning." Next I suggested that he transform the mistake he wanted to avoid into a movie of *what he wanted to do* instead, and put this movie on his future timeline, rather than the mistakes to avoid.

"Yes, I can do that," commented Ray after remaining thoughtful for a time, "but my timelines seem to want to go back together."

"OK, instead of moving what you want straight across from your past, and over to your future timeline, try doing it differently this time. Notice a past mistake, make a movie of what you want to do instead, and move it up your past timeline, *through your body,* and on into your future, letting it settle in wherever appropriate. Each time you do this your future will look much better than it did, because you are projecting something you *want* rather than something you want to avoid."

When he did it that way, Ray's timeline stabilized in the new V arrangement, and he was satisfied with it. I suggested that he allow himself to sort through other past "opportunities for learning," and do the same thing, so that his future would be filled with things to *do* rather than things to avoid. Most of us find it *much* easier to be motivated when we think of what we *do* want rather than what we *don't* want.

Judy's past and future also overlapped, but for a longer period. Her past and future both went straight ahead for six months before branching, the past to the left, and the future to the right. Judy complained that when she made a change, such as moving to a new place or getting a new job, she didn't really feel as if she had done it until about six months had passed. She had just been through a crisis, because her husband had had an affair. Although he had renewed his commitment to her and she had forgiven him, she was still bothered and depressed. She said, "It's always this way; even when something is all worked out, I feel depressed for about six months, and then I'm OK." She was excited when she learned how her timeline was organized, because it made sense out of something that had puzzled her for years. When she separated her immediate past and future, she felt better right away when something was resolved, instead of having to wait six months. She could tell that the past *was* in fact the past.

Learning Disabilities

A poorly organized, reversed, or missing timeline can sometimes cause learning disabilities. For example, Michele, diagnosed as dyslexic, had trouble remembering things. If she watched a movie, she couldn't fit the beginning, middle, and end of the movie together. Reading was almost impossible, since she couldn't remember what she had just read. She'd had many head injuries as a child and teenager, so it was assumed that her dyslexia was a result of brain damage. Since she couldn't do any work that required memory, she became a professional masseuse.

Fortunately, Michele went to see an NLP Practitioner who knew about timeline work. After finding out that she had no timeline, she was assisted in forming one, with her past, present, and future flowing in a U from one side to the other.

Gaining a timeline made a remarkable difference for Michele. She was immediately able to read a paragraph and remember it, a task she had previously been unable to accomplish. The Practitioner also noted that Michele had a series of traumatic memories between ages 5 and 13, and utilized other NLP methods to assist her in dealing with these (See chapter 7, Phobias, Traumas and Abuse for methods you can use with this). Michele found that her dyslexia vanished in almost all contexts. The only task she couldn't perform after this change was typing, because she had trained herself to type successfully while dyslexic. After gaining a timeline, Michele needed to relearn typing in a "straightened out" way. She did this successfully, and is now doing computer-assisted drafting. Michele found her life so different as a result of having a timeline that she decided to go back to school in engineering—something she never would have attempted when she was "learning disabled."

I called Michele for her personal report and to find out more about how she had previously organized time. Michele's story confirmed what the NLP Practitioner had told me, and I learned more. Instead of the sequence of events most of us have, Michele described her previous sense of time as a "mass of seaweed." "It was like having strands of seaweed in front of me, coming up from the bottom of the ocean floor. You know how seaweed has floating pods on top? In the pods were my past, present, and future."

"Were they sorted out, with the past in some pods, and the future in others?" I asked.

"No, it wasn't organized at all. They were kind of all around in a jumble. It was hard for me to remember anything because it wasn't sorted out. I'd just have to search for memories. I could never remember the things I said to people, or what I did the day before. That's all completely changed now. I can remember things. Another thing that's different is that I hear people better now, and understand what they are saying better. I can write, and read, and make sense out of movies."

As I talked further with Michele, I found that her future now went off to her left, and her past to her right. Since this is the opposite of the way most people organize time, I wanted to check to find out if it was right for Michele or not. "How did you decide to put the future on your *left* and your past on your *right?*" I asked.

"When I made the change, I just sort of stood up and pulled the seaweed into a line. That's just the way it went—past on the right, and future on the left."

"Do you want to find out if there is a better timeline arrangement for you?" I asked.

"Sure," she responded.

Since I couldn't test Michele's eye accessing cues very well on the phone, to find out if she was reversed, I decided to have Michele simply try out an opposite timeline, and find out which one worked better for her. I gave Michele very careful instructions on how to experiment with having her future to her right, and her past off to the left. "Just notice what it's like," I added.

"My future is brighter now. It's like white light. I like it better, and my past feels less like a burden. It's also a little smaller than it was before."

"Now imagine going through next week with this timeline, while checking for several things. Do you have any objections? Do you want to shift this timeline in some way to make it better? Are there any situations in your life where your old timeline will work better?"

"No. I get the answer to the last question right away," Michele responded quickly. Michele also noticed a place in her past timeline where there was a kink that she wanted to straighten out.

"My brain likes this timeline better," Michele continued. "The first time I got a timeline, I felt like I birthed a brain. Now I feel like I have access to it. This makes a big difference. My whole brain feels more connected now. . . . I feel the shift in my body now, too. My right and left sides feel connected now. It's like they are receiving information properly. I feel like my brain is all white inside."

We did a little more testing to make sure this new timeline was ecological for Michele, and I made sure she had my phone number in case she thought she needed to shift anything later on.

When I checked with Michele later, she told me she had made additional changes in her timeline. Filling in the space where her old timeline had been with white light made her comfortable that her timeline wouldn't go back there. With this security, she felt comfortable allowing her timeline to be much more flexible, and experimented with a back-to-front timeline, which she liked even better.

Michele's experience illustrates how it can sometimes be useful to make a *series* of timeline shifts. Ideally, we end with flexibility to use several alternate timeline arrangements for different situations in our lives.

Rex had also been labeled dyslexic when young. Though he had become successful at many things, he remained confused about right and left and which way to turn a water faucet. After noticing that Rex's timeline was reversed, I had Ray experiment with flipping his timeline around to the usual orientation. Several months later Ray said, "I really like my expanded future from that timeline work! Now I can easily tell left from right, and I automatically know what direction to turn a faucet."

A Key to Personal Uniqueness

Since discovering timeline codings we have been utterly fascinated by the ways in which our personal timelines influence our personalities. At first we wondered if people were just "making this stuff up." However, it immediately became clear that when someone tried out another person's time organization, he literally became very different. The world seemed different to him, and he responded differently. Obviously, these time codings were subjectively real and impactful. We will share a few more examples with you, to give you an even greater sense of this exciting area.

Mark, a therapist, first found out about timelines through our book, *Change Your Mind—and Keep the Change.* After reading the timeline chapter, he decided to do timeline work with all his clients that week. He reported that of about 30 clients, he was able to help all but two of them make significant changes by making timeline adjustments. Several of Mark's clients were particularly interesting.

One woman complained of depression, explaining she felt like something was holding her back. She felt weighed down, and couldn't move on in life. Her future was a line going straight in front of her, and the past straight behind. What was unusual was that the past went about a foot straight behind her, and then lowered and *dragged on the ground* on into the past. When she lifted her past so that it didn't "drag," she felt much better, and as if she could move on in life. Her past had literally been "holding her back" by this dragging. It still seems bizarre to us that such a simple change in a person's way of thinking can make such a profound difference, but we have become convinced by many other examples.

Another man had been to many well-known therapists. Although he was generally intelligent and competent, his personality problems had remained the same. It turned out that his timeline had a large, colorful past that was easily visible to him on his left. His future, however, was a series of tiny postage-stamp sized slides, about a foot and a half apart. Since his future was so unimpressive, it wasn't very compelling. Developing his future into a larger movie of connected events resulted in major changes in his life. His friends started asking him what had happened to make him so different.

The Value of Unusual Timelines

We've mentioned that there is no single best timeline. Some unusual timeline arrangements work very well for people, and are the basis for unique skills or abilities. For example, Tom's future went straight out in front of him in a pathway. We asked him if he was always focused on the immediate future, thinking that was all he could see. Tom said, "No, My future is a series of transparent, colorful slides. If I want to think about something happening farther in the future, I just enlarge the slides closer to me so I can see *through* them more easily into the distant future." Tom's image of his immediate future literally *colored* his more distant future. This provided a continuity that gave him an exceptionally rich ability to plan sequentially.

One man's timeline went from the floor to the ceiling in a straight vertical line. When I asked him to try out a *horizontal* timeline like most people have, he didn't like it as well. Even though he wasn't clear on the advantages, he knew he preferred his up-and-down timeline.

If your timeline is unique, ask yourself, "What are the benefits of this timeline arrangement?" If everyone had exactly the same timeline arrangement, we would tend to have similar strengths and weaknesses. The infinite variety in coding time provides a basis for diversity of talent and personal uniqueness.

Although we have been doing timeline work since we first began exploring time in early 1984, we continue to find other interesting ways of organizing time. We invite you to join us in this ongoing discovery. If you'd like to learn even more about timelines, read the first two chapters of our previous book, *Change Your Mind—and Keep the Change.*

Engaging Your Body's Natural Ability to Heal

20

Several weeks after our first baby was born, I found myself with a sore lump in my left breast. At first I assumed it would go away on its own, and didn't do anything about it. The lump continued getting worse, and soon was accompanied by a bright red patch of skin. A high fever soon followed. I finally recognized that I needed medical help. My doctor immediately diagnosed my symptoms as a breast infection, and put me on antibiotics. Within 24 hours my fever was gone, and the lump vanished several days later.

Over the next several years, this became an all-too-familiar scenario. I nursed our first child for 16 months, and frequently found myself getting the lump in my breast, followed by a bright red skin patch, followed by a high fever and antibiotics. I didn't like using antibiotics, since I like to avoid medication whenever possible, yet it seemed necessary. Each time I got an infection, I went through the same sequence. As I became familiar with the early warning signs, I went to bed immediately with a hot pad, "hoping" that my body would heal itself this time, so I wouldn't have to once again resort to antibiotics.

I was trying to use "positive thinking" to encourage my body to heal on its own. What happened, however, was that each time the symptoms continued to worsen. Each time I held out for a while, hoping my fever would subside on its own, clinging to my heating pad and drinking hot liquids. When my fever remained at 104 or 105 for too long, I became concerned and went to the doctor for a prescription, which always worked.

By this time, I'd discovered that women in my family had a history of breast infections. A number of physiological factors seem to make some women more prone to them. However, I wanted to become healthier, and be able to recover on my own. Each time I went on antibiotics for 10 days, our baby's digestion got poorer, and his diapers looked strange. I guessed that the antibiotics he received through my breast milk were harder on his tiny body than on mine. Given the recent research on the overuse of antibiotics, I expected that these frequent doses of antibiotics weren't good for the baby's long-range health either.

When our second child was born, I went through the same experience. In fact, I found myself on antibiotics even more frequently. When I looked at my calendar, I was annoyed to find that those first several months I had been on antibiotics more days than I'd been off. In my struggle to find a way to recover from breast infections without drugs, I utilized almost every NLP technique I knew. While I was lying sick in bed, I attempted many of the methods in this book, and others, with no success.

A New Discovery

Finally, as the familiar symptoms had set in again and I was in bed "hoping" as usual to recover, I experimented with something else. My personal experience that day led to developing a method which has since helped many others regain their health more rapidly.

First I asked myself, "How do I think about what will happen to me?" I knew I *hoped* to recover without drugs, but what did I actually imagine in my mind when I thought about recovering? I noticed that I saw myself lying in bed, looking ill. I saw this as if it were a still snapshot of myself that was in black-and-white, but the photograph had grayed quite a bit. I saw this image off to my left. "No wonder I haven't been getting well," I thought to myself. Even though I've been *hoping* to get well, unconsciously I've been seeing *illness.*"

Next I asked myself, "What do I know absolutely that I will recover from automatically? What do I assume my body will heal on it's own, without my doing anything?" I first thought of things like getting a cut or scrape. If I get a cut, I know my skin will heal automatically, over the course of several days. A flu or a cold is even more similar to the breast infection, because it affects my whole body more than a cut or scrape does. I know that if I get the flu, all I need to do is rest, and my body will recover on its own.

Tapping My Body's Ability to Heal

When I noticed how I thought about getting over the flu, I saw myself in a short movie, off to my right. I saw myself first lying down in bed, and then gradually becoming more and more upright and healthy. The movie was a bit like time-lapse photography where time goes by very quickly, so that in a matter of a single second in my mind, I saw myself moving from lying down ill to recuperating and standing up healthy.

I was curious what would happen if I began to think of my breast infections as "like the flu." We had already been working with many other NLP methods involving "brain codings" for beliefs (See chapter 3). I took my slide of being sick with the breast infection, moved it over to the location of my movie of automatically healing from the flu, and made a similar movie of automatically healing from a breast infection. I made it *exactly* the same: the same size, same coloring, same speed of movement, and in the same location. As I did this, my body immediately felt different. I wasn't well yet, but I felt as if I *would* be soon.

To "lock in" the change, I made up another example of having already healed automatically from a breast infection, and put it in my past. I made this movie exactly like the other experiences in my past, and put it on my past timeline. Now I felt *much* better. I felt almost certain that I would recover without drugs. Even though I knew I had just made up that experience, my body experienced it as *real.* "Since I've done it before, of course I'll be able to do it again now."

I continued my rest and heat pad routine, noticing what happened. My temperature returned to normal, without reaching the 104 level that I had experienced every time before. The lump and red spot gradually went away over the next day or two. I was ecstatic that I hadn't needed antibiotics!

After that, I never again needed to use antibiotics for breast infections during another year of breast-feeding our second child, and about 15 months of breast-feeding our third child. The pattern of my breast infections had been so frequent, so clear, and so repetitive, that there was no doubt in my mind that something was very different. It was as if my body now knew how to reverse breast infections immediately, almost before they began. From that time on I rarely even experienced the preliminary symptoms of a breast infection. During the two-and-a-half years that I nursed after this, only twice did I experience preliminary symptoms, and they went away without my ever getting a high fever. In one instance I got a high fever while away on vacation. I even ordered antibiotics, so I would have them in case I needed them. However, my fever went back down, rather than remaining high the way it had previously. This was quite a welcome contrast to my previous experience. Things were very different than my previous pattern of recurrent serious breast infections.

A Method for Regaining Health:

Since this method had made such a difference for me, we began guiding others through the process. We wanted to find out if the same method that worked for me would work for others—perhaps with many other kinds of physical problems. Since the method is so rapid, there seemed to be nothing to lose, especially since we offered this method as an *addition* to standard medical practice, *not* as a substitute. Since then, many people have found it useful with a wide range of stubborn medical problems, and we want to cite several examples.[1]

Eric and Arthritis

Eric suffered from arthritis. He experienced constant pain in many of his joints, with the worst pain in his finger joints. He had already curtailed some of his physical activity due to this pain when he volunteered as a demonstration person in a seminar.

When I asked him to think of an illness that was similar to his arthritis, but that he knew he would automatically heal from, he thought of a sprain in his wrist. When he thought about a wrist sprain healing, he imagined the area pulsating with blood bringing in healing nutrients. The healing area was more colorful, larger, and brighter than the surrounding area. Then I guided him in recoding his arthritis exactly the same way that he had already coded healing from a wrist sprain. Eric made his image of his arthritis exactly the same, with all the affected joints pulsating, etc. As soon as Eric had done this, his hands actually looked pinker from the outside.

After completing the process, Eric said, "I'd like to tell you what's going on now. One at a time, each joint is getting very hot and intensely painful in one burst, and then all the pain is gone in that joint. It's a good thing it's not happening all at once, or it might be too much for me." This

---

1. The method presented in this chapter is not to be considered a treatment for the purpose of alleviating any specific disease or physical disorder, but rather is intended as a general technique for the promotion of health with respect to illness in general. Examples are included to illustrate the personal experience and reports of individuals who have utilized the method.

process continued over the next week, with one joint after another experiencing this burst of heat and intense pain, then no pain at all. After the burst, that joint felt fine—in contrast to Eric's previous chronic pain.

Eric's symptoms of arthritis had almost completely vanished when his wife was killed in a car accident. After his wife's death, Eric's symptoms immediately returned. Two weeks later Eric attended one of our seminars where the grief resolution process was taught (See chapter 11). After resolving his grief, he became symptom-free again.

April's Chronic Back Pain

April approached me at a national conference on Health and Well-being, where I was presenting this method, and asked me if I would assist her.

"I've felt an approach-avoidance towards you all weekend about doing this," she said, "because I've gotten my hopes up before, and then had them crushed, and I don't want to be disappointed again. There's a lot wrapped up in this. I've had chronic pain for years, seven surgeries, and four miscarriages because of this."

I didn't find out the details of April's background then, because I only had about 15 minutes, so I needed to move quickly. "It sounds very important to you *not* to build up any expectations," I assured her, "And it's really not necessary for this to work. It doesn't matter at all what you consciously think or expect. We can change the way your brain thinks about this by coding it for automatic healing. If it works, it works; if it doesn't, it doesn't. That will just happen. If this is what will get your back to heal itself, that will just occur. You don't need to expect anything for healing to occur, so I suggest that you *not* expect anything." April's shoulders relaxed; she seemed relieved not to have to get her hopes up.

I needed to make several adjustments in the method to make it work easily and comfortably for April. First she couldn't find anything that seemed similar that she assumed would heal on its own. A cut or blister seemed so trivial and small compared to what was wrong with her body. "I've had surgery and pain up and down my spine, and on my stomach. There's a lot of damage," she explained.

I asked April to pick just one small spot on her body that she wanted to have heal itself, so that it would seem more *like* a cut. This worked for April. She picked the site of most of her back surgeries, and we went ahead. We discovered how to make April's unconscious image of part of her back just like the way she thought about a cut healing. She added a white glow, and made it three-dimensional. Once she had done this with one site on her body, I had April extend this same coding to all the other areas on her body that needed healing. "Just as if you had a lot of cuts in different places, each one would heal by itself." April felt much better, but something still seemed to be missing, since she didn't have quite the same feeling about her back and stomach healing as she did about a cut. What finally worked was taking her image of her cut healing automatically, moving it to her stomach area, and then "spreading" this image around her entire stomach and back area. When she did this, April broke out in immediate goose-bumps all over her body, and her face flushed. Her body was clearly making an important shift. As she looked over at me, I could see that she was very moved by the experience.

When I asked April to make up an experience of *having healed* once before from something like this in her past, she told me she couldn't do that step because of her grief over the pregnancies she had lost in the past. Since I had limited time, I suggested that she get our "Resolving Grief" videotape (See Appendix II) and use that method to help her get over her grief and then do the final step on her own. I asked her to contact me if she needed assistance completing the process.

When I checked back with April a week and a half later, she said she'd just been thinking of writing me a note, to let me know the results. She sounded excited. "I'm so glad!" she said. "When you worked with me, as soon as I got the goose bumps, the pain was gone. Then I watched your grief tape, and that helped me with my losses. Then I was telling my Dad about the healing process, and as I was telling him the steps, I got goose bumps all over again. I know it's healing."

I took time to get more information about April's history, as well. She'd had a congenital back problem which was discovered at age 21. After experiencing chronic pain, she'd had a myelogram done. She also had a degenerative disc disease, and some spinal deformity. Over the years, April had gone through seven back surgeries. She'd had laminectomies, a spinal fusion, and had a dorsal column stimulator implanted in her back. The first surgery in 1971 resulted in a wound that remained open for a year and a half. "When it finally healed, I still had pain. No relief. I had even more pain than before, because of more surgery and more scar tissue. Then I tried a number of methods to get rid of the pain." One of these was having a dorsal column stimulator implanted at Johns Hopkins. The stimulator was supposed to block her constant pain, but it didn't work, and instead created more problems including uncomfortable electric shocks, bladder trouble, and soreness in her vaginal muscles. The stimulator was turned on and off from an external power source, and since it caused problems, April stopped using it.

"After that, I tried medication for 2 or 3 more years, and became quite addicted. I went back to the Johns Hopkins pain clinic, where I did biofeedback, exercise, and was on a drug withdrawal program. A year later, I started having problems with my stomach, and was told my stomach had been eaten up by the pain medication I had taken. I had about half of my stomach removed in another operation. Then I had a series of miscarriages, and I was told that I lost them due to my back problems. Finally I had a full-term pregnancy, and a healthy child, with a second coming along later.

"For several years I didn't have chronic pain—only sometimes when I did more strenuous things like mow the lawn. Then I developed chronic back pain again. I told myself I was going to try a different approach this time, so it was perfect timing that you came along. What we did is working for me, and I'm able to support that by taking care of myself better. It was an emotional release for me, and very comforting. I noticed an immediate difference in the pain level. It went away immediately when I had those goosebumps. What's neat about the work that we did is that I feel that I have some control and some tools now."

Peter's Skin Cancer

When Peter attended a seminar where I was teaching this self-healing pattern, he had a skin cancer on his nose which had begun about two months earlier. It was about an eighth inch in diameter, and growing. He'd had two previous skin cancer growths, the first in 1983, so it was a familiar experience for him. When he first got one, he thought it was a funny mole. Since it itched, grew larger, and "felt tingling and creepy inside," Peter had it checked out by his doctor, who diagnosed it as cancer. The doctor told him his options were surgical removal, or a cortisone creme. He recommended first trying the cortisone creme, and if that didn't work, using surgery. Over a period of about 6 months, the creme did cause the cancerous spot to become healed. Peter used this same method with a second cancerous mole later.

When Peter got a third cancerous growth, this time on his nose, he got the same "ugly" feeling he had with the others and planned to use the medicine soon to get rid of it. However, it turned out that Peter had no need for the medicine this time. He sat in the audience while I demonstrated the self-healing pattern with someone else. Rather than just observe the demonstration, Peter followed the instructions for himself, and then thought no more about it. "I didn't expect anything," he told me later.

About two weeks after that seminar, Peter's wife was the first to notice that his skin cancer had changed. "She turned me sideways and said, 'It's about to fall off!'" Peter explained. "I said, 'Leave it alone,' and it fell off two nights later! Now it's gone!"

I asked Peter how he had visualized his cancer during the seminar. "I imagined it as being very warm. I thought of a bandaid over it, holding the heat in."

Ted's AIDS

Ted, a man in one of our seminars, had been diagnosed as having Aids-related complex (ARC). Ted didn't accept this as a death sentence, and he began seeking ways to improve his health and life. With his strong motivation to overcome AIDS, he utilized every method he could find to assist him in his recovery process. He utilized many of the methods in this book, and others, to decrease stress in his life, and to create a state of integrity and personal well-being. His approach made sense to us, and we encouraged him in his efforts.

When we work with someone in Ted's situation, we are only willing to promise that we can improve the quality of his life, not that we can prolong it. Nevertheless, there are many examples of people who have succeeded somehow in ridding themselves of "terminal" illness, and it seems probable that psychological changes play a large part. Bernie Siegel's fine book, *Love, Medicine and Miracles,* (1) is an impressive collection of successful cases, as well as summaries of preliminary scientific evidence about some of the psychological-physiological links that make this possible.

If a person is completely healthy—not dealing with AIDS, or another serious illness—he may be able to handle being tense, nervous, angry, and "off-balance" in a variety of ways. However, if a person wants to recover from a serious illness, it is an opportunity to make sure our personal life is in order, so that our body has maximum resources available for healing. Ted made use of many NLP methods to do this.

In addition, Ted used the method in this chapter to code AIDS like the flu. He wanted his body to respond to AIDS as something from which he would automatically recover. None of us knew whether this was possible or not, but he had little to lose and much to gain.

About a year later, Ted had himself retested for the AIDS virus. He tested positive to the antibody test, but negative to the test for the presence of the virus! They could not culture the virus from his blood. Ted's interpretation was that his body had gained immunity to AIDS. He now had antibodies to the AIDS virus (since he tested positive to the antibody test) as we would from a flu from which we have recovered. However, the virus itself was gone. "My doctors didn't believe it, so they had me retested in another lab," Ted wrote us. "Those tests came out the same, but they still wouldn't believe it was possible. I'm now the subject of intense medical curiosity."

A recent article in *Science* (2) reports that researchers have discovered that Ted is not alone. Four out of 1,000 men in a Johns Hopkins long-term study show the same pattern that strongly suggests recovery from the virus.

We don't know exactly what happened physiologically for Ted that changed the way his lab tests came out, and can't be certain that those changes are related to the change work he did. However, Ted is clearly healthy and symptom-free at this point.

Self-Healing for You

Everyone has times in their lives when they would like to be able to heal more rapidly from some injury or illness. You may be able to engage your own ability to heal through the method described in this chapter.

Certainly this method will *not* stimulate *everything* to heal. However, it takes only a little investment of time, and doesn't require you to accept any beliefs or exotic life-style changes. With nothing to lose and so much to gain, we think it's worth doing. If you're not successful doing it yourself, you might consider seeking assistance from someone specifically trained in this NLP method.

Frequently people initially overlook something to use to try out this process, because they first *assume* it can't be healed. If you have something you assume can't be healed, it may be particularly appropriate to use for this process. Since you definitely don't believe that illness or injury is something that can heal on its own, thinking about it differently could make a tremendous difference. One man in a seminar said to me, "Oh, I can't do this process on my arthritis, because that can't be changed." Then he realized that he had been *thinking* of his arthritis as something that would only get worse, and got very interested in finding out what would happen if he used this process to change his unconscious thinking.

People have reported good results from using this process with a wide variety of problems. You've already read several examples of how this process has helped people engage their body's ability to heal. Our range of examples gets broader each year as we explore what's possible with this method. Of course the more serious the illness, the greater the possible benefit.

Utilize Medical Resources

Make sure you are receiving appropriate medical attention for any physical difficulty. When I am ill, I want to obtain *all* the information available to me about what is going on. For some things, a simple medical solution may be more advantageous than attempting to do something in your mind. For some other problems, the medical profession has little to offer but dangerous drugs and surgical procedures, with little assurance that these will be successful. In those cases, you have nothing to lose and everything to gain by trying other approaches, as long as they don't preclude medical solutions. I used this approach with my breast infection, knowing that if I didn't get results within a certain time period, I would use antibiotics. Even when someone decides on a "traditional" medical solution such as surgery, it's likely that utilizing this method can assist them in healing more rapidly from the surgical procedure.

Bernie Siegel's book, *Love, Medicine and Miracles,* (1), offers many tips about forming a respectful and beneficial partnership with your doctor. I always ask a lot of questions so that I can gain from my doctor's expertise. I ask, "What is known about this illness?" "How accurate are the tests?" "What kinds of treatment are recommended?" "What are the benefits and risks of treatment?" "What are the benefits and risks if I don't use that treatment?" If the problem is something fairly serious, I may want a second opinion from another doctor.

I think of my doctor as an important consultant who has in-depth knowledge and training about physical maladies. I also remember that my body belongs to me, and recognize that medical knowledge changes over time. At least some of what is accepted as truth today will someday be superseded by new and better understandings of how to create and maintain health. Steve was medically diagnosed as having a bleeding peptic ulcer in 1956. *Everything* he was told to do then has now been found to make ulcers *worse!* Recently it has been discovered that ulcers are caused by a bacteria, and often can be successfully treated with antibiotics. Our doctors are doing the best they can with what is known today. We can make our own best decisions given this input and what we know about ourselves and our bodies. We are more respectful of doctors if we don't expect them to be God and know everything. When I have made decisions that were different from my doctor's advice, I have been fully willing to take responsibility for the consequences of my decisions. Norman Cousins' two books (3,4) provide an excellent model for intelligent participation in your own treatment and healing.

Self-Healing Outline

This method will guide you through a process that will teach your brain how to "code" an injury or illness for automatic healing. While of course there are no guarantees that this will produce healing, many people have reported phenomenal progress toward health. We do not yet completely understand the physiological mechanism through which this process stimulates a healing response in many people. It seems to do so by creating unconscious messages of healing that your body then responds to 24 hours a day. These messages are not some generic "subliminal suggestions" or other mass change methods, but are messages specifically adapted to the way *your* brain works. Having these messages in place seems to be one of the key elements that allows some people to experience remarkable recoveries from "hopeless" illnesses, when many others with the same illness did not.

Step 1. Identify what you want to heal automatically. This may be either an illness or an injury.

Step 2. Establish your personal evidence for how you will know when it is healing or has healed. Ask yourself, "After this has healed, what will be different in my experience?" "What signs will I have that this is healing?" "What will look or feel different after this has healed?"

Step 3. Find a personal experience of automatic self-healing. Think of something similar to the illness or injury you want to heal, that you know your body *automatically* heals on its own. Pick something that you know will heal no matter what you do—something you can't avoid healing. Some common examples are cuts, scrapes, blisters, sprains, a cold, or the flu. Most of us have experienced these, and we know they just heal automatically. Think of something that *you* consider similar to what you want to heal automatically.

Step 4. Think of your automatic self-healing experience as if it were happening NOW. "So if you had a cut (or whatever you picked in Step 3) *right now,* you would know that it would heal automatically, right?" Notice how you imagine the cut *if you had it now, knowing that it will heal on its own.*

Step 5. Identify your coding differences between your automatic self-healing experience (from Step 4) and your illness or injury (from Step 1). How do you *see* each of these, and how are they different?

Start by noticing *where* you see them. When you think of your illness that hasn't healed, what do you see in your mind, and where do you see it? Is it right in front of you? Is it on your body? Is it off to the side?

Ask these same questions about your automatic self-healing experience (from Step 4). When you think of what it would be like if you had a cut right now (or whatever you picked), where do you see it? Most people see it in a *different* location.

Do you see one of these two experiences *on your body* while the other one is in front of you in space? For example, you might see a cut healing *right on your hand,* while you see your injury that hasn't healed as if it were on a *picture of yourself out in front of you.*

Now check for any other coding differences. Notice if one is in color and the other in black and white. Is one a slide and the other a movie? Is one larger or closer than the other? You are checking for how your mind identifies one as something that will heal automatically, and the other as something that won't.

In your self-healing experience, is there a way in which the healing area *looks different than the area around it?* For many people, the healing area is larger, more colorful, pulsating, glowing, or in some way *marked out for healing.* It is important to notice this, because this is the way your brain knows that this area of your body deserves special attention.

You may want to write down the way you picture your automatic healing experience, to be sure you remember it.

Step 6. Now make your "unhealed" experience like your automatic self-healing experience. Now you are going to recode your injury or illness in the same way your brain already codes things for automatic self-healing. This means you will make your "unhealed" experience *like* your automatic self-healing experience. You will be picturing your injury or illness using the codes your brain recognizes as meaning that something will heal on its own. Use the information you got from Step 5 to do this.

If your unhealed experience was a slide of *illness,* or a movie of *getting worse,* first let that change into an image of *getting better* just like the one you already have for your automatic self-healing experience.

Then move your "previously unhealed" experience into the location of your automatic self-healing experience: Here's how.

If you see your automatic healing experience on your body in the appropriate spot, then see your "unhealed" experience on your body in whatever location is appropriate for it. In other words, if you see your cut healing on your hand, and you want your spine to heal, imagine your spine healing, as if you could see it right there where it is in your back.

However, if your see your cut healing in a picture of yourself out in front of you, then see your spine healing on a similar picture of yourself out in front of you in the same location. Some people have both—they see the healing *on* their body, *and* on a picture of their body out in front of them.

Now make your image like your automatic self-healing experience in every other way. If your healing experience has a glow around it or is colorful, make your unhealed experience that way, too. By doing this your mind/body will now respond to your injury/illness as something that is specially marked out to heal automatically.

Step 7: Test to be sure your injury or illness is coded for automatic self-healing. Take another look at your automatic self-healing experience and how you *now* see your injury/illness. Are they the same? If not, notice what is still different and make the injury/illness the same as the automatic self-healing.

When the unhealed experience is coded for healing, many people notice significant and immediate changes in how they feel about the injury/illness. This is a sign that a change has successfully been made at a physiological level. Does your image of your injury or illness seem as real and compelling now as your automatic self-healing experience? If not, look again for differences and make the two experiences the same.

While most people find that how they *see* the injury makes all the difference, you can also check what you *hear* inside or say to yourself. If you have a voice or sound that goes with your self-healing experience, make sure you create a similar voice, coming from the same location, for the illness/injury that you want to heal.

Step 8: Locate your past timeline. Make up another example of automatic healing and place it in your past timeline. You'll find information on finding your timeline in the previous chapter. A skilled NLP Practitioner can usually help you find your timeline in a few minutes.

Make up another example of your body *having already recovered from this kind of injury or illness once before,* and then place it in your past. Make sure you make this new "made up" memory, just like all your other past memories, so that it seems subjectively as real to you. Since most of our beliefs about what is real and possible are based on what we think has happened in the past, this step adds significantly to the power and impact of this method.

For many people, the eight steps above are all that is needed to allow healing to occur on its own. Steps 1 through 8 reorient your body toward healing at both conscious and deep unconscious levels. However, often two additional steps are helpful, and sometimes they are necessary. There is nothing to lose and a lot to gain by taking the time to go through these additional steps. After describing the steps, I'll present some examples illustrating their importance.

Step 9: Create personal ecology: check for internal objections to healing. Close your eyes and turn inward. Ask yourself, "Does any part of me have any objection to my *healing automatically?*"

If the answer is "No," you are done with this step.

If the answer is "Yes," the methods described in chapter 8 can help you find ways to satisfy internal objections while allowing your body to heal. Learning to lovingly and accurately "read" your own inner signals is a skill of phenomenal value in every area of your life.

Objections typically arise because some part of you recognizes that if you simply got well, you would lose something that is important to you. A particular illness, or a series of illnesses, may accomplish something useful and important in our lives. Some psychological theories have talked about this as "secondary gain." This tends to be a derogatory way of thinking about something that is actually of great value to us, and is well worth preserving. An illness or injury can result in getting love and attention from others, a vacation from work or other responsibilities, a chance to catch up on letter-writing, or any number of other worthwhile outcomes. When this is the case, it's important to identify other ways of achieving these positive outcomes, so that the illness or injury is no longer needed.

Check particularly carefully for objections if: 1) you have a serious illness; 2) you've had an illness for a long time and have needed to make many lifestyle adjustments due to this illness; or 3) your illness significantly affects the lives of others around you.

Step 10: Access your inner wisdom for ways to support healing. Turn inward and ask your unconscious, "Is there anything else I can do to support my automatic self-healing?" Wait for whatever images, feelings, or thoughts come to mind. It's amazing what wonderful advice we can offer ourselves, if we ask and listen. Sometimes it's even the same advice we have received from others. Yet when we are receiving it from ourselves, we usually trust it more and *want* to follow it.

In particular, check for *lifestyle changes to support healing.* When your personal habits are in order, your body has a much better opportunity to heal itself. Ask "Does my inner self have suggestions about my diet, rest, exercise, work habits, etc.?" Sometimes the "typical suggested protocol" for people with a particular illness will not be right for you. Your inner, less conscious, self will often know this before your conscious mind is aware of it.

For any major illness, it is useful to do this step on a daily or weekly basis until healing is complete. Some days you may get no advice, or simply "Keep on doing what you're already doing." Other days you'll get important input from your inner self.

This step offers you a gentle way to make sure your personal habits support healing. If you are eating a poor diet, not getting enough sleep, or overworking, your self-healing will be much more difficult. If you have a cut, you don't rub dirt in it and expect it to heal. You keep it clean and take care of it by putting on a bandage. In the same way, taking especially good care of yourself allows any injury or illness to heal more rapidly. Sometimes utilizing this method helps create motivation to develop personal habits that support the healing process. You may find yourself wanting to be more responsive to your physical needs, now that you know your body is oriented toward healing.

You can also develop better and better ways to respond to life's difficulties so that you experience resourcefulness rather than stress. For instance, simply taking five minutes to close your eyes and relax several times a day can allow healing to occur more easily. Even when circumstances are difficult, changing the way you *respond* to situations can reduce stress significantly. Many of the methods in this book will be useful for this.

Illness Can Achieve Personal Wants and Needs:

When I asked Earl to make his illness look like the automatic self-healing, he frowned and said, "When I try to do this, my whole body feels stiff and I hear a loud 'No.'"

When we explored Earl's objection, he discovered that getting ill was the only way he knew to attempt to meet some of his wants and needs. He had been trained as a child that to be a good person, it's important to "do for others." As a result, Earl never felt right about saying "No" to others or just doing something for himself. Earl found himself getting ill frequently, and through this process learned that illness was an effective way to say "No." One way of describing Earl's situation is that he found himself in conflict between wanting to satisfy his own needs and wanting to please others. First I used the conflict resolution method presented in chapter 13. Then I used the Six Step Reframing process described in chapter 8 to assist him in having other choices for meeting his own personal needs, so that he no longer needed to become ill.

Sally, who attended one of our seminars, had been ill much of her life. She had thought of this as a "health problem" that she couldn't do anything about. When a part of her objected to her healing, she learned that getting sick was a way for her body to tell her to slow down. Sally felt a need to be very active and busy, and loved "getting things done," so she hadn't paid attention to bodily signals like being tired. It was as if her body knew she wouldn't respond and really rest until she got sick. Once Sally became aware of the need to respond to these "early warning signals" from her body, she no longer got ill very often.

The "Death Wish"

Some experts on illness and healing speak of a "Death Wish." This is the idea that some people *want* to die and this "wish" creates terminal illness. This kind of thinking is not very useful in creating solutions for people. Even when people do have parts of themselves that "want to die," death is never an end in itself. Typically they want to die because they're tired of a struggle, and death is the only thing that promises an end to it. They *really* want a better way to live, but have given up on finding it.

Carol told me that she had been through many surgeries for a variety of problems. She continued having many illnesses, and spent much of her time in hospitals. Her skin was pasty white, and she looked quite ill. By doing Six Step Reframing with Carol (chapter 8), we learned that a part of her indeed wanted her to die. I asked the part what it's positive purpose was. The part said, "I want peace for her." Death was the only way this part had known to obtain peace. Six Step Reframing allowed me to assist her in finding other choices for experiencing peace that didn't require her to die.

Getting Sick to Preserve Good Relationships

Sometimes illness fulfills a positive function in our relationships with others. Children can learn that illness is a sure way to get love and affection from Mom and Dad. Love and affection is very important, particularly to young children, and most people will do whatever they perceive as necessary to get it.

This doesn't mean it's good to withdraw love and affection when your child is sick. However, if you have a child who is frequently ill, you may want to be sure you are offering *extra* love and affection when your child is *well.* Make sure your child can experience positive connections with you when you are both really healthy. You can also make sure that other well children in your family get plenty of nurturing.

Occasionally children get the message that "You have to get sick to get love around here" by observing others. If you notice that *you* learned from your own past experiences to use getting ill as a way to get love and attention, you have learned something important. Noticing the positive purpose is the first step to finding other choices. We never tell people to give up this method, but rather assist each person in *finding more satisfying ways* to get love and affection.

It's easy to think of these examples as *negative*. Some people think, "I shouldn't want to get love and attention this way," and just try to get rid of their behavior. Others think it's insulting to think that they are getting love and attention in this way, and deny it. It's important to realize that these are actually very positive and useful parts of ourselves. Having ways to experience love, or ways to care for ourselves, are things all of us want. It's only a matter of finding *better* ways to get these important experiences.

Objections that Surface Later

No matter how carefully you ask for objections, sometimes they only emerge later. Two weeks after working with Jennie, she called saying she had gotten worse. After our work together she had stopped taking her Tylenol, thinking she no longer needed it, but then had experienced more and more pain. Finally she went back on an intensive Tylenol schedule (one every four hours) to combat her pain, and she still wasn't able to lift the things she could previously. Her symptoms had definitely worsened.

I said to Jennie, "When this happens, it's usually because an internal part objects to your getting well. Since you've had such a dramatic response, clearly this is a powerful part of you that can also heal you, but that's not appropriate yet."

I asked a few questions to find out what objections she might have to healing. The information came pouring out. "I've always felt that I'm not good enough. I'm not as good as my sister. My mother always told me that when I was growing up, and it was true. My sister was 18 months older than me, so she could do everything before I could. My sister has arthritis now, and is very deformed and in a lot of pain. I have MS, but my symptoms weren't as bad as my sister's. I thought, 'I don't deserve to have better than she has.' This sounds strange, but I felt guilty for not having more pain than her. I haven't told anyone this, because I couldn't face it. It was about a year after that that I got arthritis too."

This sounded like a very important belief to deal with. When I asked her how she knew *now* that she wasn't good enough, Jennie said, "I just hear voices saying, 'You're not good enough. You're not good enough!'"

I said, "To a small child, the belief you formed makes a lot of sense. In fact, it's a measure of your intelligence that you were able to notice that your 18-month-older sister was in fact more capable. Of course it was beyond a child's ability to know that this was because she was older. So I'd like you to go back there with that understanding. Seeing it that way, what is it like?"

"I still hear, 'You're not good enough.'"

"OK. Then what I'd like you to do is go back and get a very different experience. You grew up as a second child, and your mother didn't know how to help you understand that experience of always being behind your older sister in a *positive* way.

"That's an understatement!" said Jennie.

"Now I'd like you to have the experience of growing up as the older child. You'll have an opportunity to find out the perspectives of an older child, because you will be 18 months older than your sister. You can let yourself go way back to just being born. As you are growing up, at 18 months there is a new baby born: your younger sister. Notice what it's like to grow up this way, always being able to do things first. You can walk first, talk first, cut first, run first, and do everything first. Some of this experience you can notice consciously, and your unconscious can provide a richness and depth to this experience that you don't have time to consciously track.

"I can't do it," she said. "I just get confused."

"What is your objection to doing it?" I asked.

"It's like I would lose my self. I'd lose my whole way of making sense out of things."

This was a sign that Jennie would get a very useful new perspective when she went through this process, but that I needed to find a way for her to do it safely. "OK. And that's important. You can take your way of making sense out of things now, and put it on a shelf, or set it aside in some location so that it is protected and safe. Then you can take it back when we are done with this if you want to."

"OK." This satisfied Jennie.

"And now you can be a baby and grow up this way. Notice what different perspectives and beliefs about yourself you form as you grow up this way.

"I still can't quite do it. I just see myself in my older sister's body, and her in my body. I can't do it as me."

I thought Jennie's experience would be much more powerful if she did this as *her,* so I explored what would make this possible. "OK, so rather than doing that, you can let your sister be her own age, and instead of you taking her place, it's just that you are 18 months older. You were born ahead of her in time." This simple change made it possible for her to follow the instructions. An important part of NLP is finding a way to *adapt* a process so that each individual can do it easily, safely, and usefully.

Jennie came out of this with a very different set of beliefs and perspectives. "I know I can do things. It's like, 'I can do it,'" she said.

"And now you can find whatever is valuable from your old perspective, and add that in, because there are some important understandings that second children learn. And you can keep those in a way that they amplify and strengthen your sense of your own ability. . . . Now think about yourself. Are you as good as everyone else?"

"Yes." she said calmly.

"Do you deserve to have things?" I asked this because Jennie had previously said she didn't *deserve* to have better than her sister.

"I don't know. I still don't know if I deserve things."

I explained that it may be just a matter of recognizing that it's pretty hard to decide who deserves what in this world. Personally, I think it's impossible to determine. Plenty of people work hard and are good people, but they live in third-world nations where they don't receive much for that. Others have lots, but according to my values they don't "deserve" it or make good use of it. For myself, I think figuring out who deserves what is irrelevant. Given that my goals and outcomes also include other people, the more I get my goals, the more others will also benefit. For example, I want to be better and better at doing NLP. The more I get this, the more others will also benefit. So it's not really a matter of what I deserve, it's just finding ways to get more of what I want, so that I can benefit more and those around me will benefit more too.

This made sense to Jennie. She was ready to eliminate the word "deserve" from her inner language.

I tested more to make sure she felt good as a person, so that it was OK to get well. This seemed to be taken care of.

"Do you have any other objections?" I asked. "Check inside."

Jennie did. "If I get well, I'll have to give some things up. I have a sticker that says I'm handicapped, and some days I feel better than other days. I remember one day when I looked pretty good, and I got out of my car and someone said, 'You don't look handicapped.' I kind of thought, 'I'd better look worse.' Intellectually I know I don't need to look worse, but that's the thought that came to my mind."

Jennie recognized that these thoughts were a little bit strange. Yet many of us make similar decisions for similar reasons. We sometimes hang on to symptoms or bad feelings because a part of us thinks we'd be losing something if we just got better. Fortunately, Jennie had the wisdom to acknowledge these "crazy" concerns, so that we could deal with them.

Already as Jennie was talking, she was beginning to sort out her own experience differently. Bringing old beliefs into consciousness allows us to reexamine them. Sometimes we realize that these beliefs just don't fit for us anymore. At other times, more is needed to change a belief, as with Jennie's next objection:

"And I don't want to lose money. I'm getting child support because of my disability. If I were to get well, I might lose the year-round child support, because I'd be capable. I like the security of having the support, and it's important for my child."

"So how much are you getting?"

"$200 a month."

"And you'd lose this if you were healthy?"

"Well, I might."

"So it's $200 a month. You might ask the part of you that wants the security of having the support to think about whether it would really be possible to lose that, or whether you'd actually be *more* secure being healthy. Because you wouldn't really be able to lose that money until you were capable of making *more* money, and be more secure in being able to do it yourself."

"OK. Yeah. That makes sense."

"Does it also make sense to that part of you? Does that part like this idea?" I wanted to make sure I was satisfying her *emotional* logic, not just her conscious mind's way of thinking.

"Yeah," Jennie's voice tone let me know she fully agreed.

"Any other objections?"

"Well, I'm also getting a disability pension of $12,000 a year because of having MS. When I got on disability, they told me I didn't really have enough symptoms to qualify for the pension yet, but given the typical course of MS, they would go ahead and give it to me. So that also contributed to my getting arthritis so I would have more symptoms and deserve the pension. I was also in a job I hated, and it was really nice to get the pension and not have to work. It's nice to have the money. And if I were well, I don't know if I should keep the money."

"And would you lose your benefits?"

"Well, no. That's the ridiculous part. I wouldn't really. Once you qualify for the benefits, you have them for life. If I make more money, though, my disability would be reduced by a third of the amount I make. So if I make $9,000, my disability would be reduced by $3,000."

"So you would get to *keep* two-thirds of anything you make." I refocused Jennie's attention on what she would *gain,* rather than what she would lose.

"Yeah."

"So make sure that part of you understands that if you get well you can make *more* money. If it's nice to have the money from your disability check, it will be even nicer to have more money, won't it?" I offered each of these new ways to think about things playfully, waiting for her response to know if it would be useful for Jennie. I always listened for a *full* response that would let me know I was satisfying her emotional logic. It's usually quite easy to "convince" someone's conscious mind, but usually that's not who needs convincing.

"Yes," (laughing)

"And I suggest taking your time in thinking about what to do about your pension. You have a lot of choices. I don't know what will work for you, but if I were in your situation, I think I would take my time exploring what I wanted to do to earn money, and how I was going to get the skills. I suggest giving yourself a lot of time *after* being well before you finish sorting all of that out. Since you were disabled for a long time, I think it's fair to take time with that to be sure you're really healthy. You can think it through in a way that works for you. If I were you I might consider doing several things. I might keep the pension money, and when I had more money than I needed, use it for some kind of charity myself—maybe to help someone in need become more self-sufficient. Or I might eventually decide I didn't need it because I was already *much* better off financially, and give it back.

"And do you have the sense that given who you are now, you'll be able to find a more satisfying way of making a living than what you were doing before?"

"Oh yes."

Jennie liked the idea of having choices—and having time to make them. She wasn't locked in to having to do anything.

"Any more objections?" I asked.

"Well, this is stupid, but I wanted to win with my ex-husband. By having a disability, I won; I got the child support. It took a long court battle and a lot of money to win it, but I won."

"So you might ask the part of you that wants to win, 'How will you win *better* by being totally recovered?' 'What will you win that's even *more important* when you're well?' Because then you'll be winning something a lot more important than what you won before."

"That's true." Although I couldn't see her face over the telephone, Jennie's voice was smiling.

"And does that part like that idea?"

"Yes."

"Ask inside, 'Are there any remaining objections to my automatically healing?'"

"I just feel peaceful. It feels all OK."

"Great. And you have certainly demonstrated that a part of you knows how to impact your health quickly. If you can get worse quickly, you can also get better quickly. That part clearly knows how to make that happen."

Jennie laughed.

"And I don't know if we have taken care of *all* the objections now, or if one or two more will come up over time. If any more objections arise, your unconscious might want to have a better way to signal you and get your attention than by making you worse all over. Your unconscious might select one small joint to give you a little twinge—just enough to get your attention so that you'll know to take some time to turn inward and find out what that objection is, and find a way to satisfy it."

In the next several weeks Jennie noticed another objection. Her illness had given her a way to escape the control of her ex-husband. She was very glad to have noticed this, because she recognized it as a family pattern. Her teen-aged son had already been using illness as a way to avoid being controlled by someone else. Noticing this pattern allowed Jennie to offer her son other ways to keep control of his own life.

Jennie does not expect complete healing to be immediate, but she considers herself on the road to both better physical *and* emotional well-being.

While much of my interaction with Jennie may seem like simple conversation, it demonstrates the careful use of language which can make belief changes possible.

Additional Pointers

If the healing process occurs most easily and thoroughly over a period of time, it may be useful to identify a series of markers that will let you know the healing is progressing appropriately. Don't *assume* that because a disease is serious that it will necessarily take a long time to heal. I suggest allowing your body to take all the time it needs to heal completely and thoroughly. You don't need to push your body, and there's no need to hold it back, either. *Your inner wisdom will usually know what timetable is best for your healing to be most complete and full.*

Notice the Results and Act Accordingly

Now that you have coded your illness for automatic healing, and checked carefully for any objections to healing, you can just let your body do what it knows how to do. You may experience positive results immediately or over time.

Occasionally (rarely) someone experiences a worsening of symptoms immediately after utilizing this method. If any worsening were to occur, we suggest immediately considering whether medical help would be useful. When I did this myself with my breast infection, I rested and observed my body's response carefully. *If* my fever had become dangerously high, I was prepared to immediately get a prescription of antibiotics and follow it. I knew I could rely on this as a backup method. However, since my fever only went up a bit, and then went back to normal, I did not need to rely on medical help.

If a person's illness has been in a stable state, and then suddenly gets worse after using this self-healing process, this is often due to an inner objection to healing that was not adequately dealt with in Step 9, as with Jennie. It's also possible that this is just the natural course of the illness. For example, flu usually gets worse before it gets better.

Sometimes no change is apparent for awhile. It may be that your body is healing appropriately and just needs more time for this to become noticeable. Some people and some illnesses have healed very rapidly after using this method, while others have taken longer. It's important to let your body heal in the way that's most appropriate for you. Sometimes it's useful to go inside and ask your inner self, "What will be the first sign of my healing?" so that you can have a marker along the way.

Another possibility is that some step of the process needs to be done more thoroughly in order to get the physiological shift to healing. You can test by again checking *how you imagine your injury or illness now.* Do you imagine it the same way that you imagine your automatic self-healing experience? Do you have the same positive feeling about it? Also check that you have an example of *having healed* in your past.

Another possibility is that this method is not the right one to make a difference for this particular illness. At this point we have no idea how much we can accomplish by changing our thinking. New research in this area emerges each year, as we discover that more is possible. However, there probably are some things that we'll never find a way to heal. For example, if someone's leg has been amputated, I certainly do not expect this process to grow a new leg! We recommend being open to healing, but not insisting upon it.

If you notice improvement fairly quickly, you can congratulate yourself on your natural ability to heal, and the wisdom of your body. This is also a time to be sure you *continue* with the lifestyle habits that will support your continued healing, and prevent recurrence of this injury or illness.

How to Utilize Information from Your Doctor:

Doctors have professional guidelines specifying that they must warn patients of all the bad things that could happen to them, and the likely progress of their illness. However, it's important to notice the difference between information and opinions. If a doctor says "Four out of five people with this illness die in two months," that's a statistic; that's information. However, if a doctor says "*You* will die in two months," that's an *opinion*. There's no reason you can't be that fifth person who lives longer or gets well! If your doctor predicts that you won't get well, or that you have only six months to live, that's a time to be very skeptical.

Even the *way* your doctor presents information can make an important difference. If your doctor says, "And when *you* take this medicine, *you will* probably feel sick to your stomach in about ten minutes," the doctor is talking about these unpleasant events as if they *will happen* to *you*. When listening, most of us automatically visualize, feel, (and sometimes smell) this happening to us, as a way of understanding what the doctor says. By imagining this happening to ourselves, we make it much more likely that it will happen. Doctors who have gone through our trainings now speak about unpleasant side-effects as something that *could* happen to "a person" rather than something that will happen to *you*.

You can benefit from your doctor's knowledge by deliberately imagining any possible negative side-effects on *someone else*. I can see a "generic person" having nausea out in front of me. Now I can understand my doctor without programming myself to have the problem.

Affirmations

Many people advocate repeating positive statements in order to improve health. However, making simple statements like "Things are getting better and better" will usually not do much good, because it is only an overlay that doesn't transform the underlying experience. Like "whistling in the dark," it doesn't get to the foundations of experience. Covering over an unpleasant experience with a positive experience can bury the unpleasant experience deeper.

Instead, with NLP, we directly *transform* the negative experience into something positive. Sometimes finding the positive purposes in the negative experience makes this easier. When we make this *transformation to something positive,* it sticks. There is no longer any need to constantly repeat positive affirmations to ourselves.

In addition, most "affirmations" are much too general. In order for suggestions to be helpful, they need to be specifically connected to your experience, such as the following examples:

"Knowing that the slight tingling sensation you feel is part of a natural healing process can let you become more and more comfortable and relaxed. This is a sign that your body is continuing a process that will allow you to have greater health."

"The swelling and throbbing means that your body is sending blood in to the cut, carrying healing nutrients and carrying away damaged tissue and debris, so that it can heal faster."

"That high fever is your body's way of making the appropriate adjustments to battle the infection and heal this illness."

"Giving my body the time to heal well now will help me reach my other outcomes and goals. Resting completely now will help give me more energy later."

Many people feel the sensations of illness and begin to worry about disastrous consequences, causing muscular tension and all the other elements of stress. By linking the specific symptoms and sensations with a positive outcome, the person can relax and allow maximum opportunity for natural healing to occur.

Any self-suggestion should also be adjusted to fit with the person's preferences. Each of us has certain words or phrases that we respond especially positively to, and other words or phrases that we respond to with annoyance or disbelief. Self-suggestions can be carefully edited to maximize their positive impact.

Voice tone is even more important than the words that are said. Try saying to yourself something like, "I'm getting healthier" in a high-pitched, squeaky voice that rises at the end of the statement, and notice what kind of impact that has! The tone of voice and tempo needs to be congruent and convincing to you.

Self-healing and Surgery

When surgery seems like a wise choice, you can still use the self-healing method to prepare for it and to recover from it. Some people dread surgery because they think of it as a vicious "attack" upon their body. By transforming this imagery into something more positive—such as a helpful and needed repair of something that has been damaged—you can rally all your responses toward a positive result.

You can also use positive statements to aid your rapid recovery from surgical procedures, or for other kinds of healing. A friend of ours, who was recently scheduled for a hysterectomy, asked what she could do to promote rapid healing after surgery. I suggested that she create images in her mind of healing, and say things to herself presupposing healing.

Since research has now demonstrated that people do respond to what they hear while apparently unconscious under anesthesia, I also suggested that she have someone with her in the operating room to make sure the surgeon, anesthetist, and others were saying only positive things about her or to her during the operation. I told her how some of our trainees have been anesthetists who utilized these methods with their patients, making positive healing statements as their patients went in and out of anesthesia. They reported to us that the other hospital staff members started commenting that "their" patients were different—they had fewer adverse reactions and healed more quickly.

Our friend went one step further and met with her anesthetist ahead of time, asking him to make healing suggestions to her as she was going under. He was interested in experimenting and was glad to accommodate. Our friend recovered from her hysterectomy in record time, surprising the medical staff with both the speed of her recovery and her complete lack of pain.

If The Self-healing Works, Does it Mean I'm to Blame for Having Been Ill? Should I Feel Guilty?

People frequently confuse *cause* with *cure.* They mistakenly think that if we can heal ourselves by changing our thinking, that means our thinking *caused* the illness. Not so. If a child falls out of a tree and gets a broken leg, we don't fix the broken leg by putting the child back up in the tree. That would obviously be futile. The doctor may decide to use a cast to correct the problem, something completely unrelated to the cause. Being able to heal something with our minds doesn't mean we caused it with our minds, any more than the child's cast *caused* the broken leg.

Guilt and blaming ourselves do *not* help us recover and heal more rapidly. Doing what we can to support healing, and observing our body's response usually does aid recovery. The method in this chapter offers us something new and powerful we can use to assist our own healing, no matter what the cause.

Most illnesses probably have multiple causes. A person may have a genetically inherited "predisposition" to the illness. Environmental factors such as pollutants, additives, or past injuries and illnesses may have contributed. Stress resulting from a difficult life may or may not have contributed. If we have coded our illness for worsening rather than healing, that can also be a contributing factor.

Gaining the "How-to's" for Healing

The important thing is to do everything you can to have your illness coded so that your body automatically will heal without intervention. If I take *my* way of thinking of healing, and give you a guided fantasy, it may or may not be compelling to you. But if I take the time to find out how *you* think of healing, it *will* work for you. And when it's coded in your brain that healing will happen, that impact will continue all the time. You don't need to set aside time for affirmations, or to meditate, because that's the way you think about it all the time.

Recently I was at a seminar given by a well-known author who encourages people to heal their lives, so that their bodies will then heal. It was wonderful advice and very motivational to listen to. I was sitting in the middle of a large room filled with people who had a wide range of life-threatening illnesses. They were all listening intently, hoping to find something they could use to recover. Someone from the audience finally stood up and said, "It's been very useful to me to hear you talk about learning to love yourself, and giving up old resentments, and so on. But I really need to know *how* to do that." The speaker had nothing to offer. He continued to read letters from people who said things like "I learned to love myself and others, and now I am getting well."

Not one of the people at that seminar got the "How-to's" that the woman had sense enough to ask for. They learned nothing specific about *how* to learn to love themselves, or how to learn to love others. That's where NLP offers something no other field has yet provided: specific methods to implement this kind of good advice. This book includes many *ways* to do this better.

Research Now Supports Mind Influencing Body

In recent years, researchers in the new field of psychoneuroimmunology have made discoveries which have begun to clarify how our thinking influences our health and well-being. We have already referred to some of this research at the end of chapter 5. While earlier medical thinking was that mind and body were separate, it is now known that our central nervous system (the seat of thought, memory, and emotion) communicates directly and routinely with our immune system and our endocrine system through a family of neurotransmitters and biochemicals. These researchers are carefully beginning to map out how our state of mind impacts our state of health on the molecular level. A recent article (5) summarizes some of these research findings.

As early as 1964, a study demonstrated a link between emotional conflict and the onset and course of rheumatoid arthritis. Emotionally healthy women in this study remained free of the disease, even when they had a genetic predisposition for it.

More recently, other researchers have identified nerve threads that run from our central nervous system to two key organs of the immune system— the thymus and the spleen. Other research reveals that certain brain cells communicate directly with immune system cells through neuropeptides, and that other brain cells respond to the state of the immune system.

Another study measured the impact of stress on the immune systems of medical students. Just before and during exam week these students experienced a significant decrease in immune system functioning.

More and more is becoming known about the physiological mechanisms connecting our thoughts, emotions, and physical condition. While research keeps coming in on the physiological mechanisms of mind/body connection, the field of NLP is moving rapidly forward to identify exactly what kind of *subjective thinking* has a useful impact on our bodies.

Research Support for Inner Wisdom:

In another study, Robert Ader demonstrated that the immune system can act as an unconscious sensory organ, gathering information that helps our bodies regulate themselves. Rats with overactive immune systems were given sweetened water along with a chemical that is unpleasant because it produces nausea, but which also suppresses the immune system. Most rats will not drink this mixture because of the nausea. These rats, however, continued drinking the water. Ader commented, "The animals know it's 'good' for them. . . . Signals generated by the immune system are being read by the central nervous system" (5).

This kind of research is beginning to lay the groundwork for what many have already experienced through the methods described in this chapter. We often have ways of knowing what is good for us that our less-conscious sensory systems such as our immune system gather information about. We can become conscious of this wisdom by turning inward and attending more carefully to the subtle messages our body is continually sending.

As these researchers offer the scientific basis for understanding how our thinking affects our health, the automatic self-healing method gives you a specific way to use your thoughts to influence your health positively.

References

1. *Love, Medicine and Miracles,* by Bernie Siegel.
2. "Losing Aids Antibodies," by Deborah M. Barnes. *Science,* 10 June 1988, p. 1407.
3. *Anatomy of an Illness,* by Norman Cousins.
4. *The Healing Heart,* by Norman Cousins.
5. "A Molecular Code Links Emotions, Mind and Health," Stephen S. Hall, *Smithsonian,* July, 1989, pp. 62-71.

21 *Knowing What You Want*

 The previous chapters in this book are filled with examples of people who were able to get more of what they wanted with NLP. *Knowing what you want* is equally important. Even more important is being sure that you want something that is worth having, so that you are satisfied when you actually get it. You may find it very useful to go through the series of questions below to assist yourself in developing personal goals or "outcomes" that are worth having, and that will fit with the person you want to be.

Step 1. Select a Goal.

First, ask yourself, *What do I want?* Pick one goal or desire. If you think of several goals, are they alike in some way? For example, if you want to be able to motivate yourself to clean your house, to get your reports done on time, and to finish some task, these all relate to being *motivated.* If you think of several goals that aren't alike, pick any one of them to begin.

NLP has discovered that the *way* you think about your goal makes a big difference. You can think of the same goal in a way that makes it *easy* to achieve, or in a way that makes it almost impossible. The next questions are to make sure you are thinking of your goal in ways that will make its achievement easier.

Checkpoint A. *Make sure your goal is stated in terms of what you DO want, not what you don't want.* For example, if my goal is "I want my child to quit whining," or "I want to stop feeling bad when my plans fall through," or "I don't want to eat so much between meals," I am thinking of what I *don't* want.

You can easily turn this into what you *do want instead.* "I want my child to ask for what he wants in a pleasant tone of voice." "When my plans fall through, I want to feel challenged—as if I have an opportunity. "I want to eat only vegetables between meals, and to eat a full, balanced meal three times a day."

When people think about what they *don't* want, or what they want to avoid, they often produce that in their lives, because that is where their minds are focused. Changing your thinking to what you *do* want is a simple shift that can make a tremendous difference.

Checkpoint B. *Make sure your goal is stated in a way that you can get it yourself, no matter what other people do.* If your goals require other people to make changes, even if those changes would be a good idea, it places *you* in a more vulnerable and helpless position. You won't be able to get what you want unless you can get *other* people to shift their behavior. While we all want things from other people, it's important that *we are able to get our primary goals ourselves, no matter what other people do.*

This may sound impossible at first, so let's go through several examples. It can make tremendous difference in experiencing our own abilities and strength. Let's say my goal is "I want my husband to quit criticizing me." Since this requires my husband to change, it is not something within my control. Having this as a major goal puts me in a vulnerable position.

"What can I do/have/experience that will give me what I want, no matter what my husband does?" Perhaps I want to have a sense of my own worth even when my husband criticizes me. Perhaps I want to feel resourceful when my husband criticizes me, and to be able to sort out what parts of his criticism *I* agree with and what parts I disagree with. (See chapter 6) This puts me in a more powerful position, because I can get what I want even if my husband continues to criticize me.

Now let's take another example. Let's say my problem is, "My girlfriend broke up with me and I want her back." Since I don't have control over whether she comes back, I can ask myself "What would having her back do for me?" Perhaps my relationship with her was the best I've ever had. She brought out my sense of humor, I liked having the warm connection to another person, and I felt more worthwhile.

Now I have a list of goals that *are* under my own control. I can find other ways to develop my sense of humor. I can get better at developing warm connections with people in my life, and I can find ways to feel worthwhile. I can do all of these things whether my girlfriend comes back or not.

Step 2. Know the Evidence for Your Goal.

"How will you know when you have achieved your goal?" Some people have no way of knowing if they've reached their goals. This means they never get to feel satisfied by achieving something. In addition, they don't have ways to measure whether their day-to-day behavior is taking them closer or farther away from their goal. For example, my goal might be, "I want to be more successful." If I don't have any evidence for what "successful" means, I may work at being successful all my life and even achieve a great deal, without ever feeling any fulfillment. You can define success as getting someone to smile, getting a job, or anything else specific.

Checkpoint. *Does the evidence relate closely to the goal?* Make sure your evidence provides you with good, realistic feedback about whether you are reaching your goal. Let's say my goal is to be an effective teacher, and my evidence for effectiveness is that I feel good at the end of the day. Feeling good at the end of the day is nice, but doesn't necessarily have anything to do with being an effective teacher. Better evidence is that I can observe the students in my class doing much better at a variety of tasks than they did when they started.

Let's take another example. Let's say my goal is to be an effective parent, and I feel that I am a good parent when my children tell me I am doing a good job. Again, this is far from the best evidence for me to use. If I want my children to tell me I'm great, I am likely to be too lenient as a parent, and not take charge in ways that would be better for my children in the long run. Again, better evidence is to watch and listen for their progress and development.

Step 3. Select Where, When, and With Whom You Want Your Goal.

It's very important to think about when you do and don't want your goal. For example, if your goal is "to feel confident," do you want to feel confident *all the time?* Do you want to feel confident about flying an airplane if you've had no flight training? You probably don't want to feel confident about walking a tightrope 100 feet above the ground unless you can actually do it. Where, when, and with whom *do* you want to feel confident? Perhaps you want to feel confident only when you have the skills and training to make confidence appropriate. When you *don't* already have skills, you may want a *different* feeling, such as "caution," "curiosity," or "knowing I can use my mistakes to improve my skill."

It will be much easier for you to achieve your goal if you are very careful about deciding where and when it is appropriate. When a person tries to feel confident without having any skills, they usually don't succeed.

Checkpoint. Be specific. *"What will you see, hear, or feel that will let you know it is time to have your goal?"* For example, "When I see my husband doing X, I want to feel compassionate."

Step 4. Check for Obstacles.

"What stops you from already having your desired goal?" Perhaps nothing stops you. If so, you can go on right to Step 5. However, sometimes another goal conflicts with the goal you want to achieve. When this is true, it is important to find a way to reach *both* goals. Usually two goals that seem in conflict can actually support each other. If not, they can usually be scheduled so they don't conflict. See chapters 8 and 13 for methods that can help you resolve conflict.

Step 5. Find Existing Resources.

"What resources do you already have that will assist you in reaching your goal?" If your goal is to feel a sense of self-worth, knowing when you *already* feel that way can give you a lot of information about how to achieve it. If your goal is to be able to speak in public, what parts of that goal can you already do? You can probably already speak, stand up, and look out at the audience, etc. Realizing how much you can already do provides a positive sense of accomplishment and a solid basis for learning the additional skills you need.

Step 6. Additional Resources.

"What other resources or skills do you need in order to reach your goal?" Knowing what parts you can already do makes it easier to zero in on the parts that you need to learn. Perhaps you need to access a feeling of confidence when you're being observed speaking in public. Perhaps you need a way to keep track of an outline of what you plan to do, or ways to respond to the audience more warmly.

Step 7. Make a Plan.

"How are you going to get to your goal?" *"What will be your first*

step?" Some simple goals can be achieved immediately, but more often it will take a number of steps, and some time, to achieve them.

Checkpoint A. Make sure the first step is specific and achievable. If your goal is "I want to weigh 125 pounds," ask yourself, "What will be my first step toward accomplishing this? What can I do now that will take me in that direction, and what feedback will let me know I am moving toward my goal?" We call this "chunking down." If your goal seems overwhelming, "chunking down" to a first step can make it manageable or even easy.

Checkpoint B. You may have found that just going through this self-questioning process has helped you zero in on exactly what you need to do to reach a worthwhile goal for yourself. Part of your plan may be utilizing some of the methods in this book to assist you in reaching your goal. However, if you have gone through all the previous steps, yet still find yourself well short of your goal, the next section may be useful and important for you.

What Do You REALLY Want?

Sometimes we pick goals that are almost guaranteed *not* to happen. For example, Some people have the goal of never making any mistakes. Others would like everyone in the world to compliment them or love them. Some *have* to be the absolute best at some sport or the richest person in the world.

Even if it is possible to achieve these goals, the effort and sacrifice required may make them not worth attaining. Many people find that if they do achieve these kinds of goals, they *still* aren't satisfied—the goal they pursued wasn't what they *really* wanted. Knowing what we *really* want can help us have much more flexibility in obtaining it more easily.

If we start by picking "unrealistic goals" such as these, we don't need to just abandon them. Instead, we can discover the "goal of the goal." We can ask ourselves the important question, *"What will this goal get for me?"* This can lead to having more basic and worthwhile goals, and to moving towards them more directly.

For example, Frank's goal was to gain acceptance from other people. He felt a strong desire for this and hadn't been very successful in getting it. Most of us want to have good relationships with others. However, Frank wanted to gain acceptance *so that* he could then feel good about himself. He was focused on the goal of "gaining acceptance." The goal of this goal was to "feel good about myself." Frank hadn't realized that feeling good about yourself is really a separate goal. In fact, it's much *easier* to gain acceptance from others by *starting* with feeling good about yourself. By shifting goals from "gaining acceptance from others" to "realizing my own self-worth," we shift to something more attainable and more worthwhile.

Some famous people—movie stars, etc.—go through the great effort (and sometimes personal compromise) of becoming famous because they think it will get them what they want. Yet movie stars seem to be one of the most unhappy groups of people in our culture. Fame didn't get them what they *really* wanted. Usually when people are driven to gain vast sums of money, power, fame, etc., it has to do with *believing* that if we get these things, then we will feel worthwhile, or loved, or something else very basic. When we identify this basic goal, we can find ways to have it that are more direct—without going through the effort of achieving another goal that may not really be relevant.

If your goal is to get a certain job, this could be a way for you to achieve many personal goals. You may want this job because you find the work enjoyable, or it might be a way for you to accomplish something worthwhile. This job might give you financial independence, or allow you to be around a certain kind of people. Your "goal of the goal" for this job could be to continually learn more, or to be creative. Many *different* kinds of jobs can provide enjoyment, accomplishment, financial independence, learning, creativity, or whatever *your* goal of the goal is.

For example, let's say you want to be a professional basketball star, but you're only 4'8" tall. That is a serious practical obstacle to being successful at basketball. However, when you ask "What would being a professional basketball player do for me?" you may realize that what you really want is to have a job where others respect you, and you can make money. There are literally thousands of jobs that will bring you money and respect, yet don't require you to be seven feet tall. When you focus on what you *really* want, you have many more possibilities for success.

It may be even more useful to go a step farther. If you want money and respect, you can again ask yourself, "What will money and respect do for me that's positive?" "What do I *really* want by having money and respect?" Most people want at least enough money to enjoy a comfortable life. Most of us also want to be respected. However, when goals such as money and success consume someone's life, it's usually because a person thinks that money and success are ways to get something more essential. By asking ourselves, "What will getting that do for me?" we often find that it is something like being loved, feeling worthwhile or OK, feeling safe, or survival. Essential goals or outcomes like these are important enough that they are worth going for more directly.

Sometimes you need to ask "And what would that really do for me?" several times before you get to a core goal. For example, getting a particular job could be a way to be successful. Being successful could be a way to gain the respect of others. If we go one step further, the "goal" of gaining respect from others could be to feel OK as a person.

Getting a job could be a way to avoid taking any responsibility. "I want to just do what I am told." The positive purpose of this, or the "goal of this goal" might be to "feel safe." "If I don't have to make any decisions, I feel safe."

Once we know the core goal of safety, or of feeling OK as a person, we have much more flexibility in attaining the goal. It might be that we will really be safer if we make some decisions. It might be that we can feel OK about ourselves more easily *without* trying to gain the respect from others first. When we know what we *really* want, we're much more likely to get it. Take one of your goals now, and ask yourself, *"What will having this do or get for me that's positive?"* Take the time to get down to what's really important to you.

Individual Sessions and Workshops

If you still feel stuck after exploring what you really want, you may want to consider consulting someone well-trained in NLP to help you discover what you want and how to achieve it. Sometimes it can be much easier to achieve our personal goals or outcomes with the assistance of someone with more experience in these methods. While some of our readers have written to tell us of the valuable changes they made on their own, others find it much easier to experience results personally when they are being guided by someone else. This can happen in a seminar, in an atmosphere of assistance from the trainer and other participants, or through private sessions. Everyone responds somewhat differently, and part of using NLP skillfully is being sensitive to those differences and dealing with them. There are many subtleties to doing NLP well, and many adaptations that a skilled NLP trainer or practitioner will be able to make with any particular method so that it fits for each unique person.

If you are considering a workshop or private work to get more benefits for yourself, we'd like to suggest some guidelines so that you get the most for your investment of time and money. The field of NLP currently has no universal standards or licensing procedures, and quality varies dramatically from person to person, and from one center to another. Here are some ways you can gather information before making an investment:

Client Work

1. Does your therapist or change agent spend lots of time gathering information about what has gone wrong in the past? While some of this can be useful, devoting a lot of time to gathering information about what went wrong will seldom lead to solutions. What leads to solutions is finding out how you or other people *solve* similar difficulties. Effective NLP practitioners will spend much more time gathering information about your positive goals and your personal abilities and resources.

2. Are you moving toward your goal or outcome? Some goals are typically achieved in one session by NLP practitioners, while others take more time. Even with goals that take more time, clients typically experience *some* movement in the desired direction within the first two or three sessions. If you don't, it may be time to work with another therapist or change agent. Even if you are working with a skilled person, they may be missing something, or your goal may lie outside their area of expertise. Noticing movement towards your goals is the single most important criterion to use.

3. Does your therapist or change agent give you labels telling you what is wrong with you, rather than spending time helping you get what you want? This is a sign that another person may be a better investment for you. Diagnostic labels are not solutions; they usually provide little or no direction for you—or the practitioner—to know what to do to help you get what you want.

4. Make a distinction between feeling good or feeling understood by the therapist, and whether you are getting the changes you want in your life. Ideally you can have both in a counselor. However, some warm and wonderful people do not have the skills to help you get the results you want. If you have a wonderful therapist but *you* aren't getting your desired changes, we suggest you try someone else.

Seminars

If you're interested in a seminar or workshop, here are some brief recommendations to help you select training that will offer you the most.

1. Get Personal Experience of the Trainer. This can happen through attending a free preview, or through a videotape or audiotape. Trust your first-hand experience more than brochure quotes, endorsements, certificates, or degrees.

2. Staying Power. Does the trainer have a good track record for repeat seminars over a period of time? Those who have both personal integrity and ability (rather than just flash and charisma) can get results that satisfy people over time.

3. Information vs. Demonstrations. In a good training, you will get live *demonstrations* of the methods being taught, not just words describing methods or results.

4. Exercises. After demonstrating, does the trainer provide you with carefully-designed exercises that allow you to immediately *practice* new skills? Observation and *practice* are what will make new skills a part of *you.*

5. Evidence. Do you learn how to *know* whether what you've learned is working? A good trainer will teach you what nonverbal signs to watch and listen for.

6. Personal Integrity. Does the trainer act in ways that are congruent with what is being taught? Here are some of the qualities *we* look for in trainers:

a. An effective trainer will presuppose that anyone can learn—it's matter of finding a way for each person to learn most easily. If a trainer acts like a "guru" who wants to razzle-dazzle you, watch out. Participants usually learn less from this kind of training (even though they're sometimes impressed more!).

b. A good trainer will respect and honor questions and objections from participants.

c. A good trainer will follow through on any promises she makes to participants.

d. Effective trainers can easily admit mistakes and will welcome suggestions to improve the training.

7. Skill. This may be difficult to detect before going through a lot of NLP training, but is very important. Some checks are: Can the trainer *demonstrate* getting results? Do you *observe* nonverbal shifts in the demonstration client? Do you notice your own skill improving, or does the trainer just *say* "Your unconscious is getting it," or "You feel confused *now,* but six months from now you'll notice the difference." Insist on observable results.

8. Sense of Humor. The single best aid to learning is a sense of humor—the kind that is infectious, laughing *with* others or at the human condition, *not* at anyone's expense. If you find a trainer who has this along with the other qualities we've listed, you've found someone you're likely to be pleased with.

These seminar recommendations are condensed from a more complete article, "A Consumer's Guide to Good Training," which is available free from our office. You can get a copy by sending a stamped, self-addressed envelope to: NLP Comprehensive, 2897 Valmont Road, Boulder, CO 80301.

Afterword

In this book we have presented many examples of rapid personal change to demonstrate to you what is possible with NLP patterns and understanding. We have also described some of the methods we use to gather information and make changes, and some of the understandings that guide us in using those methods. We hope we have been able to give you some indication of the comprehensive breadth and depth that NLP represents. In contrast to some "new approaches" that are just a single gimmick, or a bag of tricks, NLP offers a systematic set of concepts and methods for understanding and changing human experience. It is the beginning of a true science of the mind.

We can often deal with most of the problems described here as quickly as we have indicated, once we have identified how the problem works. However, identifying the structure of a difficulty also takes some time. In addition, getting a single result may require a number of the kinds of changes illustrated in the cases we have presented.

A "single" problem such as being overweight may involve the need for any or all of the following: better self-image, the Naturally Slender Eating Strategy, learning effective ways to motivate and decide, resolving a phobic response to childhood abuse, or learning better social or coping skills. A single successful intervention of the kind demonstrated here will often only solve part of a problem configuration.

In addition to knowing *what* to do, the *way* we do it is equally important. The instructions we give people can't just be read in a monotone. Our nonverbal gestures, congruence, tone of voice, tempo, etc. are essential components if those words are to create a compelling experience that leads to change. An artist may have a magnificent image in his mind and know exactly what colors are needed to create the desired effect, but he also needs the skills to be able to put the paints onto the canvas.

In the same way, a violin is a very simple instrument, yet it takes considerable practice and skill to get a clear, sweet sound out of it. If you are interested in learning how to do this kind of work with people, we hope you realize that it's as difficult to learn to do NLP well from a book as it would be to learn to play a violin that way. In either case, "hands-on" practice and guidance from someone skilled makes a tremendous difference. A good violin teacher can show you in seconds how to adjust the position of the violin to improve the sound, something that might take you years to discover on your own. The case descriptions in this book, like a musical score, are only outlines or summaries of what can be accomplished. The actual doing of it often takes considerable practice and skill that can't be conveyed in words.

We've also noticed that we can usually get results more quickly with people who have attended some of our seminars. These people have a lot of background experience that we can quickly utilize to assist them in reaching their goals, and they have fewer limiting beliefs to get in their way. As they learn more and more about how their own minds work, they have more mental skills and resources available to resolve problems and make desired changes.

There are also occasionally times when everything we try doesn't work. This is true of every field of knowledge, including those with much longer histories than NLP. When the existing methods don't work, this marks the growing edge of the field, where we need to create new understandings and new interventions. We have used these occasions to stimulate us to develop new methods. There is so much we can do now that we couldn't do a year ago; by the time this book reaches your hands even more will be possible.

In closing, we'd like to point out something that the cases in this book demonstrate over and over again. People become more capable and more human by *adding* alternative perceptions, responses, behaviors, and ways of thinking, not by subtracting or inhibiting them.

For thousands of years, societies have used disapproval, punishment, prisons, and other forms of coercion to prevent behavior that they didn't like by reducing the options available to people. Coercion always signifies a failure to effectively teach people better alternatives. Sometimes that failure is in turn a sign that some of a society's goals are inappropriate to being human, and could be changed. However, if a society's goals are appropriate, there must be something lacking in education and socialization if people have to be coerced into desirable behavior. By teaching additional effective choices and alternatives (and how to think of more choices when you run out of them) people can have more and more enjoyable and fulfilling lives. When people have choices, they don't need to be controlled, because they have effective ways to get what they want without controlling or harming others.

The methods illustrated here all *add* to our internal abilities and capacities. This expanded internal sense of ourselves also makes us more sensitive, resourceful, responsive and creative in our relationships with others.

Many experts state that we use only a small percentage of our brain, the estimates usually ranging from 5% to 15%. Although people may not use most of their brains, that's not the major problem. The major problem is in *how* we use whatever fraction of our brain we do use. No matter how you think about it, the mind is truly an uncharted frontier, full of valuable resources that are now barely utilized. You can use NLP to make better use of more of your mind, and get much more of what you want in your life.

Some of those who are using NLP are people who already possess many abilities and who have a positive sense of their own self-worth. These people are using NLP to gain even more. Others come from more painful beginnings, and are utilizing the heart of NLP to turn their lives around in a positive direction. One woman wrote to us a little over a year after her first training with us:

"When I came to your Practitioner training, I had very little hope left in life. I could no longer deal with the pain and was ready to give up. I went through major, very rapid transformation, and finally was able to build a foundation of my own strength. I took every NLP training I could this past year and have grown so much that at times I am overwhelmed. I've seen dramatic changes in the lives of my clients, and I now know I can make a difference in this world. The work you represent has changed my life and given me so much. Thank you and bless you for touching my life."

We feel similarly blessed with NLP, and in being able to pass on this blessing to others. NLP has opened doors for us that we didn't even know were there. And when we bump up against a situation we don't yet know how to deal with, NLP understandings and skills provide a firm basis for discovering new solutions.

We hope this book has opened a few doors in your mind about what it is possible for you to have in your life, and how to accomplish it. We wish you well in your journey.

Appendix I

Eye Accessing Cues

While most people lump all of their internal information processing together and call it "thinking," Richard Bandler and John Grinder have noted that it can be very useful to divide thinking into the different sensory modalities in which it occurs. When we process information internally, we can do it visually (sight), auditorily (hearing), kinesthetically (feeling), olfactorily (smell), or gustatorily (taste). As you read the word "circus," you may know what it means by seeing images of circus rings, elephants, or trapeze artists; by hearing carnival music; by feeling the hard seats, or the child on your lap, or by feeling excited; or by smelling and tasting popcorn or cotton candy. The meaning of a word can be perceived in any one, or any combination, of these five sensory channels.

Bandler and Grinder have observed that people move their eyes in systematic directions, depending upon the kind of thinking they are doing. These movements are called eye accessing cues. The chart (below left) indicates the kind of processing most people do when moving their eyes in a particular direction. A small percentage of individuals (about 5%) are "reversed," that is, they move their eyes in a mirror image of this chart.

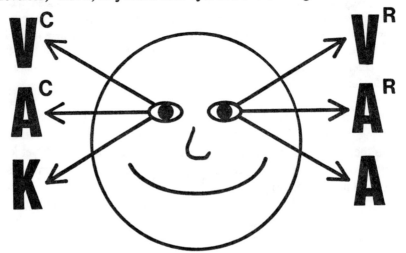

The chart is easiest to use if you simply superimpose it over someone's face, so that as you see her looking in a particular direction you can visualize the label for that eye accessing cue.

V^r   **Visual remembered:** seeing images of things seen before, in the way they were seen before. Sample questions that usually elicit this kind of processing include: "What color are your mother's eyes?" "What does your coat look like?"

V^c   **Visual constructed:** seeing images of things never seen before, or seeing things differently than they were seen before. Questions that usually elicit this kind of processing include: "What would an orange hippopotamus with purple spots look like?"

A^r   **Auditory remembered:** remembering sounds heard before. Questions that usually elicit this kind of processing include: "What is the sound of your alarm clock?"

A^c   **Auditory constructed:** hearing sounds not heard before. Questions that tend to elicit this kind of processing include: "What would the sound of clapping turning into the sound of birds singing sound like?" "What would your voice sound like an octave lower?"

A^d   **Auditory digital:** Talking to oneself. Questions that tend to elicit this kind of processing include: "Can you say something to yourself that you often say to yourself?" "Recite the Pledge of Allegiance internally."

K   **Kinesthetic:** Feeling emotions, tactile sensations (sense of touch), or proprioceptive feelings (feelings of muscle movement). Questions to elicit this kind of processing include: "What does it feel like to be happy?" "What is the feeling of touching a pine cone?" "What does it feel like to run?"

Eye accessing cues are presented in more detail in *Frogs into Princes and Solutions* (see Selected Bibliography).

Appendix II

Audiotapes & Videotapes

For a fuller experience of some of the methods in this book, choose from our audiotapes and videotapes.

Audiotapes
"Introducing NLP," by Connirae Andreas.
A down-to-earth, example-filled introduction to NLP in its current form. Experience how your thoughts create your life, and some quick and effective ways to change them. Features a complete demonstration of a generative method for changing habits into a desire to become more of the person you want to be (the Swish Pattern). (67 min., $9.95) See chapters 17 & 18.

"Using Your Brain," by Richard Bandler.
Experience the genius of Richard Bandler, co-developer of NLP. In a tape that is by turn humorous, sensitive and thought-provoking, Richard guides you through exercises to increase your expressiveness, see the ludicrous side of a problem, learn how people fall in and out of love, understand others and more. These are selections from the best of the NLP Comprehensive Bandler training videotapes. A useful complement/supplement to the book. (60 min., $9.95)

The "Decision Destroyer" by Steve Andreas.
Richard Bandler's "Decision Destroyer" allows you to create robust personally compelling resources, and put them in your past before you needed them, so that later problem experiences are reevaluated in a positive way. (75 min., $16) See chapter 4.

Videotapes
Resolving Grief.
Connirae Andreas guides a man who had recently lost an infant son and other loved ones in previous years to peaceful and resourceful resolution. Developed by the Andreases for any loss; a person (divorce, separation, or death), a job, valued object, etc. (57 min., $50) See chapter 11.

Six-Step Reframing.
A powerful pattern for accessing and organizing a person's unconscious resources to change undesired habits, feelings and behaviors. Connirae Andreas demonstrates with a woman who wanted to stop smoking. (71 min,. $65) See chapter 8.

Eliminating Allergic Responses: retraining your immune system.

Tim Hallbom and Suzi Smith demonstrate with clients who learn to eliminate their allergic responses to food (wheat and milk), cats, and darkroom chemicals. (55 min., $50) See chapter 5.

A Strategy for Responding to Criticism.

Learn a pattern developed by the Andreases that allows you to take feedback comfortably without getting angry or feeling bad. Demonstrated by Steve Andreas in an NLP Comprehensive Training. (40 min., $50) See chapter 6.

The Swish Pattern.

A rapid, powerful intervention for changing habits and feelings. Steve demonstrates by eliminating one client's nailbiting habit. Connirae demonstrates with another woman's response of anger when her daughter used a particular tone of voice. (71 min., $65) See chapters 17 & 18.

The Fast Phobia/Trauma Cure.

Steve Andreas helps a client eliminate an intense, 20-year phobia of bees in 7 minutes. Also includes a 15-minute follow-up interview with a Vietnam veteran whose "post-traumatic stress disorder" (PTSD) was completely relieved in one session with this method. (42 min., $50) See chapter 7.

ORDER these tapes by sending check or money order to NLP Comprehensive (see address below). Visa and MasterCard accepted. 15% off for orders of three or more videotapes. All orders are shipped UPS within the U.S. Add $2.50 for the first 2 tapes and $1.00 for each additional item. All foreign orders will be shipped airmail; call for prices. All listed videotape prices are for U.S. (NTSC) format. Videotapes in PAL and SECAM are $25 more than the listed price for each tape. All titles are also available in ¾″ U-matic format (NTSC, PAL, SECAM) by special order. Please specify format and system. Orders not specified will be shipped NTSC-VHS. Please make payment in U.S. dollars drawn on a U.S. bank.

NLP Comprehensive
2897 Valmont Rd.
Boulder, CO 80301
1-800-233-1-NLP

A wider range of NLP resources is available from NLP Comprehensive. Call or write for your complete catalog of videotapes and audiotapes, including those featuring NLP co-developers Richard Bandler, John Grinder, Leslie Cameron-Bandler and David Gordon.

Appendix III

Trainings & Certification

Do you want more for yourself, your relationships, or your work? Are you ready to learn more about making that happen for yourself? There have always been people who have been able to achieve what others only dream, who have learned to use their abilities in exceptional ways. What is new about NLP is the ability to systematically study human excellence in ways that make it easily available to others.

Our purpose is to find, and communicate to others, ways that people can use to manifest the potential they feel inside—to further our growth as human beings and develop richer and more fulfilling lives. NLP Comprehensive conducts personal and professional seminars on topics ranging from personal development and parenting to enhancing health and the treatment of addictions and codependence. We also offer the full range of NLP Certification programs: Practitioner, Master Practitioner and Trainer. We are committed to offering the highest-quality NLP trainings available, constantly updating them as this groundbreaking human technology continues to develop. For a current listing of seminars, write or call:

NLP Comprehensive
2897 Valmont Road
Boulder, CO 80301
(303) 442-1102

When people are first introduced to Neuro-Linguistic Programming and begin to learn the techniques, they frequently become cautious and concerned with the possible uses and misuses of this knowledge. We fully recognize the great power of the information presented in this book, and wholeheartedly recommend that you be gentle and cautious as you learn and apply these techniques, to protect yourself and those around you.

Connirae and Steve Andreas continue their research into applying NLP to the problems and difficulties that beset people from all walks of life. They also design and supervise the NLP Comprehensive Certification trainings. They accept a limited number of speaking engagements.

Selected Bibliography

Andreas, Steve; and Andreas, Connirae. Change Your Mind—and Keep the Change. 1987
The sequel to *Using Your Brain—for a CHANGE* features Timelines and time language: how people mentally and verbally code their past, present and future and how to use them to rapidly produce profound change. Also includes methods for eliminating compulsions, a strategy for responding to criticism, aligning your values with who you want to be, "going over threshold" so you never do something again, and how to adapt interventions. ($8.50 paper)

Bandler, Richard. Using Your Brain—for a CHANGE. 1985
A witty introduction to NLP Submodalities by the renowned NLP co-developer who first explored them. Includes how to relieve phobias and traumas, positively motivate yourself, increase your understanding, change core beliefs, and turn a habit into an urge to become more of who you want to be. ($7.50 paper)

Bandler, Richard; and Grinder, John. Frogs into Princes. 1979
NLP's originators doing NLP while teaching its fundamental principles and patterns. Includes how to build rapport, recognize thinking patterns from nonverbal cues, transfer resourceful feelings from one part of your life to another, and a method for turning limitations into solutions. An immediate and well-rounded introduction to NLP, created from live seminars. ($7.50 paper)

Bandler, Richard; and Grinder, John. Reframing: Neuro-Linguistic Programming and the Transformation of Meaning. 1982
Changing the meaning of an event or behavior is a powerful way to create new choices. Included in this book are meaning, context, and advanced Six Step Reframing as well as reframing for couples, families, organizations and individuals with addictions. Also includes a section on negotiating conflicts both internally, between couples and within groups. ($8.50 paper)

Cameron-Bandler, Leslie. Solutions. 1985
This book on improving relationships, sex, and intimacy is also a systematic handbook of the fundamentals of NLP. Includes establishing rapport, quality information-gathering, getting well-formed outcomes, NLP change techniques, using metaphor therapeutically, falling in and out of love, and re-evaluating relationships. ($11.95 paper)

Grinder, John; and Bandler, Richard. Trance-formations: Neuro-Linguistic Programming and the Structure of Hypnosis. 1981
Discussions, demonstrations and exercises build your experience of the skills of Ericksonian hypnosis and hypnotherapy. Learn to utilize the natural thinking processes underlying all hypnotic techniques, and how to apply NLP techniques in trance states. Includes both basic and advanced methods of induction as well as self-hypnosis. ($8.50 paper)

All the above books, as well as other NLP titles, can be ordered from:

Real People Press
Box F
Moab, UT 84532
(801) 259-7578

40% discount on orders of 10 or more books (any combination of titles).

Index

About the Authors

Connirae and Steve Andreas have been studying and teaching Neuro-Linguistic Programming since 1977, and have been certified NLP Trainers since 1980. They have edited four of the most widely-read books by the co-developers of NLP, Richard Bandler and John Grinder: *Frogs into Princes, Trance-formations, Reframing,* and *Using Your Brain—for a CHANGE.* They are authors of the advanced NLP book *Change Your Mind—and Keep the Change,* as well as the comprehensive *NLP Practitioner Training Manual,* and *NLP Trainer Training Manual,* both of which apply NLP technology to the teaching of NLP. Founders of NLP Comprehensive, they have produced over 50 NLP training videotapes and audiotapes by the NLP Co-developers and others in addition to their own work.

For the last ten years Steve and Connirae have devoted their professional lives to providing the highest quality NLP information through seminars, books, articles, videotapes and audiotapes. Active in developing new NLP change patterns, they continue to study the mental processes of people who have exceptional skills, in order to create additional models of human excellence.

Connirae and Steve live with their three young sons in the foothills of the Rocky Mountains near Boulder, Colorado.